REMAKING S

The Future of World Capitalism
Series editors: Radhika Desai and Alan Freeman

The world is undergoing a major realignment. The 2008 financial crash and ensuing recession, China's unremitting economic advance, and the uprisings in the Middle East, are laying to rest all dreams of an 'American Century'. This key moment in history makes weighty intellectual demands on all who wish to understand and shape the future.

Theoretical debate has been derailed, and critical thinking stifled, by apologetic and superficial ideas with almost no explanatory value, 'globalization' being only the best known. Academic political economy has failed to anticipate the key events now shaping the world, and offers few useful insights on how to react to them.

The Future of World Capitalism series will foster intellectual renewal, restoring the radical heritage that gave us the international labour movement, the women's movement, classical Marxism, and the great revolutions of the twentieth century. It will unite them with new thinking inspired by modern struggles for civil rights, social justice, sustainability, and peace, giving theoretical expression to the voices of change of the twenty-first century.

Drawing on an international set of authors, and a world-wide readership, combining rigour with accessibility and relevance, this series will set a reference standard for critical publishing.

Also available:

The Birth of Capitalism:
A Twenty-First-Century Perspective
Henry Heller

Remaking Scarcity

From Capitalist Inefficiency to Economic Democracy

Costas Panayotakis

PlutoPress
www.plutobooks.com

Fernwood Publishing
HALIFAX & WINNIPEG
www.fernwoodpublishing.ca

First published 2011 by Pluto Press
345 Archway Road, London N6 5AA
www.plutobooks.com

Distributed in the United States of America exclusively by
Palgrave Macmillan, a division of St. Martin's Press LLC,
175 Fifth Avenue, New York, NY 10010

Published in Canada by Fernwood Publishing
32 Oceanvista Lane, Black Point, Nova Scotia, B0J 1B0
and 748 Broadway Avenue, Winnipeg, MB R3G 0X3
www.fernwoodpublishing.ca

Fernwood Publishing Company Limited gratefully acknowledges the financial support of
the Government of Canada through the Canada Book Fund, the Canada Council for the
Arts, the Nova Scotia Department of Tourism and Culture and the Province of Manitoba,
through the Book Publishing Tax Credit, for our publishing program.

Library and Archives Canada Cataloguing in Publication
Panayotakis, Costas
    Remaking scarcity : from capitalist inefficiency to
economic democracy / Costas Panayotakis.
(The future of world capitalism)
Includes bibliographical references.
ISBN 978-1-55266-461-2
    1. Sustainable development--Citizen participation.
2. Economic policy--Citizen participation. 3. Capitalism--
Social aspects. 4. Scarcity. I. Title. II. Series: Future of
world capitalism (Winnipeg, Man.)
HD75.6.P35 2011   338.9'27   C2011-903614-2

British Library Cataloguing in Publication Data
A catalogue record for this book is available from the British Library

ISBN   978 0 7453 3100 3   Hardback
ISBN   978 0 7453 3099 0   Paperback (Pluto Press)
ISBN   978 1 55266 461 2   Paperback (Fernwood)

Library of Congress Cataloging in Publication Data applied for

This book is printed on paper suitable for recycling and made from fully managed and
sustained forest sources. Logging, pulping and manufacturing processes are expected to
conform to the environmental standards of the country of origin.

10 9 8 7 6 5 4 3 2 1

Designed and produced for Pluto Press by Curran Publishing Services, Norwich
Simultaneously printed digitally by CPI Antony Rowe, Chippenham, UK and
Edwards Bros in the United States of America

CONTENTS

FOREWORD

In *Remaking Scarcity* Costas Panayotakis expertly dissects a capitalist system in the agonies of intractable crisis and gives a radical
yet practicable guide to its transformation. But what is special about
the book appears in the title. For Panayotakis, to re-make scarcity
means to overcome the illusion socialists have foisted on themselves,
that once the workers have taken power, a new age of abundance
will have dawned. This is an ancient notion, perpetually resurrected.
One of its lineages leads to Arcadia, a real place in the Peloponnese
peninsula that came to symbolize a Golden Age of abundance. In the
American folk tradition we find the "Big Rock Candy Mountain,"
a cornucopia overflowing with goodness and plenty. In Britain and
the Continent, the land of Cockaigne served the purpose. Similar
ideas crop up wherever exploitation and repression set into motion
the hope for a better world.

We are not talking here about the salutary impulse to undo the
hardships and insults imposed by a ruthless class society, from
hunger to lack of shelter and health care – in short, the provision
of a decent life for all, or what one might call redistributive justice.
There is however a way that the rational and just demand for a
better world can come bundled with the boundlessness of desire; and
it is this latter factor, useful as it may be for stirring up the enthusiasm needed to get a social movement going, which has weighed
heavily upon socialism by compromising the all-important question
of superseding capital. Capitalism is by far the most productive
system humans have ever devised, and promotes itself as such by
promising limitlessness and instant gratification. Bemused by the
dazzling collection of toys the dominant consumerism rains down
upon us, progressives and socialists all too often succumb to the
argument that capitalism may be a disaster, but at least it has solved
the question of production; why not, therefore, get rid of the bad
aspect of capitalism and retain what's good? Why not build upon
capital's productive genius and produce our way to happiness? The

whole complex is conditioned by the economic orthodoxy which holds that what is wrong with society today is insufficient demand.

Costas Panayotakis sets out to disabuse people of this idea, and powerfully succeeds, with a sophisticated reading of political economy, sociology and, thanks to his work on the journal *Capitalism Nature Socialism*, radical political ecology. He understands the lessons of the ecological crisis and is unafraid to draw the tough but essential conclusion, that capital's productive genius is precisely the instrument of its disaster: it only, truly, knows how to produce things and force humanity to live by them – or die. As Che Guevara once said, under capitalism we get to choose the razor blade with which to cut our throat. Capitalism would collapse if it made people happy; it runs on discontent, competition, addiction: that is, by evoking the evils latent in human nature. Capitalist production and the idea of endless growth are joined at the hip. And since endless growth will bring the planet and our civilization down, it follows that all our energies and resources need to be dedicated to the making of a post-capitalist world.

Panayotakis recognizes that a survivable post-capitalist world means a world of sufficiency, not endless expansion of production. Its realm of freedom is built on a foundation of material limit – the necessary understanding that we can't always get what we want. Indeed, the very need-structure of humanity, its 'wanting,' needs transformation. We need to turn away from the present addictive/consumerist model to one respectful of limit as the condition for creativity. Thus scarcity becomes a framework for building a worthwhile society, as a building is constructed upon the firm, limiting foundation of matter and not the fickle sands of desire.

Panayotakis sees this in terms of democracy, no longer confined to the political sphere but as the reigning principle of economic activity. Thus we can build a humanly worthwhile, sustainable world by expanding the notion of democracy into the sphere of production. This is the chief conclusion, illustrated fruitfully in the latter part of his book. It comprises an important maturation of the left as society confronts the breakdown of its reigning mode of production.

However the notion of socialism may have been battered throughout the nineteenth and twentieth centuries, the present crisis with its ecological dimension endows it with new life. 'Economic democracy' is a good description of Panayotakis's vision of a sustainable world. But it is a method directed toward definite ends. The logic is inexorable: society based upon individualized ownership of the means of production – and all the exploitation and aggression entailed by this – is unsustainable, indeed, a recipe for extinction. Economic democracy, therefore, means the return of collective ownership and a society of mutuality, or it means nothing at all. The name's not the thing, but an index of the thing. Call it 'commoning'; call it a 'co-operative commonwealth'; call it 'ecosocialism'; call it 'economic democracy.' But remember this: the old world is dying; here is the shape of the new one waiting to be born.

Joel Kovel

PREFACE

This is the work of a recovering economist. When, over 20 years ago, I decided to make economics the focus of my undergraduate studies, it was out of a sense that the economy has a big impact on people's lives. I was therefore surprised and dismayed to find out that the economics I was taught did not seem to increase my understanding of the real world around me. Schooled, like most undergraduates in the United States, in the dominant neoclassical perspective, I was also disappointed by how uncritical this perspective was of a capitalist economic system which even back then seemed so obviously flawed in so many different ways.

At the risk of sounding provocative, I would even say that studying economics was the closest I have ever come to experiencing totalitarianism. The problem was not just that my teachers, at a prestigious institution that counted Nobel laureates among its faculty, did next to nothing to expose me to any alternatives to the neoclassical approach. The main problem was that they did not really inform me that such alternatives did in fact exist. For example, although I was vaguely aware of the existence of Marxist economists, the message conveyed to me from practically all my teachers was that such creatures were odd and distasteful throwbacks to a distant past that one need no longer worry about. So it was that, upon completing my undergraduate degree in economics, I decided to pursue a doctoral degree in sociology.

Although most of my sociologist friends like to joke that they are not true sociologists and that they stand at the margins of the profession, to me sociology was a breath of fresh air. To begin with, it is much harder to find mainstream sociologists insufferable once one has had the pleasure of studying under mainstream economists. Beyond that, however, not only did sociology seem more tolerant of a diversity of theoretical approaches, it in fact made Marx required reading for every single graduate student! As if this was not enough, I also found, somewhat to my surprise, that switching to sociology did not mean giving up my goal to understand the economic world all around me. Instead, it proved a necessary step in the direction of achieving precisely that goal.

My doctoral dissertation focused on the implications of Max Weber's concept of rationalization for Marxist critical theory. In the course of writing my dissertation I became more and more interested in the position that the concept of scarcity held in the Marxist emancipatory project. Underlying my dissertation was the assumption, shared by other Marxists before me, that the possibility of a better, non-capitalist future stemmed from the potential to abolish scarcity that capitalism had created.

I completed my dissertation about ten years ago and have worked on this book ever since. While my distaste for capitalism has not abated, my approach to the question of scarcity has evolved in important ways. This evolution partly reflects the debt I owe to a large number of people who have over the years informed my thinking and enriched my understanding of the world. The year I finished my dissertation was also the year that my association with the journal *Capitalism Nature Socialism* (*CNS*) began. Interacting and working with Joel Kovel, Karen Charman, Salvatore Engel-DiMauro, George Martin, Maarten de Kadt, and everybody else in the CNS crowd quickly alerted me to the need to integrate the ecological question into any discussion of the relationship between capitalism and scarcity.

Another group that played a pivotal role in the development of this book's argument were the faculty members from across the City University of New York system who participated in the 2005 Faculty Fellowship Publications Program. I would therefore like to thank Sharon Zukin, Samir Chopra, Marcia Esparza, Jordi Getman, Janet Johnson, Anru Lee, Frederick Wasser, and Richard Wilkins for their insightful response to what at the time I thought would be the opening chapter of my book. Their comments led me to confront neoclassical economics in a systematic fashion rather than just shrugging it off as a discourse that obscured the possibility of eliminating scarcity altogether. Taking up this challenge has shaped my current view that the problem is not scarcity per se but rather the inhumane and ecologically unsustainable configurations of scarcity that capitalism creates.

My thinking has also benefited from the constant intellectual stimulation I have received from a number of other New York City circles I am fortunate to be a part of. My participation in the editorial collective of *Situations*, a journal seeking to radicalize our collective imagination, has, both directly and indirectly, nurtured my interest in and commitment to the project of economic democracy, which plays a central role in the argument of this book. For this I have to thank Stanley Aronowitz, Peter Bratsis, Ric Brown, Bill DiFazio, Jeremy Glick, Andrew Greenberg, Michael Pelias, Sohnya Sayres, Dominic Wetzel, Betsy Wissinger, Ivan Zatz, and Mark Zuss. Equally important for my thinking has been my regular participation in the Marxist Theory colloquium, which is organized by Bertell Ollman at New York University and co-sponsored by the journal *Science and Society*. Having learned a lot over the years from the speakers and participants in the colloquium, I was also delighted to present the ideas discussed in this work in the colloquium's April 2011 meeting.

Given the scarcity of time that my heavy teaching load at CUNY's New York City College of Technology entails, I would have been unable to do the research and writing for this book without successive PSC-CUNY grants and a fellowship leave in the 2008–2009 academic year. This was the year that capitalism's current crisis erupted. In making sense of this crisis I have greatly benefited from the talks and educational programs offered by the Brecht Forum, one of the most vibrant political and intellectual spaces in New York City. I have heard a number of the thinkers and scholars whose work I discuss in this book at that space, and have particularly benefited from Rick Wolff's emphasis on the importance of the question of surplus for Marxist theory, as well as his insistence that we should respond to this crisis by struggling not for a regulated capitalism but for a genuinely democratic economy.

As I was beginning my manuscript in spring 2009, I met for the first time Radhika Desai and Alan Freeman. After having a conversation with Radhika about my book as well as the book series they were starting, I decided that I would send them a book proposal, which I did a few months later. In the last year and a half they have been the most thorough and insightful critics and editors that any author could hope to have. At least as important has been the contribution of the anonymous peer reviewers who read and provided feedback regarding both my book proposal and my manuscript. Thanks to their work this book is much stronger than it might otherwise have been.

I also owe a debt to my brothers and sisters at the Professional Staff Congress, the union representing the faculty and professional staff of the City University of New York. Struggling and agitating alongside them has taught me not only to analyze but also to fight the configurations of scarcity that capitalism creates. I would also be remiss if I didn't thank my students whose daily confrontation with low-paying jobs, rising tuition, relentless budget cuts, and lack of enough time to combine work, family, and study is a constant reminder of the need to remake scarcity through radical social change.

I should also thank my parents Yannis and Voula, and my brother Alexandros, as well as all my friends who have cheered me on in the long years when I worked on this project. One of these friends, Austerity Nut, has taught me that the good fight requires not only sharp analysis and fierce determination but also a zany sense of humor. Equally inspiring are the struggles, "now hidden, now open," against capitalist brutality in my country of origin, Greece, in the Arab countries, and in every other corner of this world. It is to this noble fight for social justice and human liberation that this work is dedicated.

1 CAPITALISM, SCARCITY, AND ECONOMIC DEMOCRACY

This book's main arguments had started to crystallize by the time the current economic crisis began. The outbreak and development of this crisis have confirmed, while also adding urgency to, the multiple messages that this book conveys. First of all, the armies of the unemployed that the crisis has created clearly refute the claims of mainstream neoclassical economics and neoliberal opinion-makers that capitalism uses scarce resources efficiently. Second, capitalism's failures are inseparable from its undemocratic nature. There is no better illustration of this undemocratic nature than the fact that those most responsible for this crisis are doing as well as ever, while workers and ordinary people around the world now find themselves paying dearly for the sins of others. Third, this paradoxical turn of events highlights the need for a different society based on economic democracy, or the principle that all citizens should have equal say over the goals and operation of their society's economic system. Fourth, the undemocratic nature of capitalism gives rise to resistance, which generates hope for a future that is more democratic than our woefully undemocratic present. The sudden and rapid spread of revolt throughout the Arab world highlights both the volatility of the present moment and the possibilities for democratic movements of all kinds that this volatility creates.

Having formulated in my mind some of these ideas, I began writing the book itself soon after the global economic meltdown hit in the fall of 2008. The world at that time looked in many ways different from the way it looks as I write these lines in the spring of 2011. With even staunch conservatives, such as then-US President Bush (2008) declaring in public that "the market is not functioning properly," there was a general sense that free market fundamentalism and the neoliberal consensus of the last three decades was coming to an end. Adding to this belief was the massive government intervention into the collapsing economy that marked both the waning months of the Bush administration and the policies of many other governments around the world. The main purpose of this intervention was to bail out and support the financial institutions in Wall Street and around the world that caused this crisis.

One of the immediate effects of this crisis was the election of

1

Barack Obama to the presidency of the United States. Having during his presidential campaign blamed the crisis on the failures of trickle-down economics, Obama seemed to suggest that, once elected, he might break with the neoliberal policies of his predecessors (*New York Times* 2008).[1] In fact, even some radical commentators, such as Walden Bello (2008b), saw in Obama a possible carrier of a new global social democratic project that would mitigate the inequalities and ecological destruction that neoliberal globalization had produced.

A little more than two years later, all this seems ancient history. Obama has failed to rise to the expectations of his liberal and progressive supporters, and has allowed the political right, including the notorious Tea Party, to benefit from people's pain and understandable anger. In particular, the political right was able to exploit the fact that Obama continued Bush's Wall Street friendly policies, while also passing a fiscal stimulus package that was too small to prevent a rapid increase of unemployment. As I have argued elsewhere, progressives and the Left may have contributed to this turn of events through their unfortunate description of bailouts as 'socialism for the rich.' Instead of presenting both the crisis and the outrageous bailouts following it as a classic example of capitalism's undemocratic nature, this term in fact shifted blame from the true culprit behind these phenomena, namely capitalism, to 'socialism.' Departing from the simplistic equation of capitalism with markets and of socialism with government intervention, this term made it possible to interpret the deepening economic crisis as the result of an unfortunate deviation from true and authentic capitalism (Panayotakis 2010c).

As a result, austerity is spreading around the United States like wildfire. While official unemployment is over 9 percent, government policy from the federal to the municipal level is not one of creating jobs and stimulating the economy but of laying off public sector workers, while attacking their salaries, pensions, and labor rights. Accompanying this shameless attack on public sector workers are deep cuts in education, health care, and other essential social services (Krugman 2011, Wolff 2011).

This situation is not unique to the United States. Brutal austerity policies are spreading throughout Europe, as the European Union more and more openly turns into a vehicle of neoliberal policies that deepen the economic crisis, while also dismantling welfare states and a social model that had supposedly tamed and humanized capitalism. Ireland, a country that neoliberals celebrated until recently as a Celtic tiger whose example others should emulate, is in deep crisis, having turned to the International Monetary Fund (IMF) and the European Union for support after assuming the debt of private banks.[2] Another country that has turned to the IMF and the European Union for loans, Greece, is also in dire straits, as its government uses the crisis to reduce salaries, wages, and pensions, to destroy long-standing labor rights, and to attack a welfare state that was quite rudimentary to begin with.[3] Just as in the United States, European political and economic elites are clearly determined to 'solve' the crisis on the backs of those least responsible for it. Let teachers and firefighters, students and retirees, workers, and the unemployed pay! After all, someone has to finance the successive support packages going to banks and financial institutions around the world.

Thus, scarcity is the order of the day. Governments, the argument goes, have to cut back because they simply don't have any money. This argument is one example of the ways that economic and political elites use the concept of scarcity to legitimize a capitalist economic system that enriches the privileged few even as it impoverishes and humiliates everybody else. The ideological use of this concept is not unique to the present time. As I argue in this book, this ideological use permeates neoclassical economics, the theoretical approach that shapes the conventional wisdom regarding economic affairs. It is the intention of this book, therefore, to demystify the concept of scarcity by relating the social and economic realities it describes to the operational logic of the capitalist system.

A related purpose of this book is to discuss the social struggles that result as capitalism creates wealth and distributes scarcity among the different classes and social groups both within nation-states and internationally. There are growing waves of social protest in the United States, Europe, and around the world. There are also the inspiring struggles of people around the Arab world, who are rising up against both political repression and the immiseration that neoliberal policies and the current crisis have inflicted on them (Hanieh 2011, McNally 2011b, Prins 2011). Many of the Arab leaders under challenge have been long-time allies of the United States and the West, and are now increasingly turning to military repression of their citizens (Slackman 2011). Looking the other way as their allies unleash violence on protesters in Iraq, Yemen, and Bahrain, the United States and the West have chosen to attack another Arab leader facing challenge, Colonel Gadaffi of Libya. These developments, moreover, add another complication to the ongoing global economic crisis, as they threaten to raise oil prices (*Economist* 2011).

As this quick overview of the world's evolving situation makes clear, economic crises highlight the importance of understanding capitalism's management of scarcity and of refuting the main claim which mainstream economists, journalists, politicians, and opinion makers of all kinds make on its behalf. Throwing millions into unemployment, starving thousands of millions, while wasting or destroying productive and natural resources, capitalism can neither serve human well-being and environmental sustainability nor make rational use of its unprecedented technological potential. There is an alternative: economic democracy. Under it, all citizens would set society's economic goals in accordance with their desires and values, instead of leaving such decisions to a capitalist class that is only concerned about profit. This book explains why capitalism misman-ages scarce resources, how economic democracy can manage them better, and how the transition to a society consistent with economic democracy can be achieved.

The concept of scarcity lies at the core of neoclassical economics, the theoretical approach that not only reigns supreme within the disci-pline of economics but also informs public discourse and legitimizes our capitalist economic system. Underlying this concept is the idea that the resources people can use to meet their needs and desires are limited, making it necessary for people to make hard choices. Scarce resources include not only goods, tools, land, and natural resources, but also time (see Frank 2003: 3–4; Krugman et al. 2007: 6). After all, free time to relax, pursue one's interests, engage in cultural activ-ities, exercise, spend time with friends and family, and participate in community activities can be as essential to one's happiness and welfare as the consumption of goods and services (Frank 1999). The mission of neoclassical economics then becomes to show that the capitalist economic system is efficient because "markets are usually very good at making sure that resources are used well" (Krugman, Wells and Olney 2007: 15).

I do not deny that scarcity exists. But neoclassical economics forgets that society constructs the individual needs, which give rise to it, and, under capitalism, generates inequalities, which prevent the market from handling that scarcity efficiently. Rather than serving consumer desires efficiently, capitalism encourages the pursuit of profit and capital accumulation. In so doing, it leads not to the satisfaction of human needs but to immense human suffering for billions of people around the world, a toxic consumerist culture that fails to satisfy even the fraction of the world's population that can partake in it, and a deepening ecological crisis.

Though inspired by many of the insights of the Marxist tradition, this book also takes issue with Marxists who assume that a socialist society will eliminate scarcity altogether.[4] Instead, it argues that abolishing scarcity is not an end in itself. Scarcity is not inherently problematic if it merely reflects the fact that humans refine their needs and desires, enriching human life even as they perpetuate gaps between these desires and their society's productive capacity. An economically democratic society does not have to abolish scarcity per se, but it does have to manage it in accordance with ecological sustainability and people's autonomously formed desires.

Since it understands scarcity as the gap between people's desires and the material means at their disposal, this book examines both the 'demand' and 'supply' dimensions of scarcity. Unlike neoclassical economics, this work focuses both on the social and economic processes, which on the demand side shape human needs and desires, and on the ways that exploitation and social and economic inequalities affect, on the supply side, the distribution of scarce resources that different groups and individuals can use to pursue their objectives and desires.

Because scarcity has a demand and a supply side, the configurations of scarcity that confront any given individual reflect their position within society. In particular, they reflect the economic, political, and cultural processes that constitute people in their position as desiring subjects who tend to have some needs and desires rather than others. Equally, the configurations of scarcity they face reflect the material resources that people in their position can use to satisfy their needs and desires. Since, moreover, individuals are members of groups, such as classes, nations, ethnicities, and genders, they engage in struggles against class and other social inequalities which shape both the distribution of material resources and the configurations of scarcity that different individuals and groups face.

Since scarcity stems from the gap between what people want and what they have, its configurations are closely connected to the daily problems that people face, such as poverty, unemployment, racial and gender discrimination, war, crime, disease, and the deepening ecological crisis. These problems in turn affect these configurations. Discrimination will affect an individual's ability to get a job and hence determine how well they can meet their needs. Unemployment and poverty may lead to crime or create a pool of people desperate enough to become mercenary soldiers or terrorists. This poverty and desperation may result from deteriorating ecological conditions that destroy people's traditional modes of subsistence. In short, the configurations of scarcity that people face constantly result in, are shaped by, and in general, interact with a wide range of social problems.

In a classic discussion of the contribution that sociology can make to the illumination of social problems, C. Wright Mills (1961: 4) emphasized over 50 years ago the need "to grasp the interplay of man and society, of biography and history, of self and world." As Mills pointed out, the link between large-scale social processes and the problems that ordinary people face in their everyday life is not always transparent. This often leads people to feel trapped. One of the purposes of sociological analysis, Mills suggested, was to empower people by helping them both to see the links between their troubles and the social structures producing them and to realize that others, who are in a similar social position as they are, face similar problems. In making these connections clear, sociological analysis also makes clear the dialectic between people and the society they live in. If there is interplay between people and their society, this is because people are as much a product of the society they live in, as their society is the product of the actions that people take.

Mills's emphasis on this point was, in part, a reaction to American individualism and its belief that individuals get what they deserve. As Mills pointed out, the fact that people sometimes behave in ways that land them into difficulties does not mean that all their everyday problems are self-inflicted. Such an assumption not only lets social structures off the hook but also prevents people from recognizing that, when social structures are to blame for their problems, these problems call for collective action that can bring about social change.

The same is true for the configurations of scarcity facing ordinary people in capitalist societies. Consisting of the gap between their desires and material means, the configurations facing different individuals depend, in part, on individual effort and talent. This book argues, however, that to a large extent these configurations are also shaped by the logic of profit. Because this logic leads to configurations of scarcity that entail widespread hunger, poverty, involuntary unemployment, and rapid ecological degradation, only a society based on economic democracy can manage scarcity in a rational and humane fashion. This suggests, however, the need to challenge the undemocratic capitalist system in which we currently live and labor.

PLAN OF THE BOOK

Because neoclassical economics represents contemporary society's conventional wisdom regarding economic life in general, and the question of scarcity in particular, Chapter 2 explains both how neoclassical economics approaches the question of scarcity and how this approach legitimizes capitalism. By contrast, Chapter 3 argues that the configurations of scarcity that capitalism generates are shaped by the logic of profit and capital expansion, a logic that escapes human control and subordinates all human beings to its dictates.

As Chapter 4 makes clear, a portion of capitalist profits is devoted to the construction of a consumerist culture that, as psychologists and other social scientists have pointed out, not only aggravates environmental degradation but also undermines human well-being. In this respect, this consumerist culture contributes to capitalism's inability to translate its tremendous productive potential into a richer, happier life for all human beings. This inability bears witness to the capitalist system's irrationality. Far from using scarce resources efficiently, capitalism wastefully drives people to ever-higher levels of consumption which usually fail to increase their sense of happiness. Chapter 4 also links capitalism's irrationality in this respect to capital's exploitation of workers. Indeed, I argue, capital's creation of a consumerist culture undercuts the ability of workers to derive maximum satisfaction even from the part of their product that returns to them as wages and salaries. This sheds light on a qualitative implication of capitalist exploitation that scholars have grappled with in the past without being able to fully understand.

As Chapters 5 and 6 show, a multiplicity of social and economic inequalities in contemporary capitalist societies, along with the social struggles which these predictably generate, shape the configurations of scarcity facing individuals and social groups around the world today. Chapter 5 deals with class, gender, and racial inequalities as well as with the implications of capitalism's partiality for long working hours. Recognizing households as major sites of labor in our society, it also argues that economic democracy requires the democratization of households and the abolition of gender inequalities that prevent all adult members in the household from having equal say over the economic decisions within the household. Chapter 6, by contrast, examines capitalism's global dimension as well as the connection between the pursuit of profit and the stark global inequalities responsible for the inhumane configurations of scarcity faced by billions of people the world over.

Chapter 7 focuses on the deepening ecological crisis and its implications for the configurations of scarcity facing people around the world. It discusses the connection between economic inequality and ecological degradation, and argues that their control of the economic surplus allows capitalist elites to shift the environmental costs of their economic activity onto the general public, devastating in the process most of the planet's ecosystems. Chapter 7 also offers a critique of the concept of externalities that neoclassical economics uses to understand ecological degradation. Against neoclassical economics, I argue that ecological degradation is not the result of market failures that go against the main thrust of the capitalist system. Instead, so-called 'externalities' efficiently pursue capitalism's true objective, which is not to satisfy consumers' demands but to maximize profit.

After dissecting in the first few chapters the dangerous irrationality of the configurations of scarcity that capitalism creates, Chapters 8 and 9 make concrete the concept of economic democracy. Chapter 8 discusses the debate between supporters of market and non-market post-capitalist models, and explores the extent to which David Schweickart's market and Michael Albert and Robin Hahnel's marketless models are consistent with the principle of economic democracy. Chapter 9 sketches a strategy of economic democratization that couples the pursuit of progressive reforms that alleviate capitalism's inhumane and ecologically destructive configurations of scarcity with the building of alternative economic institutions, such as democratically run worker cooperatives, that challenge the logic of capital and nurture ordinary people's democratic skills. While the first component of this strategy presupposes an effort to democratize the state, the latter focuses on the building of alternative economic institutions and spaces that cultivate ordinary people's ability to govern themselves. A virtuous circle between these two components is possible, as the democratization of the state can facilitate the spread of democratically run economic institutions, while the democratic skills ordinary people acquire in such institutions can equip them to fight more effectively for progressive social change that democratizes the state even further. The creative tension between reforms aimed at democratizing the state, on the one hand, and building autonomous institutions, such as worker cooperatives, on the other, can therefore trigger a process of social change with the potential to transform the debate between competing visions of a non-capitalist, economically democratic social order from an academic question to an issue of immediate political relevance.

In a sense, Chapters 8 and 9 complement each other. Indeed, convincing visions of a non-capitalist future can add to the conviction of popular movements that 'another world is possible' and that the kind of movement to democratize the economy that Chapter 9 discusses is worth pursuing. Conversely, the more such a movement develops, the more people's democratic skills and appetite for economic democracy will increase the political salience of visions of an alternative socio-economic order. While appeals to economic democracy may now seem utopian, the radicalization of human needs that a process of economic democratization would trigger can fuel the desire for change and transform economic democracy into a widely embraced alternative to a capitalist system that continues to exact an intolerable toll on humanity and the planet.

To summarize, after an introductory overview of the book's argument in Chapter 1, Chapters 2 and 3 describe two contrasting approaches to the question of scarcity, the neoclassical approach that views capitalist markets as efficient mechanisms of allocating scarce resources, and an alternative Marxist-inspired approach that understands prevailing configurations of scarcity in terms of the logic of profit and capital expansion. Chapter 4 focuses on the demand side of scarcity, with special emphasis on capitalism's construction of a consumerist culture. Chapters 5 to 7 focus on the supply side of scarcity and on the ways that cross-cutting (class, gender, racial, and global) inequalities as well as the deepening ecological crisis affect the material means that people and social groups can bring to bear when they try to satisfy their needs and desires. While Chapters 2 to 7 offer an analysis and critique of capitalism and neoclassical economics, Chapters 8 and 9 explore the possibility of an alternative social system based on economic democracy. Finally, the book's concluding chapter briefly recapitulates the main elements of the relationship between capitalism, scarcity, and economic democracy that this work hopes to illuminate.

2 THE NEOCLASSICAL APPROACH TO SCARCITY

The question of scarcity is central to neoclassical economics, the theoretical tradition that dominates the economics profession (see Cato 2009: 30–1, Weintraub 2002, Keen 2001: 157–8), and which, through its influence over politicians, bureaucrats, and opinion-makers around the world, shapes conventional wisdom regarding economic affairs (Keen 2001: xiii–xiv). After touting for decades the virtues of markets, many neoclassical economists now interpret the current crisis as a 'market failure,' to be addressed through vast bailouts of capitalist interests and a little more regulation by the government. In so doing, neoclassical economists continue to provide ideological justification for the growing economic inequality, human misery, and ecological degradation that capitalism is inflicting on people around the world. This book discusses how capitalism produces these problems, as well as how neoclassical economics obscures their causes.

Neoclassical economics views scarcity as a challenge to human society that capitalist markets, with some help from the state, can meet. Although there is room for debate within it regarding the degree of government action necessary to correct occasional market failures, neoclassical economics portrays capitalist political economies as generally benign systems, which allow people to satisfy their needs and wants as fully as possible in a world of scarce material resources. Since this work offers a critique of the notion that capitalism manages scarce resources efficiently and in accordance with the common good, a discussion of the neoclassical approach is a natural starting-point for its analysis. This chapter does not, of course, offer an exhaustive discussion of neoclassical economics. Instead, it provides a general overview of that theory, leaving the discussion and critique of some of the theory's more specific claims to later chapters.

Neoclassical economics understands scarcity as a lack of suffi-cient material means to provide all the goods and services that people desire. It is the presence of scarcity, moreover, that provides economics with its object of study. Indeed, in his classic statement of this position, Lionel Robbins (1962: 16) defined economics as "the science which studies human behavior as a relationship between ends and scarce means which have alternative uses."[1] In other words, economics focuses on the choices that individuals and societies have to make when the scarcity of material means precludes simultaneous pursuit of all their ends (Robbins 1962: 15). As time, material resources, and the services of others are all scarce, every choice we make in favor of one end is simultaneously a sacrifice of another. Thus the economist, Robbins (1962: 30) points out, is 'a true tragedian' because he studies "that conflict of choice which is one of the permanent characteristics of human existence."

In studying these choices, economists only make what Robbins (1962: 78–9) views as self-evident and uncontroversial assumptions. One such assumption is that individuals are capable of ranking their ends in order of importance. This means that individuals weigh all their ends against each other, and in so doing, treat them as means to the ultimate end of achieving as high a level of satisfaction as possible (Robbins 1962: 15).

For Robbins, economists have to view the ends that people pursue as exogenous conditions to be treated by other disciplines. For example, economists do not seek to understand how individual preferences become what they are, leaving the matter to "psychologists or perhaps even physiologists" (Robbins 1962: 85–6).[2] Instead, they adopt a 'humanist' approach which, as Wolff and Resnick (1987: 259) point out, attributes economic phenomena to individual traits and human nature. Thus, they do not see that individual preferences are inseparable from the structure of social and economic relations in which individuals become who they are. Nor do they admit that individual preferences are, for that reason, a product as well as a motivating cause of economic activity.

For Robbins, moreover, technology is an exogenous factor on the supply side, just as preferences are an exogenous factor on the demand side. This means that:

> [e]conomists are not interested in technique as such. They are interested in it solely as one of the influences determining relative scarcity. Conditions of technique 'show' themselves in the productivity functions just as conditions of taste 'show' themselves in the scales of relative valuations.
>
> (Robbins 1962: 37–8)

The relative scarcity of various goods and services changes with changes in these two exogenous factors. The exogeneity of these factors means that the reasons for their change do not concern economics. Economics instead concentrates on how individuals respond to such exogenous changes, as well as on how this response changes prices and incomes across the economy (Robbins 1962: 126–7).

While neoclassical economists consider these assumptions self-evident, critics describe neoclassical economics as a 'degenerate' paradigm that "holds to its core beliefs in the face of either contrary factual evidence or theoretical critiques that establish fundamental inconsistencies in its intellectual apparatus" (Keen 2001: 157–8). If neoclassical economics continues to dominate the discipline of economics, this is not because of its superiority to its alternatives but because, as Douglas Dowd (2000: 198) points out, it "has become servant rather than analyst of the economic system."

The ideological function of the neoclassical paradigm consists in its attempt to provide a rigorous theoretical elaboration of Adam Smith's 'invisible hand' metaphor. According to Steve Keen (2001: 161–2), Adam Smith and the originators of classical political economy played an important ideological function by providing a rationale for the removal of the controls that constrained the ability of industrialists and merchants to accumulate capital. The emergence of political economy signified the rise of an alternative, 'humanist' outlook that understood social and economic institutions not as instances of an all-encompassing and divinely ordained cosmic order, but in their connection to human action and interests (Wolff and Resnick 1987: 259). Adam Smith's 'invisible hand' metaphor was especially significant because it undercut the view of state economic controls as guarantors of social stability. It did so by suggesting that, thanks to markets, even self-interested individuals unwittingly "promote[d] the public interest" (Smith 1909: 351). Even as they pursued nothing but their private gain, individuals were "led by an invisible hand to promote an end which was no part of [their] intention" (Smith 1909: 351–2). Rather than destabilizing social life, the removal of economic controls would, thanks to the benign influence of the invisible hand, enhance human welfare.

The emergence and rise of neoclassical economics in the late nineteenth and early twentieth centuries represented both a continuation of and a departure from classical political economy and the Smithian project. As E. K. Hunt (2002) explains in his history of economic thought, neoclassical economics turned away from classical political economy's interest in the class divisions at the basis of capitalist society. Adam Smith and classical political economists, such as Ricardo and Marx, not only acknowledged the existence of major economic classes, such as landowners, capitalists, and workers, but also placed these classes at the center of their analysis. These economic thinkers were also more open about the link between capitalist profit and the exploitation of workers, as well as the link of this exploitation to the structural advantage that capitalist employers enjoyed in their negotiation with propertyless workers. Just as they did not mistake the formal equality of capitalist employers and workers meeting in the labor market for lack of exploitation of the latter by the former, these thinkers were also more willing to recognize the consistent tendency of the state to side with the employers and against the workers. Although Marx was the political economist to develop these critical insights most clearly and consistently, such insights were not altogether absent from Adam Smith and David Ricardo (Hunt 2002).

Neoclassical economics, by contrast, replaces classes with individuals who own such factors of production as land, capital, and marketable skills. These individuals bring these factors to the marketplace, and receive in exchange a return that they use to maximize their utility or to attain as satisfying (to them) a combination of consumer goods and services as their budget will allow. The link between scarcity and the need for choices that Robbins emphasizes thus takes two forms.

First, an individual who derives satisfaction from good or service A simultaneously gives up the satisfaction they could have derived from an alternative bundle of goods and services. The consumer who spends US$15,000 on a new car, for example, forgoes the pleasure they might have derived from spending that money on traveling, home electronics, and so on. Second, the decision of an individual to part with the factor of production they control also involves a sacrifice. The individual who lends their money to an entrepreneur does so for a monetary return that will at a later date allow them to possess and gain satisfaction from a bundle of goods and services. To receive this return, however, this individual has to forgo the satisfaction that they would derive from immediate consumption. Similarly, the worker who surrenders their time for a wage is choosing the satisfaction they will derive from the bundle of goods they will be able to buy with their wage over the satisfaction they would have derived from not working for someone else and instead devoting their time to more pleasurable pursuits. It is for this reason that neoclassical economists often treat leisure as an 'economic good', viewing an individual's decision whether to work as a choice between leisure and the other economic goods that the individual can buy if they surrender their leisure for a wage. Finally, the owner of land who disposes of it for a monetary return chooses the satisfaction they will derive from consuming this return over the satisfaction of using the land for their own purposes.

In other words, all individuals struggle with the scarcity of resources, whether these resources take the form of money, time, or land. This reality forces individuals to make the most of their resources, using them to attain that bundle of economic goods and services that will maximize their satisfaction. For neoclassical economics, therefore, individuals use exchange, money, and the market to manage the scarce resources at their disposal effectively.

The result is an 'efficient' economy which supposedly does not waste resources because it allows individuals to maximize the satisfaction they derive from the scarce resources at their disposal. The neoclassical concept of efficiency owes much to the work of Vilfredo Pareto, an Italian economist and sociologist who lived in the late nineteenth and early twentieth centuries. For Pareto an economy is efficient if its allocation of resources makes it impossible for one individual to achieve what they would consider an improvement in their condition without making one or more other individuals worse off (see Layard 2005: 129–31, Bannock et al. 2003: 292, Boyes and Melvin 2005: 101, Hahnel 2002: 32–3). If, for example,[3] person A ends up with an apple, even though they prefer oranges, and person B ends up with an orange, even though they prefer apples, this allocation of resources is not Pareto efficient. In this situation a 'Pareto improvement' is possible, since the satisfaction of at least one individual can increase without reducing anyone else's satisfaction. Indeed, A and B could achieve such a Pareto improvement by simply exchanging the apple for the orange. In this way A and B would increase their respective levels of satisfaction without adversely affecting the satisfaction of anyone else in the community.

As this example makes clear, misdistribution of final goods is one possible source of Pareto inefficiency within an economy. Robin Hahnel usefully lists six other possible sources. Pareto inefficiency could result from a 'misallocation of productive resources,' which reduces output by not allocating productive resources to the productive units that could best use them.[4] Another source of inefficiency is unemployment of productive resources, which reduces people's satisfaction by reducing the output available for consumption. The equivalent of this source of inefficiency on the consumption side is letting final goods go to waste rather than distributing them to people who need them. A related source of inefficiency is wasting productive resources by using up more of them per unit of output than necessary given existing technology. Finally, Pareto inefficiency also results when the integration of the production and consumption sectors misallocates goods between consumers and producers (Hahnel 2002: 37–8).

The concept of Pareto efficiency valorizes capitalist markets by suggesting that they lead to an efficient use of scarce resources. In fact, as E. K. Hunt (2002: 381) points out, providing a theoretical justification for this idea seems to be the main mission of neoclassical economics. By showing that, under certain conditions, markets could lead to Pareto efficiency, neoclassical economics formalizes Adam Smith's claim that self-interested action in the market promotes the common good.

As critics of neoclassical economics have pointed out, however, the conditions of Pareto efficiency are so numerous and unrealistic that they make the whole concept irrelevant to the realities of contemporary capitalist economies (Hunt 2002: 388–9). To begin with, for Pareto optimality to obtain, markets have to be competitive. A large number of buyers and sellers is necessary, and none of these buyers and sellers can be large enough to control prices. This assumption has long been problematic, with the rise of large monopolistic or oligopolistic corporations that often dominate their respective markets. A related condition is the absence of increasing returns to scale. This means that increasing the scale of production should not allow a company to reduce its average costs. This condition is also not realistic in contemporary capitalist economies. In fact, the presence of increasing returns of scale is a major reason for the emergence of large corporations, which use their size to reduce costs, drive smaller businesses out of the market, and share control of the market with a handful of other equally large competitors.

Another condition is perfect knowledge, on the part of buyers and sellers alike, regarding all the economic alternatives open to them, as well as an absence of uncertainty regarding the future. Moreover, Pareto optimality requires either the absence of 'externalities' or the ability of governments to counteract their effects through such measures as "taxes, subsidies, or the creation of new property rights."[5] Externalities are present when market prices do not take into account the positive or negative effects of the production and consumption of goods and services on parties other than their sellers and buyers (Bowles, Edwards, and Roosevelt 2005: 59). Since in such cases producers and consumers do not take into account the full social costs and benefits of their choices, self-interested action will not allocate resources efficiently.

The conditions for Pareto optimality can be viewed in two ways. The first, and less convincing, way is to argue that economics shows free market capitalism to be a paragon of efficiency. Simplistic as this view is, it has nevertheless gained wide acceptance among scholars, journalists, politicians, and other opinion makers who either do not understand or choose to underplay and ignore the unrealistic conditions that market efficiency presupposes.

Long on the defensive, the second interpretation has gained more credence ever since economic crisis convinced even then-President Bush (2008) that "the market [wa]s not functioning properly." In this interpretation markets cannot by themselves ensure economic efficiency, since they are prone to a variety of 'market failures'. It is therefore incumbent on the government to take corrective action that minimizes the incidence and disruptive effect of such failures. In addition to providing public goods and addressing negative externalities, such action includes regulation of financial markets and counter-cyclical fiscal and monetary policies that prevent a downward spiral whenever a capitalist crisis erupts.

The concept of market failures endows neoclassical economic theory with some ideological and policy flexibility, which is evident in debates between liberal and conservative neoclassical economists. The former tend to be more willing to acknowledge both the threat to the general well-being that market failures pose and the need for government action that they create. The latter, by contrast, underplay market failures and warn against the risk of 'government failures,' whenever government action against market failures ends up making things worse. This ideological flexibility also accounts for the long-standing tendency of policy-makers to respond to serious capitalist crises through successive oscillations between periods of deregulation and relatively less government intervention, and periods when the government steps in to clean up the wreckage that free market capitalism leaves in its stead.[6]

As a number of theorists have pointed out, moreover, the concept of market failure is broad enough to accommodate a wide range of social and economic policy regimes, including the extensive welfare states that have in the past characterized the affluent countries of North and Western Europe (see Block 1994b, Esping-Andersen 1994). All in all, neoclassical economics illustrates what sociologists might describe as a functionalist approach to the question of scarcity. Just as sociological functionalism often assumes that social institutions are designed to meet people's needs, neoclassical economics tends to view capitalism as an effective and rational response to the challenge of material scarcity. While neoclassical economists may disagree on which mix between markets and government intervention makes it possible for capitalism to respond to scarcity in an effective and rational manner, none of them ever doubts that such a mix exists. In this respect, what E. Roy Weintraub (2002) says about economists in general may be more appropriate for neoclassical economists in particular:

> Economists publicly disagree with each other so often that they are easy targets for standup comedians. Yet non-economists may not realize that the disagreements are mostly over the details – the way in which the big picture is to be focused on the small screen.

And, as Weintraub (2002) also makes clear, this orthodoxy is defended fiercely indeed:

> The status of non-neoclassical economists in the economics departments in English-speaking universities is similar to that of flat-earthers in geography departments: it is safer to voice such opinions after one has tenure, if at all.[7]

No wonder, then, that, when it comes to the question of scarcity, it is neoclassical economics that represents the conventional wisdom which informs the thoughts and actions of economic elites and ordinary citizens alike.

While this chapter provides a first overview of the fundamental elements of this conventional wisdom, the critique of neoclassical economics will be an important theme in the chapters that follow. I will undertake this critique from the standpoint of an alternative theoretical approach that highlights the crucial influence of the logic of profit and capital accumulation on the configurations of scarcity that people around the world have to navigate and struggle over. It is, therefore, to the relationship between this logic and the configurations of scarcity that it brings about that I now turn.

3 SCARCITY AND CAPITAL ACCUMULATION

Unlike neoclassical economics, this work does not view capitalist markets as benign mechanisms that efficiently respond to the challenge of material scarcity. One purpose of this chapter is to begin to challenge the idea that scarcity is a pre-existing, 'exogenous' datum which is a cause but not also an effect of economic dynamics.[1] Another is to connect people's experience of scarcity in today's society to the search for profit that has long driven social, economic, and technological change in capitalist societies.[2] While this chapter provides a first overview of the connection between the search for profit and the configurations of scarcity facing individuals and groups the world over, the ones that follow discuss in greater detail both the demand and the supply side of this connection.

This chapter places special emphasis on the impact that capitalism's crisis tendencies have on the configurations of scarcity that prevail within capitalist societies, and argues against the view that a post-capitalist society has to abolish scarcity altogether. Scarcity is not problematic in itself, since it may accompany the enrichment of human needs and desires that a post-capitalist society may well promote. What is problematic is the undemocratic determination of the configurations of scarcity that people live under. This is the reason for the inhumane and ecologically unsustainable configurations of scarcity in capitalist societies, and this was, as this chapter also argues, one of the problematic features of twentieth-century Soviet-style regimes. An economically democratic society, by contrast, will give rise to configurations of scarcity consistent with human well-being and the ecological integrity of the planet.

THE SOURCE OF CAPITALISM'S TECHNOLOGICAL DYNAMISM

As Marxist and neo-Marxist economists and social scientists have long argued, capitalist profit stems from the ability of the capitalist class to extract surplus labor from workers (see Marx 1977, Bowles et al. 2005: 143–5, Sweezy 1942: 59–63). This extraction of surplus labor is not unique to capitalist society, but present "[w]herever a part of society possesses the monopoly of the means of production"

(Marx 1977: 344–5). This monopoly gives the owning class leverage over the direct producers, who have to give up part of what they produce to the owners. Owning classes in the past have used this surplus in a variety of ways. In addition to using part of the surplus to support the affluent lifestyles of their members, they have also used this surplus to erect public and religious monuments (Bowles et al. 2005: 101), construct public projects, such as "canals, dykes and other hydrographical works essential for irrigation" (Mandel 1968: 41), and so on.

What sets capitalism apart is not just the difficulty of recognizing the extraction of surplus labor in a system that gives workers the option of not signing the labor contract offered to them by their employer. Even more important for the purposes of this work is the effect of market competition on the use of the surplus. To remain members of the owning class and continue to enjoy the advantages of that position, capitalists have to stay ahead of the competition. To do so, they can only consume a small part of the surplus they extract from workers because only the capitalist who reinvests can hope to remain competitive.[3]

Capitalists, on the other hand, who respond to 'the desire for enjoyment' more than 'the passion for accumulation' (cf. Marx 1977: 741) will soon find themselves "eliminate[ed] from the ruling class" (Sweezy 1942: 339).[4] It is out of this systemic pressure to accumulate wealth by reinvesting the surplus that workers produce but don't keep that the peculiar economic and technological dynamism of capitalist society arises (see Bowles, Edwards, and Roosevelt 2005, ch. 7).

Even critics of capitalist society, such as Marx, have recognized and celebrated its dynamism (see Marx and Engels 1978). One manifestation of this dynamism is the dizzying increase in the productivity of labor that capitalism has made possible. Illustrating the magnitude of this increase, Bowles and Edwards (1993: 8) report that "it took 1430 times as long to spin yarn in 1750," while Bowles and colleagues (2005: 7) add that agricultural labor in the United States is 100 times more productive today than it was in 1830. Another effect of this dynamism has been the increase of the world's per capita output by a factor of ten since 1820 (Bowles et al. 2005: 12). This dynamism is promising insofar as it creates technical means that could drastically reduce both human suffering around the world and the time people spend working. While, as I argue below, these technical means do not necessarily make it possible to eliminate scarcity altogether, they do raise the possibility of using

scarce resources in ways far more conducive to human well-being
and enjoyment than is currently the case.

As I will argue in later chapters, capitalism cannot use scarce
resources in a rational, humane, and ecologically sustainable fashion
because of its undemocratic nature. Capitalism is undemocratic
insofar as it does not allow all human beings to have an equal say
over the economic decisions that profoundly affect their lives. The
fact that workers do not control the surplus they produce does
not just lead to economic inequalities, poverty, and great levels of
unnecessary human suffering. It also has profound implications for
the kind of culture we have, for the natural environment we live
in, and for the democratic integrity of the political system we live
under. As I will argue, the exclusion, under capitalism, of the many
from important economic decisions, including decisions regarding
the use of the surplus, predictably leads to great human suffering,
a deepening ecological crisis, and a consumerist culture that fails
to satisfy. All these phenomena form part of the configurations
of scarcity that capitalism creates. All these phenomena, in other
words, form part of the combination of human needs and wants,
on the demand side, and of the distribution and employment of
material resources, on the supply side, which has developed under
the long-term influence of the logic of profit.

Linking the configurations of scarcity prevailing in today's
world to the logic of profit leads to an understanding of scarcity
that is different from, and more dynamic than, that of neoclassical economics. As Richard Wolff and Stephen Resnick (1987:46)
point out, neoclassical economics views both people's productive
abilities and their tastes as extra-economic factors. As a result, this
view obscures and ignores the tendency of capitalist economies to
generate perpetually changing configurations of scarcity.

The search for profit constantly changes the prevailing configurations of scarcity because the constant reinvestment of the economic
surplus revolutionizes both the productive forces, and the goods and
services that workers produce and consumers desire. Insofar as the
dynamism of the capitalist economy keeps unsettling the universe of
commodities and needs, it also keeps reshuffling the parameters and
constraints within which individuals and economic agents pursue
their objectives. Thus, technological developments do not just greatly
increase the production of wealth and bring change to the supply
side parameters of the configurations of scarcity that capitalism
generates. By contributing to the creation of new commodities,
they also contribute to the rise of new desires that also change

the demand-side parameters of these configurations. Increasingly, moreover, these changing configurations involve the creation of new forms of scarcity, such as the environmental scarcities emerging out of the rapid ecological degradation that accompanies the endless pursuit of profit.

ECONOMIC CRISES AND THE CYCLICAL NATURE OF CAPITALISM'S CONFIGURATIONS OF SCARCITY

The constant change in capitalism's configurations of scarcity is not just a function of the long-term effects of the single-minded search for profit. In affecting every individual's access to the material means of subsistence, capitalism's boom and bust cycles also affect the configurations of scarcity they are faced with in their everyday lives. It is this cyclical dimension of the configurations of scarcity facing people in capitalist society that is the focus of this section.

Marx and Engels (1978: 478) have pointed out the paradoxical nature of capitalism's "epidemic[s] of overproduction" which periodically create the appearance that "a famine, a universal war of devastation ha[s] cut off the supply of every means of subsistence." "In all earlier epochs," Marx and Engels (1978: 478) add, such epidemics "would have seemed an absurdity," since they result not from a lack of resources but from the existence of "too much civilization, too much means of subsistence, too much industry, too much commerce." This paradoxical phenomenon is a manifestation, Marx and Engels thought, of the contradictory nature of capitalist society and the tendency of its relations of production to fetter the further development of the forces of production.

While Marxist economic literature has long debated the different mechanisms that result in recurrent capitalist crises,[5] Marx and Engels's discussion in the *Manifesto* points to something that all capitalist crises have in common, namely the waste that results from capitalism's periodic inability to fully employ available productive resources. This inability is not surprising. As the motivation for production in capitalist society is profit, anything that undercuts profits can trigger the outbreak of a crisis. When this happens, the configurations of scarcity facing individuals deteriorate, as the material means at their disposal shrink. More importantly for our purposes, they do so not because of a lack of resources or a reduction in the economic system's productive potential, but because of the operational logic of a system based on profit.[6]

This means that under capitalism there is more to scarcity than a gap between people's material desires and society's productive potential. The most salient feature of the configurations of scarcity that capitalist crises create is the suffering that results from the capitalist system's periodic inability to put people and productive equipment to work. This periodic inability cannot be blamed on people's wants, on society's productive potential, or on the gap between them. This inability stems from the overriding influence of the logic of profit over the configurations of scarcity that capitalism generates.

In this sense, capitalism's configurations of scarcity are marked by a perpetual oscillation between periods of relative economic prosperity, in which economic insecurity and unemployment stay at a 'normal' level, and periods of economic crisis, in which skyrocketing levels of economic insecurity and unemployment wreak havoc with people's lives. A recent study by a researcher at the Harvard School of Public Health concluded, for example, that

> Workers who lost a job through no fault of their own ... were twice as likely to report developing a new ailment like high blood pressure, diabetes or heart disease over the next year and a half, compared to people who were continuously employed.
> Interestingly, the risk was just as high for those who found new jobs quickly as it was for those who remained unemployed.[7]
>
> (Rabin 2009)

The negative health impact of capitalist crises is, moreover, not unique to those losing their jobs. Describing people's response to the economic crisis, a 2009 *New York Times* article was reporting that "[a]nxiety, depression and stress are troubling people everywhere, many not suffering significant economic losses, but worrying they will or simply reacting to pervasive uncertainty" (Belluck 2009). As a result, a Washington therapist reported, "People are coming in more with severe anxiety or more marital strife, some domestic violence, some substance abuse" (Belluck 2009).

Given the regularity of capitalism's economic crises, the toll these crises inflict on human beings is integral to the process through which people's experience of scarcity is socially constructed. This toll partly stems from the limited control that, under capitalism, most people have over their economic lives. The experience of Anne Hubbard, one of the people interviewed in the *New York Times* article just mentioned, illustrates this basic fact. Ms. Hubbard, a graphic designer from Massachusetts, experienced panic attacks as a result of the current crisis and had to turn to therapy and medication, even though she and her family were not facing any financial problems. Recounting her ordeal, Ms. Hubbard "said the weakening economy made her 'fear that even if you do everything right, something bad can happen to you'" (Belluck 2009).[8]

These examples show that capitalist crises inevitably change both sides of the neoclassical scarcity equation (or inequality, since the side of wants is always greater than that of the productive potential). By undercutting people's health, family life, and self-esteem, capitalist crises create the need or desire for health care, medication, therapy, substances such as alcohol and drugs (and then professional health to kick those harmful habits), family counseling, and so on. The effect of unemployment on people's health as well as on their skills also diminishes the productive resources that society can call upon to meet the increased needs and desires.[9] Thus, to the extent that the search for profit triggers recurrent economic crises, it also bears responsibility for the devastating configurations of scarcity that such crises entail.

SCARCITY AND THE LONG-TERM EVOLUTION OF THE CAPITALIST SYSTEM

We have so far discussed capitalism's long-term technological dynamism as well as its cyclical nature. As we saw, both these features of capitalist development have an impact on the configurations of scarcity we all face in our everyday lives. At least as important are the ways in which capitalism as a social and economic system evolves over long periods of time. Such long-term evolution also has important implications for the configurations of scarcity people face. This section illustrates this point through a discussion of Paul Baran and Paul Sweezy's *Monopoly Capital* (1966). My choice to pay close attention to this work does not signify complete support of its analysis. On the contrary, one reason I chose it is so that I can discuss and criticize an assumption Baran and Sweezy share with many other Marxist theorists. This is the assumption that the abolition of scarcity is already possible, and that it only requires transition to a socialist society that would use the productive forces already in existence more rationally than capitalism ever could.

The other reason I discuss Baran and Sweezy's work is because it demonstrates the attention we need to pay to the qualitative aspects of the configurations of scarcity within capitalist societies. In analyzing and evaluating these configurations, it is not enough to compare the quantity of wealth actually produced to people's material desires or to society's productive potential. Such quantitative dimensions of the prevailing configurations of scarcity are undoubtedly important, but they do not tell us everything we need to know. As my discussion below suggests, Baran and Sweezy's analysis shows the need to see the quality of the wealth produced within a society as an important dimension of its configurations of scarcity, as well as to examine possible links between this qualitative dimension and its quantitative counterpart.

Baran and Sweezy's analysis responds to the tendency of neoclassical economics to downplay the important ways in which capitalism evolved throughout the twentieth century. According to Baran and Sweezy (1966: 53), the small firms with no power to control prices that are the mainstay of neoclassical economic models no longer dominate contemporary economic life. Such firms now labor in the shadow of giant corporations "producing a significant share of the output of an industry, or even several industries, and able to control its prices" (Baran and Sweezy 1966: 6). Possessing "attributes which were once thought to be possessed only by monopolies," contemporary capitalism flies in the face of the competitive neoclassical model (Baran and Sweezy 1966: 6). This development completely invalidates the Smithian and neoclassical assumption that capitalist markets can be trusted to produce outcomes conducive to human "welfare and happiness" (Baran and Sweezy 1966: 56).

In Baran and Sweezy's (1966: 58) view, the oligopolistic structure of the economy allows the dominant corporations in each industry to become price setters and avoid cut-throat price competition. Instead, companies compete for market share only in ways that do not reduce prices and profits to the levels that would prevail in a truly competitive market. Thus, competition does not disappear and its persistence creates "a strong positive incentive for the large corporation in an oligopolistic industry not only to seek continuously to cut its costs but to do so faster than its rivals" (Baran and Sweezy 1966: 69). Indeed, companies that successfully reduce costs are well positioned to pursue non-price forms of competition, such as "advertising, research, development of new product varieties, extra services," and to make a bid for an increased market share. Conversely, companies that fail to do so are "soon in trouble" (Baran and Sweezy 1966: 69).

Since, however, the exclusion of price competition prevents cost reductions from lowering prices, the race to reduce costs leads to a rising surplus. As the sustainability of this surplus, however, depends on consuming and finding investment outlets for this surplus, the fact that such outlets are not forthcoming undercuts aggregate demand, thus giving rise to a major contradiction.[10] "Since surplus which cannot be absorbed will not be produced, it follows that the normal state of the monopoly capitalist economy is stagnation ... this means chronic underutilization of available human and material resources" (Baran and Sweezy 1966: 108). In this context, the experience of scarcity 'by the ordinary citizen' takes a form that directly contradicts the experience of scarcity assumed by neoclassical economics.

> To him, the economic problem appears to be the very opposite of what the textbooks say it is: not how best to utilize scarce resources but how to dispose of the products of superabundant resources .... If he is a worker, the ubiquitous fact of unemployment teaches him that the supply of labor is always greater than the demand. If he is a farmer, he struggles to stay afloat in a sea of surpluses. If he is a businessman, his sales persistently fall short of what he could profitably produce.
>
> (Baran and Sweezy 1966: 109)

In the competitive capitalism described by Marx and Engels, Baran and Sweezy suggest, overproduction crises were "a temporary derangement ... under monopoly capitalism ... 'too much' appear[s] as a pervasive problem affecting everyone at all times" (1966: 109).

Deep economic crises, such as the present one, would therefore not have surprised Baran and Sweezy.[11] Indeed, Baran and Sweezy suggest, the only reason this kind of crisis is not permanently present in contemporary capitalism is the pervasive production of waste that bolsters economic output and employment. Part of this waste takes the form of the immense economic resources devoted to boosting consumption by manufacturing human needs (see Baran and Sweezy 1966, ch. 5). Another part of this waste takes the form of growing levels of military spending (Baran and Sweezy 1966, chs 6, 7).[12]

This implies that capitalism's crisis tendencies do not just lead to an oscillation between the configurations of scarcity specific to times of relative prosperity and those specific to times of economic crisis. Coloring even the configurations of scarcity associated with times of prosperity, capitalism's crisis tendencies shape not just the quantity of the wealth produced but also its quality. In fact, quantity and quality interact as the deteriorating quality of the wealth produced helps to avert a collapse of the quantity of wealth produced. As Baran and

Sweezy (1966: 142) put it in their discussion of government expenditure, "the uses to which government puts the surplus which it absorbs are narrowly circumscribed by the nature of monopoly capitalist society and as time goes on become more and more irrational and destructive." The fact, in other words, that government expenditure can moderate pressures of economic stagnation and collapse does not change the fact that the 'wealth' this expenditure produces would have done much more to meet human needs if, instead of financing interminable arms races and military buildups, it was channeled into education, housing, healthcare, and other valuable social services. In the configurations of scarcity that result from this process, output and employment may be greater than they would have been in the absence of government spending, but the nature of this output is not conducive to the maximization of human welfare.

In explaining why the economic output financed by government spending takes destructive forms, such as military expenditures, Baran and Sweezy (1966: 173) point out that they are more consistent with the imperative of capital accumulation than social expenditures which may be more beneficial to the general population but which also threaten capitalist profit as well as "class privileges or ... the stability of the class structure." Thus, just as Marx and Engels's discussion of crises of overproduction supplements the neoclassical understanding of scarcity as a gap between human wants and productive potential with an understanding of the dynamic and cyclical nature of the configurations of scarcity that capitalism creates, Baran and Sweezy's analysis shows that the quality of the wealth produced is as important an aspect of those configurations as its quantity. For the purposes of this book this is an insight that is far more important than the specific claims that Baran and Sweezy's theory of monopoly capitalism advances. One could counter to Baran and Sweezy's theory the fact that economic globalization may have actually "reduced economic concentration" (Bowles et al. 2005: 280). It is much harder to dispute, though, Baran and Sweezy's claim that, its contribution to economic growth and employment notwithstanding, a significant portion of the output in contemporary capitalist societies takes destructive forms that do little to add to human well-being.

DO WE NEED TO ABOLISH SCARCITY?

Going further than their insight into the need to consider the quality of the output that capitalism produces, Baran and Sweezy also argue, however, that the productive potential generated by monopoly capitalism makes it "objectively possible to eliminate scarcity" (1966: 353). With the transition from competitive to monopoly capitalism "[h]uman and material resources remain idle," thus refuting the claim that capitalist markets lead to an efficient use of scarce resources. Instead, even the resources that are employed are to an increasing extent devoted to activities the products of which are, when "judged by genuine human needs, useless, wasteful, or positively destructive" (Baran and Sweezy 1966: 344). The purpose of this section is to question Baran and Sweezy's assumption that abolishing scarcity must be one of the features of any desirable post-capitalist social order. I will argue that it is not scarcity in itself that is the problem, but rather the inhumane and ecologically destructive configurations of scarcity that capitalism generates. In an economically democratic post-capitalist society, scarcity might persist as people's wants and desire for free time continued to evolve. The crucial difference, however, would be that both the formation of wants and the distribution of resources in such a society would create drastically different configurations of scarcity that would be much more conducive to human welfare and the ecological integrity of the planet.

Explaining what they mean by the possibility to eliminate scarcity, Baran and Sweezy assert that "[i]n the United States today the means already exist for overcoming poverty, for supplying everyone with the necessities and conveniences of life, for giving to all a genuinely rounded education and the free time to develop their faculties to the full" (1966: 344), Moreover, Baran and Sweezy argue, 'automation and cybernation' have brought to an end the era in which 'the vast majority of mankind' was inevitably faced with "life-long labor and bare subsistence standards of living" (1966: 352). "Under conditions such as prevail in the United States today [continued belief in the inevitability of scarcity] is false consciousness par excellence" (Baran and Sweezy 1966: 352–3). Thus, Baran and Sweezy imply, the premise at the basis of neoclassical economics is nothing but a misleading ideology.

Baran and Sweezy's claims regarding scarcity raise as many questions as the neoclassical economics they criticize. To begin with, capitalism has generated a seemingly infinite cornucopia of machines and gadgets, all of which claim to add to our personal comfort, to save us trouble, to qualify, in short, as conveniences. Some of these conveniences, like the private automobile, are, as Baran and Sweezy (1966: 174) themselves recognized in their discussion of the impact of "the cancerous growth of the automobile complex" on cities, neighborhoods, and American society's transportation system, very destructive, and have themselves become a source of new forms of environmental scarcity. In addition, the production and consumption of all conveniences draws on the planet's resources and generates pollution that taxes the planet's 'sinks.'

In view of these facts, which are not inconsistent with Sweezy's (2004) own discussion, in later years, of environmental degradation, it is clear that Baran and Sweezy's formulation of what it would mean to overcome scarcity is much more problematic today than it was when *Monopoly Capital* was first published. Indeed, in the configuration of scarcity generated by early twenty-first-century capitalism, it may not be scarcity in the abstract that represents the most pernicious ideology, but rather the stubborn refusal in some quarters to recognize the existence of any ecological limits.

In fact, almost half a century after Baran and Sweezy's book it is increasingly obvious that capitalism's increased productivity, which led Baran and Sweezy to dismiss scarcity as a historically obsolete ideology, has been based on unconscionably high levels of ecological degradation in general, and carbon emissions in particular. Indeed, even Baran and Sweezy's followers recognize that the bid to defend US access to the natural resources necessary for economic growth and capital accumulation helps to explain the wars that US governments have initiated in recent years, as well as the persistence of high military spending even after the end of the Cold War (Foster, Holleman and McChesney 2008, Foster 2008b).

One could conceivably defend Baran and Sweezy's argument regarding the possibility of eliminating scarcity by arguing that most of the conveniences in contemporary capitalist societies do not pass Baran and Sweezy's 'genuine needs' test and thus do not deserve to be included in the conveniences that a post-capitalist society beyond scarcity would need to provide. In fact, Baran and Sweezy's own argument seems to point in that direction when they include among the people implicated in 'anti-human activities' "the tool and die makers turning out the intricate machinery needed for a new automobile model, the manufacturers of paper and ink and TV sets whose products are used to control and poison the minds of the people, and so on" (1966: 344).

One of the problems with such an argument, however, is that both the 'genuine needs' standard and its use in evaluating conveniences would probably prove to be at least as controversial as the conveniences this standard was called upon to evaluate. Any appeal to genuine human needs would raise deep philosophical questions regarding human nature, on which different people would probably take different positions.

This means, however, that, even in a future post-capitalist society, disagreements on the question of scarcity might persist. People who shared Baran and Sweezy's implicit philosophy of human nature might agree that the post-capitalist society in question had indeed overcome scarcity, while people who did not might very well disagree. Far from reflecting a false consciousness on the part of people who felt that, its advantages notwithstanding, this post-capitalist society had not eliminated scarcity, these disagreements would simply reflect a diversity of outlooks among the members of this post-capitalist society. As some theorists have pointed out, diversity of outlooks should not be seen as an obstacle to be overcome by any future non-capitalist society, but as one of the goals that such a society would seek to promote (Hahnel 2002, 2003). Indeed, to the extent that a social environment characterized by diversity of outlooks and lifestyles enriches everybody's life experience, a non-capitalist society the diversity of which prevented us from declaring that scarcity had been eliminated would arguably be preferable to a non-capitalist society that eliminated scarcity by ensuring that all its members shared a single philosophy of human nature.

One example might illustrate this point: is it impossible to imagine that even in a post-capitalist society there would be a greater desire, among people, to travel around the world than would be consistent with the ecological limits we have to respect? Any anti-capitalist from the global North who enjoys flying to Latin America, Africa, Asia, and Europe would have to admit that in a post-capitalist society they would have no more right to do that than the billions of people from the global South who would also love to do that but can currently not afford an airplane ticket. Since the traveling habits of many of today's anti-capitalist intellectuals and activists (and I include myself in that group) could not become universalized to include every single person on this planet, it is clear that in a post-capitalist society, which respected natural limits while giving everybody an equal chance to travel, the aspirations of people to travel might exceed the possibility of doing so. This gap between demand for traveling and the supply feasible given the ecological limits of the planet would signal the persistence of scarcity in a post-capitalist society which might still be infinitely more conducive to the well-being of all than the capitalist society we currently live under.

This example also illustrates the fact that scarcity in a post-capitalist society may persist precisely to the extent that this society creates the conditions for a richer life for all its members. A post-capitalist society that sought to create the conditions for a richer human life would probably also encourage the development and refinement of the needs and desires of its members, with all the material demands that such a refinement might entail. The desire of billions of people to travel around the world, for example, might very well be greater in a post-capitalist society than it is today, and result from the greater awareness of the members of such a society of the richness of cultures and the beauty of nature in faraway lands. The greater material demands that the satisfaction of people's refined desires will conceivably make on the economy and nature may in turn mean that the members of a post-capitalist society will not be able, or willing, to pursue the satisfaction of their desires up to the satiation point. Thus, while the refinement of human needs and desires will reshape the demand side of a post-capitalist society's configurations of scarcity, the satisfaction of these refined needs and desires will be constrained by a dimension of these configurations on the supply side, namely ecological limits.[13] The presence within the same society of these two opposing tendencies will both underline the continuing relevance of scarcity, and highlight the need of resolving the resulting dilemma in accordance with both the principle of economic democracy and that of ecological sustainability.

A related set of questions is raised by Baran and Sweezy's claim that the end of the inevitability of scarcity also spells the ends of "the inevitability of life-long labor and bare subsistence standards of living for the vast majority of mankind" (1966: 352). There is no question that the technological advances generated by capitalism do create the possibility of an alternative society that would allow all people both to satisfy more than their basic subsistence needs and to work less than they do under capitalism. But achieving this outcome by no means presupposes the overcoming of scarcity.

In fact, the very existence of reduced work time and increased standards of living as two distinct ways of improving human life will call for choices familiar to neoclassical economists. Indeed, one of the ways that, according to neoclassical economics, individuals negotiate scarcity is by weighing the attractions of material consumption against the 'disutility' of work. Thus, neoclassical economists assume that work is experienced as a 'bad,' while its opposite, 'leisure,' is a good that people can 'buy' by forgoing the wage they would have received if they had decided to work instead.

This view of work, which was also shared by Adam Smith, is, as both Marx and more contemporary economists have pointed out, by no means self-evident (Smith 1909: 39, Marx 1973: 610–11, Bowles et al. 2005: 286–7). Nevertheless, it certainly is the case that, as Bowles and colleagues (2005: 286) point out, work has an 'opportunity cost.' In other words, even if work does not necessarily have to be experienced as a 'bad,' it still does represent a sacrifice of time that could have been devoted to other (possibly more) enjoyable activities. In fact, this opportunity cost will increase even further in a post-capitalist society that puts an end to the poverty of leisure that, as Baran and Sweezy (1966: 348–9) so poignantly describe, prevails in contemporary capitalist societies. In other words, to the extent that it endowed people with the skills and time necessary to pursue challenging and creative activities that will make their free time more enjoyable, a post-capitalist society would also increase the sacrifice involved in devoting one's time to work rather than to alternative leisure activities.

This means that whatever could be said about the availability of material goods in a post-capitalist society, scarcity of time is likely to persist. But the persistence of scarcity of time should not obscure the great superiority of a post-capitalist society's configurations of scarcity over the configurations of scarcity confronting people around the world today. In capitalism scarcity of time often takes the form of overwork, which undermines people's health, happiness, and family and community life.[14] In a culturally rich post-capitalist society, by contrast, scarcity of time might persist because even a significant increase in people's free time might fail to keep up with the dramatically increased availability of compelling cultural and community activities that individuals could pursue in their free time.

This means that even such a society and its members may have to confront a tradeoff between consumption and work. Thus, for example, even a society that afforded everybody a comfortable standard of living by requiring them to work only three hours a day would have to decide whether to channel productivity increases into a further reduction of the workday or a further increase in people's living standards. Although such a scenario may sound utopian when compared with contemporary global capitalism's brutal realities, it is conceivable that even in this scenario there will still be many people who might have preferred both higher levels of consumption and even lower workdays.[15] To the extent that their aspirations exceeded their high standards of living and the seemingly ample free time available to them, scarcity, at least in the neoclassical sense of the term, would persist.

SCARCITY AND THE UNDEMOCRATIC LOGIC OF CAPITAL

The fact that a post-capitalist society could produce configurations of scarcity which served human well-being and protected the planet without eliminating scarcity completely suggests that the problem with capitalism is not that it does not abolish scarcity, but that its undemocratic nature predictably generates configurations of scarcity that are vastly inferior to those that could be attained through a move towards economic democracy. Indeed, it is the lack of economic democracy that accounts for the irrational configurations of scarcity that emerge out of Baran and Sweezy's analysis. Baran and Sweezy themselves highlight one aspect of the capitalist system's undemocratic character when they discuss the power of the economic oligarchy to channel the use of the surplus in ways that are beneficial to itself but irrational from the point of view of society as a whole. At least as important, however, is the fact that under capitalism all human beings, including capitalists themselves, are subordinated to the logic of capital accumulation. It is on this dimension of the undemocratic nature of the capitalist system that this section will focus.

As Sweezy himself recognizes, the pressure of capitalist competition means that, even to preserve their capital and continue enjoying the privileges, prestige and power associated with their class position, capitalists must tirelessly pursue profit and capital accumulation (1942: 79–81, 174–6, 339). Indeed, Sweezy argues,

> The objective of expanding capital is ... not one which capitalists are free to take or leave as they choose; they must pursue it on pain of elimination from the ruling class. This holds equally for actual owners of capital and for those who... come into the 'management' of capital, as not infrequently happens in the modern large corporation. Neither is in any sense a free agent. The ruling class under capitalism is made up of the functionaries of capital, those whose motives and objectives are prescribed for them by the specific historical form of their control over the means of production.
>
> (Sweezy 1942: 339)

The pressure to accumulate is, moreover, not alleviated by the fact that, with the rise of monopoly capitalism, it is increasingly corporations, rather than 'the individual businessman' that become the agents of capital accumulation (Baran and Sweezy 1966: 43). The curbing of price competition does not mean that competition disappears. As noted above, the focus of competition shifts to other areas, such as cost-cutting and the sales effort. Just as companies that are successful in these areas increase their profit and gain a competitive advantage, so does the position of less successful companies become more precarious. This is especially the case as successful companies can reinvest their higher profits to increase their competitive advantage even further through the pursuit of innovations that allow them to reduce costs even further, achieve production and market breakthroughs, and so on (Bowles et al. 2005: 257–68).

As profit and capital accumulation are conditions of corporate survival, corporate managers' ability to climb the corporate ladder depends on their contribution to corporate profitability, so that "the company man ... is dedicated to the advancement of his company precisely to the extent that he is dedicated to advancing himself" (Baran and Sweezy 1966: 38). Thus, corporate managers are ruled by the imperatives of capital accumulation just as business owners were and remain.

Baran and Sweezy correctly recognized that "[t]he ruling class under capitalism is made up of the functionaries of capital," but they did not fully appreciate the implications of this insight. To begin with, this insight means that, even though these functionaries form part of the ruling class, they only rule in the name of capital. The abstract logic of capital accumulation that governs their actions escapes human control and generates rapid economic and technological change precisely by making them more insecure than were the members of pre-capitalist ruling classes.

The capitalist ruling class thus rules only in the (admittedly important) sense that control over the means of production provides its members with a disproportionately great power to influence the terms under which they and all other socio-economic groups are subordinated to the logic of capital. In other words, their economic power allows them a greater impact over the parameters regulating the logic of capital accumulation that both they and all other socio-economic groups are forced to serve and adjust to. Recognition of this fact has important implications for how we interpret the significance of the surplus that the capitalist society generates. According to Baran and Sweezy, "[t]he size of the surplus is an index of productivity and wealth, of how much freedom a society has to accomplish whatever goals it may set for itself"(1966: 9). What this claim fails to recognize is that the unprecedented rise in the surplus that capitalism makes possible is due precisely to the fact that, as Sweezy pointed out in his earlier work on *The Theory of Capitalist Development* (1942), capitalists do not have a choice but to seek to expand their capital by any means necessary.

In this respect, however large the surplus produced by a capitalist society, its use reflects the abstract logic of capital accumulation much more than it does any independently formed goals that society and its members may have. In fact, central to the abstract logic of capital is, as Baran and Sweezy themselves point out, the 'elementality' of "a society which is governed as though by great natural forces, like wind and tide, to which men may seek to adjust but over which they have no control" (1966: 338).

Thus the large surplus capitalism produces does not increase the freedom of society but, on the contrary, reflects its subordination to the abstract logic of capital. In an economically democratic non-capitalist society a growing surplus would free humanity to pursue its freely determined goals. In capitalism this is not possible, both because of the system's oligarchic nature and because its logic of capital accumulation escapes people's control and subordinates them to its imperatives. Because of this, the irrationalities specific to monopoly capitalism cannot even be viewed as usurpation, by the capitalist oligarchy, of society's freedom to use the surplus according to its goals. These irrationalities, which include wasteful military spending and the sales effort, are simply the product of the oligarchy's adjustment to the changed conditions within which the logic of capital continues to unfold. In this respect, they serve as a reminder of a contradiction inherent in capitalism in all its forms: although capitalism increases the surplus, and therefore the potential for human freedom, it does so only by denying humanity the opportunity to control this surplus and to deploy it in a humane and ecologically sustainable fashion.

This contradiction often gives rise to social and class struggles over the distribution of resources and the contours of the configurations of scarcity prevailing at any given time.[16] The struggle against the logic of capital requires, however, not just a challenge of the privileges and advantages of the capitalist class and the socio-economic groups that wield power. A challenge that is defined in such narrow terms is likely to lead to little more than a struggle over the terms regulating the mutual subordination of the contending parties to the logic of capital. In other words, the struggle against the logic of capital cannot just take the form of fighting for changes that alleviate the burden of scarcity on the most exploited and oppressed groups in society. While such changes are important, the struggle against the logic of capital is above all a struggle for an alternative society that allows humanity to recapture control over the surplus it produces and to decide democratically how this surplus is to be used. In this sense, the struggle against the logic of capital is a struggle for a society that allows people to democratically determine the configurations of scarcity most consistent with their needs and desires.

A NOTE ON THE SOVIET EXPERIENCE

This discussion has an important political implication. To begin with, the view of the struggle against capital as a struggle for economic democracy means that it is no longer possible to accept Baran and Sweezy's endorsement of 'socialist countries' as positive examples of the "use [of] man's mastery over the forces of nature to build a rational society satisfying the human needs of human beings" (1966: 367). There have been various interpretations of Soviet-style regimes, but whether one understands them as Moshe Lewin (2005) does, as examples of 'bureaucratic absolutism,' or as Stephen Resnick and Richard Wolff (2002) do, as instances of 'state capitalism,' it is clear that these regimes did not give their citizens equal voice over the goals and priorities served by the economic system. Thus, such regimes were certainly not consistent with the concept of economic democracy I use in this work. As Resnick and Wolff (2002) have shown, moreover, the fact that the Soviet system did not allow democratic control over the surplus produced was at the center of the contradictions that contributed to the Soviet Union's eventual demise.

The struggles over the surplus that Resnick and Wolff discuss in their treatment of the Soviet experience can also be conceptualized as struggles over the changing configurations of scarcity that prevailed in the Soviet Union after the revolution of 1917. Indeed, Resnick and Wolff's analysis suggests that the expropriation of private capitalists after the revolution may have, at various times, ameliorated the conditions facing some of the most exploited and oppressed classes and social groups in the Soviet Union, but never allowed the population at large to determine democratically the configurations of scarcity they wanted to live under.[17]

Instead, as various scholars have argued, a number of factors contributed to the degeneration of the Soviet Union into an authoritarian regime (e.g. Kovel 2002: 201, Negri 2008: 12–17). To begin with, Russia did not have a strong democratic tradition, so the Tsarist legacy marked the new post-revolutionary society. Tracing the transformation of Soviet bureaucracy into an autonomous force which escaped the control of political authorities, Moshe Lewin has gone as far as to interpret Soviet history as an evolution "from a 'one-party to a 'no-party' system" and to attribute this development to the historical continuities between the post-revolutionary regime and "Tsarist traditions of state-building" (2005: 348, 380).[18]

Also important was the fact that the Soviet state that was born out of the revolution had to fight for survival against more powerful capitalist societies which initially attempted to repress the revolution, and which continued to pose a threat even after the end of the civil war that followed the revolution. The 'encirclement' of the Soviet Union by hostile capitalist powers forced the regime to industrialize at a brutally rapid pace that exacted a great human toll. Antonio Negri (2008: 14) in fact compares Stalinism with the brutal process of primitive accumulation that also marked the birth of capitalism in the West.[19] This process rapidly turned the Soviet Union into an economic and military superpower capable, as Moshe Lewin points out, to save not only itself but also Europe "from a Nazi domination that would have stretched from Brest to Vladivostok" (2005: 372). Nonetheless, Lewin adds, the Soviet Union's rise to the status of a superpower also "pushed it into an arms race that helped to perpetuate the worst, most conservative features of the system and to reduce its ability to reform itself" (2005: 385).[20]

This brief overview of the factors that contributed to the failings of the Soviet regime suggests that the configurations of scarcity that confronted Soviet citizens continued in crucial respects to be shaped by the logic of capital. The economic and technological dynamism emanating from this logic created a reality that could not be ignored, in view of the threat that a hostile capitalist world posed for the Soviet Union. To the extent that the threat posed by a dynamic and hostile capitalist bloc contributed to the authoritarian development of Soviet society, it also facilitated the emergence of a political and economic elite with disproportionate power to shape the configurations of scarcity facing Soviet citizens in accordance with its own priorities and interests. And despite the success of the Soviet regime in bringing about industrialization and modernization, the configurations of scarcity that accompanied these processes also included vast ecological destruction as one of their central components.[21]

All in all, the collapse of the Soviet Union and the transition of the countries of the Soviet bloc to capitalism have made it clear that, in addition to being undemocratic, the Soviet model of 'socialism' eventually proved incapable of meeting the challenges of an international environment that was in crucial ways shaped by the dynamic logic of capital. It is impossible to say whether Soviet society would have navigated this environment better if the strong libertarian impulse of the revolution had not been suppressed by the Bolsheviks.[22] What the Soviet experience does show, however, is that suspending or postponing the movement towards economic democracy in the name of surviving a hostile capitalist environment can no longer be considered a credible option for radical movements hoping to mount a fundamental challenge on the logic of capital.

4 SCARCITY, CAPITALIST EXPLOITATION, AND CONSUMPTION

If scarcity signifies a gap between people's material desires and a society's productive potential, understanding scarcity requires an analysis of how social and economic factors shape both people's desires and society's productive potential. While I have already noted the link between capitalism's technological dynamism, on one side, and the importance of competition and the logic of profit in that system, on the other, in this chapter I turn to the link between capitalism and the rise of a consumerist culture that has reshaped people's material desires. This is a link that neoclassical economics refuses to explore. The result is a tension that often haunts neoclassical analyses.

Lionel Robbins, for example, declares that economics is not "concerned with ends [i.e. people's desires and economic preferences] as such" but rather takes them "for granted" (1962: 31, 32). This treatment of preferences as an exogenous variable that pre-exists rather than interacting with economic life is typical of neoclassical economists (Wolff and Resnick 1987: 135). Nevertheless, Robbins himself contradicts it when he admits "in some societies there exist definite financial incentives to certain individuals to produce changes in ... the tastes of economic subjects by persuasion" (1962: 129).

Neoclassical economists, like Robbins, often justify their view of preferences as an exogenous variable by presenting economics as a value-free 'positive science' (Robbins 1962: vii, 91). The economist, according to this argument, does not and should not judge the worth of economic agents' ends. Abba Lerner (1972: 258), for example, contrasts the tasks of a social critic, who "may try to change some desires to others of which [she] approve[s] more" to that of an economist, who "must be concerned with the mechanisms for getting people what they want, no matter how these wants were acquired." Lerner rejects the idea that consumer preferences are "not genuine, because influenced or even created by advertising." For Lerner (1972: 258) telling people "what they 'really want'" is a "denial of [their] personality – a kind of rape of [their] integrity."

38

This view of the economist's task is closely linked to the neoclassical conception of economic efficiency which requires a use of scarce resources that satisfies individuals' existing preferences as fully as possible. This conception reflects the intellectual debt of neoclassical economics to methodological individualism, which views society as an aggregate of individuals rather than understanding social relations as constitutive of individuals and their desires.

As social historians, economists, and psychologists have long pointed out, however, in capitalist societies corporate interests and advertisers routinely use psychological research to manipulate consumers. They do so by targeting people's psychological insecurities and unmet psychological needs in ways that turn these insecurities and needs into fuel for the consumption of commodities (Ewen 1977, Kasser et al. 2003). Such consumption does not address these needs and insecurities, and may even perpetuate them and intensify them by inducing individuals to adopt unrealistic aspiration levels, which are likely to lead not only to dissatisfaction but also to growing levels of debt (Schor 1998). A socio-economic system that generates such outcomes may seem dysfunctional and yet, as Benjamin Barber (2007: 196) clearly recognizes, producing such outcomes is perfectly rational from the standpoint of capitalist corporations seeking to increase their sales and profit margins by any means necessary.

It is therefore not the economists and social theorists who point to the endogeneity of preferences in capitalist societies who 'rape' people's personality and integrity, but the corporate interests who use cutting-edge scientific research to manipulate the very consumers they claim to serve. The force of Lerner's conception of the role of economists stems from the appeal of "the idea of normally letting each member of society decide what is good for himself" (1972: 258). Because of its methodological individualism and 'humanism,' neoclassical economics views self-determination as an unproblematic trait of human nature, glossing over the extent to which social and economic relations can either undercut it or nurture it. In view of the real power of corporate capital over consumers, the ideal of individual self-determination requires economists who believe in it to question a system that instrumentalizes people and to contribute their expertise to the construction of an alternative system that would nurture rather than undermine people's ability to determine 'what is good for themselves.'

Two conclusions follow from this as well as from the more detailed analysis that I present in the rest of this chapter. First, the only goal that capitalism can pursue efficiently is not the satisfaction of consumers' needs but the maximization of corporate profit. These two goals do not coincide but, as I will argue later in this chapter, are often in conflict with each other. The growth of material consumption within capitalism does not enrich people's lives because it is the product of a toxic consumerist culture that is as contradictory to human satisfaction as it is beneficial to the forces of corporate capital that have long built it up and financed it. In this sense, the efficient pursuit of profit negates rather than serves the efficient satisfaction of consumers' wants.

This basic fact suggests a second conclusion. Far from promoting individual choice, capital uses the power it derives from private property and its control of society's economic surplus to shape people's preferences as well as their general culture in ways that promote the pursuit of profit. Instead of empowering people to decide what it is that they want to choose, capital reduces the concept of choice to an empty ideological slogan that helps to negate the very principle of choice it claims to support.

All in all, Lerner's distinction between the role of the economist and that of a social critic is problematic since it invests the economist with an aura of objectivity usually reserved for science, while casting any reference to the endogeneity of economic preferences as the domain of social critics expressing not objective facts but subjective values. In reality, the task of the economist, as Lerner defines it, is no more objective and ideologically neutral than that of the social critic. Given that corporate capital has both the incentive and the resources to manipulate consumers by shaping their preferences, a 'science' that focuses on the efficient satisfaction of the consumers' existing set of preferences bolsters a socio-economic system with little respect for the integrity of individuals. Affirming the value of efficiency as the only appropriate for economists diverts attention from the main threat to people's integrity, which comes from corporate power, not from social critics who could only dream of the sort of access to the general public enjoyed by corporate advertising and marketing campaigns. Thus, by implicitly casting the distinction between pro- and anti-capitalist values as a distinction between economics and social criticism, Lerner unwittingly subordinates economics to capitalism and presents the adoption of pro-capitalist values as a scientific commitment to the 'objectivity' of facts.[1] Lerner may be right to emphasize both the right of individuals to make their own decisions and the importance of economic efficiency in a world of scarce resources. His attack on critical accounts of the endogeneity of economic preferences, however, does less to advance these objectives than to bolster capitalism.

IS SCARCITY ONLY THE PRODUCT OF INFLATED NEEDS?

If neoclassical economists overlook the social construction of people's material desires, some social theorists go to the opposite extreme of treating it as the only source of scarcity. Marshall Sahlins and Nicholas Xenos, in particular, make an important contribution by emphasizing the link between scarcity and capitalism's inflation of material wants, but their conclusions are not devoid of weaknesses.

Hunters and gatherers as 'the first affluent society'?

In "The first affluent society," Sahlins takes on both neoclassical economics and the traditional view that hunters and gatherers lived a life of deprivation, which was dominated by the search for food. Alluding to Robbins' discussion of scarcity as humanity's tragic predicament,[2] Sahlins declares that "[t]o assert that the hunters are affluent is to deny ... that the human condition is an ordained tragedy, with man the prisoner at hard labor of a perpetual disparity between his unlimited wants and his insufficient means" (1972: 1). The idea of unlimited wants, Sahlins (1972: 3) suggests, constitutes a form of 'bourgeois ethnocentrism' that lurks behind the assumption that hunters and gatherers must have led a dismal existence. Once unlimited wants are assumed, no other conclusion seems possible in view of the hunters and gatherers' 'technical incompetence' (Sahlins 1972: 1).

Sahlins insists, by contrast, that scarcity is not the product of deficient technical means, but a relation between technical means and people's material desires. Defining an affluent society as "one in which all the people's material wants are easily satisfied," Sahlins points out that "there is ... a Zen road to affluence," which requires not the perfection of technical means but human wants that "are finite and few" (1972: 2). Exemplifying this alternative road to affluence, hunting and gathering societies proved that "the 'economic problem' is easily solvable by Paleolithic techniques. But then, it was not until culture neared the height of its material achievements that it erected a shrine to the Unattainable: Infinite Needs" (Sahlins 1972: 39).

In Sahlins's view, therefore, the 'economic problem' as conceived by mainstream economics only arises from the postulate of infinite needs. This postulate naturalizes scarcity, presenting 'economic man' not as a product of capitalist society but as a trans-historical prototype of rational economic behavior. Scarcity, Sahlins believes, is more intense in capitalist society because of both the inequalities it generates and the inflation of material wants that it brings about.

Hunting and gathering societies were, by comparison, affluent because their members could satisfy their needs with minimal effort. To support his view, Sahlins cites ethnographic accounts suggesting that in hunting-gathering societies "the food quest is so successful that half the time the people seem not to know what to do with themselves" (1972: 11). As a result, in these societies "leisure is abundant, and there is a greater amount of sleep ... than in any other ... society" (Sahlins 1972: 14). Indeed, many hunting-gathering groups "refused to take up agriculture ... 'mainly on the grounds that this would involve too much hard work'" (Sahlins 1972: 27).[3]

In view of his definition of affluence, Sahlins's (1972: 1) designation of hunters and gatherers as the "original affluent society" implies that hunting and gathering societies easily satisfied "all the people's material wants." This claim is still controversial in the literature since Sahlins's classic essay. Nurit Bird-David (1997), for example, challenges the empirical basis of Sahlins's argument and his attribution to hunters and gatherers of a Zen way to affluence. In Bird-David's view, hunters and gatherers are best described in terms of "a third way – the 'sharing way' – to affluence. Their way is based on assumptions appropriate to their sharing economy – that material wants are linked with material means that are available for sharing. (They want a share of however much is available)" (1997: 129). And Nolan and Lenski (1998: 101) have suggested that, in his attempt to counter the overly dismal depictions of hunting and gathering life that had dominated academic literature in the past, Sahlins's description of hunters and gatherers as the original affluent society may have veered too far in the opposite direction.

Interestingly, even Sahlins's own account contradicts this description. Indeed, there is at least one need in hunting and gathering societies that these societies did not satisfy. This is the need for mobility. As Sahlins (1972: 31) points out, hunters and gatherers have to lead a nomadic life because hunting invariably ends up decreasing "the local carrying capacity." This constant mobility accounts for the fact that hunters and gatherers are not interested in material possessions, especially bulky ones that cannot be easily transported (Sahlins 1972: 12). This is why "[o]f the hunter it is truly said that his wealth is a burden" (Sahlins 1972: 11).

The premise of Sahlins's 'first affluent society thesis' is that the impact of their nomadic lifestyle on their desire for possessions makes it easier for hunting and gathering societies to conquer scarcity. In formulating this thesis, however, Sahlins does not take fully into account the implications of the impact that this nomadic lifestyle has on those members of hunting and gathering societies who cannot transport themselves. In Sahlins's own words,

> The same policy of debarassment is in play on the level of people ... infanticide, senilicide ... etc., practices for which many food-collecting people are well-known .... The people eliminated, as hunters sometimes sadly tell, are precisely those who cannot effectively transport themselves, who would hinder the movement of family and camp. Hunters may be obliged to handle people and goods in parallel ways, the draconic population policy an expression of the same ecology as the ascetic economy. More, these tactics of demographic restraint ... form part of a larger policy for counteracting diminishing returns in subsistence. A local group becomes vulnerable to diminishing returns – so to a greater velocity of movement, or else to fission – in proportion to its size (other things equal).
>
> (Sahlins 1972: 33–4)

Clearly, this passage contradicts Sahlins's rosy view of hunters and gatherers, since a society that can only feed the majority of its members by sacrificing the less mobile minority does not truly "satisfy all the people's material wants" and thus cannot, by Sahlins's (1972: 1) own definition, qualify as an affluent society. In other words, although hunting and gathering societies reduce human needs in one respect, they also create a need for transportation that lack of adequate transportation technologies prevents them from satisfying. While Sahlins may, therefore, be correct to point out that technological advances cannot by themselves lead to the conquest of scarcity, he is certainly not correct in presenting the hunters and gatherers as proof that "the 'economic problem' is easily solvable by paleolithic techniques" (Sahlins 1972: 39).

The passage above also suggests that it is the hunting and gathering society's low technical level and its inability to overcome scarcity which force its members "to handle people and goods in parallel ways." Treating goods as disposable and easily replaceable could, as Sahlins suggests, be viewed as a sign not of poverty but of freedom from material acquisitiveness. Hunters and gatherers, Sahlins (1972:

14–15) argues, are free because their ascetic lifestyle is not the effect of an effort to restrain their desires for material goods. Such an effort is not necessary because hunters and gatherers never developed the acquisitive human nature postulated by neoclassical economics in the first place. The claim regarding hunters and gatherers' freedom is, however, less easy to defend in the case of treating people as disposable. The fact that, by Sahlins's own admission, hunters and gatherers often speak of cases of infanticide and senilicide with sadness suggests that such practices have a negative effect not just on those who perish but also on those who survive. All in all, Sahlins's otherwise provocative argument falls short of justifying the paradoxical designation of hunters and gatherers as "the original affluent society."

Nicholas Xenos and the invention of scarcity

While Nicholas Xenos also understands scarcity as a paradoxical phenomenon, his focus is not on hunters and gatherers but on modern society. His goal is to explain "why … the concept of scarcity as a fundamental aspect of the human condition was born in the relatively affluent societies of the modern west" (1989: ix). While his work is in part an intellectual history of the concept of scarcity from Hume to Keynes, Xenos also attempts to trace the experience of scarcity back to the conditions of capitalist modernity, with their loosening of the rigid pre-capitalist status order. The rise of capitalist modernity destabilized the traditional social order and ushered in changes that both enriched the bourgeoisie and precipitated the economic decline of landed aristocracy. In addition, it endowed the status order with a fluidity that was absent from precapitalist societies in which an individual's position was "defined exclusively by birth … and … the signs of one rank were out of bounds to any other" (Xenos 1989: 16). The fluidity of status that capitalism introduced stemmed from the increasing role that markets were starting to play both in consumption and in the social distribution of the marks of social position.

One effect of this growing importance of markets was a partial delinking of 'birth' and 'wealth' (Xenos 1989: 17). In particular, the bourgeoisie increasingly emulated the consumption patterns of the nobility in an attempt to lay claim to the social status that the nobility had traditionally enjoyed. More generally, by loosening the boundaries between different status groups, capitalist modernity paved the road to competitive consumption as a way of both improving one's social position and of defending one's position from pretenders belonging to social groups below one's own (Xenos 1989: 90).[4]

In this context, the growing phenomenon of ever-changing fashions did not only represent a weapon the most affluent could wield against their would-be imitators. It was also a means that could be skillfully exploited by profit-seeking producers and merchants. In fact, 'masters of salesmanship' early on developed marketing techniques that exploited such social phenomena as competitive consumption and fashion (Xenos 1989: 9–10).

It was this new social landscape of fashion, competitive consumption, the availability (thanks to trade) of new luxuries and exotic products, and new marketing methods, which, according to Xenos, gave rise to the distinctively modern experience of scarcity. The new universe of goods confronting individuals triggered desire because these marks of distinction now seemed within reach. As family name and descent were no longer a requirement for their possession, goods doubling as status symbols were available to anyone willing to pay the price. Money had become "the mediator of desire" (Xenos 1989: 10).

An opportunity for the middle classes and those willing and able to turn their newfound financial prowess into social status, this development was also a threat to those on the top of the social status order. Thus, the pressures this new money-centered landscape of consumption exerted on the individuals navigating it also helped to reproduce it. "Such a world necessitates a constant scrambling after the latest luxuries in order to keep up and to keep in front. Acquisitiveness is thus built into the desire merely to maintain one's social standing" (Xenos 1989: 19).

This pursuit of social status through consumption is as frustrating as it is appealing, however, because one's ability to play this game successfully clashes with the persistent class inequalities underlying the more fluid, and thus seemingly more democratic, stratification system of modern societies.

The struggle to establish one's identity and position is ceaseless because there are no objectively fixed statuses, but the struggle tends to reproduce the de facto statuses that do exist. The wealthier find it easier to shift their consumption from one set of objects to another than do those with less wealth. A competitive hierarchy is established, with no rest for anyone but with real upward movement forestalled.

(Xenos 1989: 98)[5]

The result is an upward spiral of consumption that not only fails to increase anyone's satisfaction, but, as other scholars have pointed out, also diverts resources from alternative uses, such as valuable public programs, leisure, and other goods with greater potential to contribute to the general well-being.[6]

Faced with the frustrating reality of scarcity that competitive consumption creates, people haplessly oscillate, according to Xenos, between attempts to reduce inequalities between themselves and those above them, and attempts to fend off the demands of those below them. Unable to envisage any credible way out of the frustrating predicament that he describes, Xenos concludes that "[p]erhaps the best we can hope for is to free our minds from the concept that has taken hold of it, but such understanding is the first stage of freedom from our self-imposed slavery" (1989: 117).

Apart from being unsatisfying, this conclusion also goes against the thrust of Xenos's argument, which locates the experience of scarcity in the social conditions of capitalist modernity, and more specifically in the distinctive form that class divisions assume during this period. This experience is, therefore, not some kind of intellectual delusion that can be shunted aside at will, but flows from the social relations of everyday life. It is, therefore, not our experience of scarcity but the social relations underlying it that enslave us. This also means, however, that it is these social relations that have to be transformed if we are to ever liberate ourselves from the frustrating experience of scarcity that Xenos describes.

In particular, Xenos explains the spread of competitive consumption in terms of the fluidity of the class system instituted by modern capitalist society. On the one hand, this fluidity democratized access to marks of distinction by making them available to anyone who had the financial wherewithal to buy them in the market. On the other hand, as Xenos also recognizes, this democratization is deceptive and partial since only the affluent can prevail in the game of competitive consumption.

In this respect, capitalist modernity represents continuity as well as a break with the pre-capitalist past: as a class society, capitalism continues to distribute social recognition in an unequal and hierarchical way that systematically favors the society's dominant groups. Unlike previous class societies, however, capitalism seems more democratic because it makes an individual's social position depend not just on birth and ascription, but to some extent also on personal achievement.

This distinction is worth noting because the fact that capitalism is a class system is at least as important for our purposes as the fact that it is a more open system than the class systems of the past. It is the combination of these two facts that explains the rise of competitive consumption as the predominant way of seeking social recognition. In other words, the rise of competitive consumption gave rise to a distinctively modern experience of scarcity because the democratization of the status order in capitalist society could not but remain partial. This is why the solution to the frustrations of competitive consumption can only lie in a further democratization of the economy through a challenge of the class divisions at the basis of capitalist society.

At one point Xenos recognizes that a more egalitarian society might be able to avoid the experience of scarcity that competitive consumption creates. He chooses, however, not to develop this insight, discounting the possibility of an egalitarian society on the grounds that its attainment "entails a laborious and probably impossible revolution from below" (Xenos 1989: 6). Had he thought through the implications of his argument, Xenos might have realized that the obstacle to human liberation is not a false conception of scarcity, but rather the conviction that the social relations responsible for the frustrating experience of scarcity that he describes are immutable and impermeable to challenges from below.

In reality, many social orders in the past have changed as a result of challenges from below. In addition, the serious ecological crisis that capitalism has created makes the fundamental social change that Xenos rules out not only possible but indeed necessary. This crisis is, in fact, a serious contradiction of capitalist society which Xenos does not discuss. This omission is especially surprising given the fact that competitive consumption encourages people to seek recognition through ever-growing levels of material consumption which inevitably inflict ever-growing damage on the planet. In short, Xenos's conclusions suffer because of his refusal to fully think through the link between the undemocratic nature of the capitalist socio-economic system and the frustrating and ecologically destructive configurations of scarcity that this system produces.

CONSUMERISM AND CAPITALISM'S CONFIGURATIONS OF SCARCITY

The spread of competitive consumption is only part of the broader process through which capitalism has, in the course of a few centuries, radically transformed humanity's culture of consumption. As Grant McCracken (1988) has pointed out, the rise and consolidation of modern capitalism has revolutionized consumption no less than production. The consumer revolution that paved the road to the rise of capitalism, only to be advanced even further by the logic of profit and capital expansion, gradually removed consumers' "tastes and preferences from the hold of convention and local tradition, and put them increasingly in the hands of ... the marketplace" (McCracken 1988: 18). In so doing, it also remade culture in the image of capital, employing advertising and marketing techniques in ways that facilitate the "collapsing [of] the cultural into the economic" (Jameson 2000: 53).

These techniques tap social, cultural and historical life worlds for meanings that are then 'transferred' onto commodities available for sale in the market (McCracken 1988). As commodities become embodiments of cherished cultural values, ideals, and aspirations, the increasingly commercial culture that results is one in which growing levels of material consumption become the defining characteristic of the good life.

In this context, companies increasingly become brokers of meaning, as their success comes to depend on the strength of brands built through lavish expenditures on marketing, advertising and public relations campaigns.[7] Financing these expenditures are corporate profits made possible by "slashing jobs," "lowering workplace standards," "lowballing ... [workers] on wages and hours" and, last but not least, ferociously fighting against any attempt by workers to form labor unions (Klein 2000: 190, 236, 240).

In fact, the very adversity of the configurations of scarcity that neoliberal capitalism imposes on ordinary people around the world makes it possible for corporations to burnish their brands even further. By reducing corporate taxes, neoliberal policies have eroded the tax base that could finance public cultural institutions, such as "schools, museums and broadcasters." As such institutions now have to turn to corporations for support, culture increasingly becomes "into little more than a collection of brand-extensions" (Klein 2000: 30). As Benjamin Barber (2007: 180–1) points out, advertisers are keenly aware of how profitable the systematic colonization of culture can be. Declaring brands to be 'the new religion,' advertisers study cults for "insights for the creation of brand worship" (Atkin 2004: xi, 202, cited in Barber 2007: 180–1). Branding then becomes the latest stage in the process, pioneered by American capitalism, of turning consumer goods into embodiments of "a distinct and eventually dominant alternative to political and even religious visions of ... life" (Cross 2000: 18).[8]

Such commercialization of culture contributes to the inhumanity and irrationality of the configurations of scarcity that capitalism produces. For example, the materialist attitudes and values that it breeds are, according to psychologists, injurious to people's physical and psychological well-being as well as to their general quality of life (Kasser 2002: 7, 11, 14, 22; Kasser et al. 2003: 57). Indeed, in his study of the high costs of materialism, Tim Kasser reports that:

> Existing scientific research ... yields clear and consistent findings. People who are highly focused on materialistic values have lower personal well-being and psychological health than those who believe that materialistic pursuits are relatively unimportant. These relationships have been documented in samples of people ranging from the wealthy to the poor, from teenagers to the elderly, and from Australians to South Koreans. Several investigators have reported similar results using a variety of ways of measuring materialism. The studies document that strong materialistic values are associated with a pervasive undermining of people's well-being, from low life satisfaction and happiness, to depression and anxiety, to physical problems such as headaches, and to personality disorders, narcissism, antisocial behavior.
> (Kasser 2002: 22)

In view of this fact, it is not surprising that rapidly increasing levels of consumption in rich countries have not led to corresponding rises in the reported levels of life satisfaction and happiness (Easterlin 1996, Lane 2000, Layard 2005: 3, 38).

The irrationality of the configurations of scarcity that capitalism produces becomes painfully obvious as that system proves unable to turn unprecedented levels of technological development and material wealth into a richer and more satisfying life even for the minority of the world's population living in the affluent consumer societies of the global North.

In fact, capitalism's contempt for human needs accounts for the phenomenon of compensatory consumption, whereby the pursuit of a consumerist lifestyle becomes an "inadequate [attempt] to obtain need-satisfaction" (Geronimo 1988: 66). Not only does this attempt fail but also, since materialism itself is a factor undermining human well-being, a vicious cycle sets in, which tends to perpetuate human misery. As the poverty, inequalities, insecurity, and alienation produced by the capitalist system stand in the way of the satisfaction of people's needs, such compensatory materialism is strengthened, thus further undermining human welfare (Kasser 2002: 27–30).

But capitalism is able to profit even from the havoc that it causes, as advertisers and marketers boost sales through cutting-edge scientific and psychological research that manipulates people's emotions, insecurities, and vulnerabilities (Kasser et al. 2003: 56, Cross 2000: 34, Barber 2007: 177, Levin et al. 2003, Kilbourne 2003: 252). As many of these anxieties are rooted in the capitalist system itself, advertising has in the past channeled people's dissatisfaction with their conditions of life (including consumerism) in ways that increase consumption and bolster capitalism with all its frustrating flaws (Ewen 1977: 64–5, Frank 2000).

One of the flaws of capitalist societies that advertising has in the past exploited is the insecurity that the absence of economic democracy imposes on people living in these societies. In his investigation of advertising practices in the 1920s, Ewen points out, for example, that "[m]en were encouraged to buy according to the categories of job security, much as women were encouraged to buy in order to secure home security for themselves" (1977: 156). Amplifying this point, later in his book he adds,

> [j]ust as men were encouraged to cultivate their appearance to impress the boss, for women the imperative of beauty was directly linked to the question of job security – their survival, in fact, depended upon their ability to keep a husband, ads continually reminded women – or more precisely, the wage that he brought home.
>
> (Ewen 1977: 177–8)

In other words, advertisers have long turned even the gnawing economic insecurity under capitalism into promises that the right kind of consumption could protect both men's jobs by making them look competent and successful and women's economic security by allowing them to attract and keep economically successful husbands.

CONSUMERISM, EXPLOITATION, AND ECONOMIC DEMOCRACY

The adverse effects of consumerism have led some scholars to conclude that consumption is as much a site of capitalist exploitation as production. This section briefly presents two forms this argument has taken, then discusses their weaknesses and offers a more compelling account of the relationship between capitalist exploitation and consumerism.

Goran Ahrne ties consumerism to capitalist exploitation by arguing that workers often receive increases in material standards of living with indifference "due to a saturation in the kinds of needs that may be satisfied through consumption" (1988: 63). Workers would be better off with shorter working hours rather than increased levels of consumption, but that would go against "the interest of capital accumulation" (Ahrne 1988: 59). This is exploitation because,

> when people do have to work they also spend their money, but this does not imply that this spending or consumption has any value at all. It may be a kind of exploitation, where people have to consume their own surplus labor. It is a strange kind of oppression. People do not really suffer, but still in the long run it is an exploitation of people's time to live.
>
> (Ahrne 1988: 62)

For George Ritzer (2005: 51), on the other hand, the growing significance of consumption in twentieth-century capitalist societies has foregrounded the exploitation of consumers as against that of workers. In Ritzer's (2005: 50) view, just as its control over the means of production has in the past allowed capital to exploit workers, its control over the means of consumption today allows it to exploit consumers. By means of consumption Ritzer means the sites at which consumers can purchase commodities. Referring to them as "cathedrals of consumption," Ritzer (2005: x, 7) describes how malls, casinos, entertainment parks, and so on spend enormous amounts to create spectacles that will lure consumers and encourage them "to spend ever-increasing amounts of time and money on consumption." In other words, it is capital's interest in controlling consumers' choices that shapes these new means of consumption. "Consumers can be said to be exploited by the new means of consumption by being led to buy more than they need, to pay higher prices than need be, and to spend more than they should" (Ritzer 2005: 52).

Clearly, both Ahrne and Ritzer recognize that the consumption patterns that contemporary capitalism produces do more to boost profit than to serve the needs of consumers. They cannot develop this insight adequately, however, since neither of them provides a compelling account of the relationship between capitalist exploitation and consumerism. As I will argue below, such an account is possible provided one recognizes the implications of the undemocratic nature of the capitalist economy.

Ritzer's account ignores what the Marxist tradition has long emphasized – that "worker and consumer, capitalism and consumer culture, wage-labor and commodity consumption are born at the same moment: separation from the means of production entails both the sale of labor as a commodity and the buying of commodities to reproduce labor (the worker's needs are met by buying consumer goods through the market" (Slater 1997: 180). This means that capital's relationship to consumers is intimately connected to its relationship to workers, so that one cannot reach an adequate understanding of consumption without relating it to production.

The spectacular cathedrals of consumption that Ritzer describes are financed by workers' surplus labor and thus presuppose exploitation in production. At the same time, capital has a history of intensifying exploitation to the point of undercutting demand for its products and giving rise to economic crises. The closest that Ritzer (2005: 136) comes to acknowledging this contradiction is in his recognition of the dependence of today's consumer culture on credit. He fails to mention, however, that the growing indebtedness of US households which fueled the building of ever more spectacular cathedrals of consumption was also a manifestation of stagnant real wages and slowly increasing family incomes.[9]

As a result, Ritzer's attempt to supplement Marx's analysis of exploitation in production with an analysis of exploitation in consumption ironically proves less dialectical than Marx's keener recognition of the contradictions traversing and fueling capitalist economies. This becomes evident in Ritzer's surprisingly rosy conclusion that "[t]he new means of consumption have, in general, succeeded in making consumption not only more fun but also more democratic" (2005: 194). The fact that, as Ritzer's book appeared in 2005, inequalities were in the process of rising to levels last seen before the Great Depression of the 1930s, does not just refute the claim that consumption has become more democratic. It has also contributed to a massive economic crisis that has started to shatter Ritzer's magnificent cathedrals of consumption into pieces.[10] Last but not least, the connection between growing inequalities and the current crisis illustrates the link between production and consumption that Ritzer glosses over when he claims that today's capitalism has replaced the exploitation of workers by that of consumers.

Moreover, Ritzer's rosy assessment of the impact of the new means of consumption overestimates the enjoyment that these can deliver.

As psychologists examining the conditions for enjoyable experience have concluded, both shopping and consumption-intensive leisure activities tend to be less enjoyable than less consumption-intensive activities (Csikszentmihalyi 1990: 99, 2003: 101–3). Thus, even in 'good' economic times, the expansion of the cathedrals of consumption does more to fuel materialist attitudes, with all their negative effects, than to promote human enjoyment. Far from providing people with innocuous and democratic fun, the cathedrals of consumption form part of a toxic cultural environment in which, according to a Stanford University report, "'up to 8 percent of Americans, 23.6 million people, suffer from compulsive shopping disorder,' an affliction associated with 'out-of-control spending' that 'rips apart relationships and plunges consumers into overwhelming debt and bankruptcy'" (Barber 2007: 239).[11]

Though Ahrne (1988: 62) clearly rejects the notion that capitalist patterns of consumption are 'democratic,' his contention that people's exploitation consists in their having "to consume their own surplus labor" obscures the issue. In the Marxist framework he claims to adopt, this idea is a logical impossibility. Being that portion of the worker's labor that exceeds the labor necessary to provide for the worker's own socially determined consumption requirements, surplus labor is, by definition, not consumed by workers. Thus, while his belief that shorter work hours, rather than increased consumption, would improve people's well-being is widely shared by scholars, Ahrne is unable to provide a compelling account of how long work hours and consumerism are linked to capitalist exploitation.

Such an account is possible if one combines the adverse effects of long work hours with the fact, recognized by both Ahrne and other scholars, that capital's resistance has long been a major obstacle to a shorter work day (Schor 1991, Basso 2003, Cross 1988: 11, Hinrichs 1991: 36–8). These two facts point to capital's ability to impose a pattern of consumption that does not serve the interests of the general population. This ability in turn stems from the economic and political power that capital derives from its control over society's productive resources and its economic surplus.

This ability also suggests that capitalist exploitation has a qualitative implication which usually escapes the attention of traditional Marxist accounts. The extraction of surplus labor does not just have the quantitative implication of denying workers part of the wealth they produce. The qualitative implication of exploitation stems from the fact that capital uses the surplus it extracts from workers to impose a pattern of consumption that is more consistent with profit than with human enjoyment. This qualitative implication means that capitalist exploitation does not just affect the share of the economic pie workers receive, but also the amount of satisfaction that workers enjoy from the portion of their product that comes back to them in the form of wages and salaries.

This formulation makes it easier to understand what Ahrne must have in mind when he misleadingly describes growing levels of meaningless consumption as people being forced "to consume their own surplus labor." What Ahrne is really talking about is the fact that the undemocratic nature of capitalist society denies workers a voice over the allocation of labor productivity gains.[12] Ahrne's point is that capital is more willing to raise wages than to reduce work hours. This means that capital prefers to translate higher labor productivity into a larger economic pie, with some of the growth going to workers, than a smaller economic pie which would mean for workers lower levels of consumption but more free time and a more satisfying life.

The problem here is not that workers are being forced to consume their surplus labor. Rising consumption in the context of rising labor productivity does not mean that workers are no longer deprived of the surplus they produce. Workers are exploited as before, so the difference that Ahrne is trying to understand is that between two different exploitation scenarios, each having different implications for workers. One is a scenario of higher consumption but longer hours, and the other is one of constant consumption but shorter hours. The difference between these two scenarios, as far as the workers are concerned, is not even one of degree of exploitation. In other words, this is not a question of whether workers receive their share of the material benefits that productivity increases generate. It is a question, instead, of the form that these benefits receive. This form makes a difference because, if shorter hours would do more to advance the well-being of workers but this option is denied them because of the structural power of capital, the adverse effect of this denial is as real to workers as the effect of having to perform surplus labor. Thus, capitalist exploitation does not just involve denying workers a part of the economic pie they produce. It also favors patterns of consumption that make even the share of the product that workers receive less satisfying to them than that share would be if these patterns were democratically determined.

All in all, although differences in the balance of forces between capital and labor mean that the length of the working day varies across the capitalist world, capital in general encourages long work hours not only through its historic resistance to any shortening of the work day, but also through the culture of consumerism that it has built with the help of the economic surplus that it extracts from workers.[13] In this sense, the role of consumer culture in the qualitative dimension of capitalist exploitation to some extent parallels the role of capital in its quantitative dimension.

In the Marxist narrative, capitalist exploitation turns surplus labor into capital, an external and alienating reality that grows at workers' expense. Similarly, consumer culture turns workers' surplus product into an alienating, if seductive, system of consumption which prevents full enjoyment of even the share of the economic pie that they receive as wages. And just as capital routinely turns surplus labor into new productive technologies that increase the quantitative dimension of exploitation, so it uses part of this surplus to build a consumerist culture which strengthens the adverse qualitative implication of capitalist exploitation.

The qualitative implication of exploitation also helps to explain what Robert Lane (2000) has described as "the loss of happiness in market democracies." Pointing to dramatic increases in "major depression and dysphoria ... in economically advanced countries, with the incidence highest among younger age cohorts," Lane (2000: 33) attributes this problem to the fact that contemporary capitalism encourages people to focus on the pursuit of money rather than the quality of their relationships with other people. This emphasis on material wealth is counterproductive because, as Richard Layard (2005: 220) also points out, the happiness that people derive from cultivating human relationships tends to be more long-lasting than the satisfaction they derive from an increase in their material standards of living.

Since it is the quality of social relationships rather than money that is more closely related to reported levels of subjective well-being, it is not surprising that capitalism has become an obstacle to a richer and more satisfying life even for the minority of the world's population living in the affluent global North. To begin with, the inequalities that capitalism inevitably creates undercut social solidarity and the quality of people's social relationships (Wilkinson 2005: 33–56). On the other hand, both capital's resistance to any reduction in the working day and its encouragement of long work hours through the consumerist culture it continues to build leave people with less time for family and friends as well as for participation in civic life (Kasser 2002: 61–2, Frank 1999: 53, Schor 1991: 15, Beem 2005: 222). Last but not least, long hours of work under-resource people for leisure.

People who are exhausted after a long day of work are more likely to engage in undemanding activities, such as watching television, which cannot provide the more substantial enjoyment that, psychologists and other social scientists tell us, comes with leisure activities that require the acquisition and development of skills (Csikszentmihalyi 2003: 95, 97; Lane 2000: 308; Schor 1991: 161; Basso 2003: 20, 95, 110; Scitovsky 1992; Lodziak 2002).

The inability of capitalism to translate the production of growing levels of material wealth into a happier, more satisfying life for all seems less paradoxical, once we recognize the impact that capitalism's deployment of the surplus has on people's desires as well as on the free time available to them. The inhumanity and irrationality of the configurations of scarcity that capitalism generates stem as much from the toxic consumerist culture that the exploitation of working people has historically made possible as they do from the material deprivation and poverty that this exploitation also entails. The ability of the working classes in the affluent global North to partake in consumerist lifestyles may have in the past discouraged a challenge of capitalist class relations (Resnick and Wolff 2003: 211–12). But, lest the quantitative increase (at least until recently) in the consumption of workers in the global North tempt us to think otherwise, the increasing futility of this increase shows that the rise of consumerism does not disprove, but on the contrary confirms, the inhumanity of capitalist exploitation.

5 ECONOMIC DEMOCRACY AND THE MULTIPLICITY OF SOCIAL INEQUALITIES AND STRUGGLES

We have now moved beyond the neoclassical conception in at least two ways. Chapter 3 discussed the ways in which the search for profit and capital expansion shapes the configurations of scarcity within capitalist societies, while Chapter 4 discussed how it also contributes to the formation of human needs and desires. This chapter focuses on the fact that not everybody is subject to the abstract logic of capital in exactly the same way. This reality constantly gives rise to social and economic struggles between classes and social groups who seek to improve the terms of their subordination to that logic. In particular, since class, gender, and racial inequalities greatly affect the configurations of scarcity that people confront in their everyday life, this chapter examines both the various social and economic inequalities present in capitalist societies and the struggles that these inequalities bring about. It also discusses the implications of the concept of economic democracy both for these inequalities and for the length of the working day. The latter question is important because economic democracy presupposes enough time for all citizens to deliberate over the goals and priorities of the economic system. Since class, gender, and other social and economic inequalities affect the amount of time people can spend on public affairs, this chapter also touches on the connection between such inequalities and the length of the working day.

STRUGGLES OVER THE PROFIT RATE

Since the pursuit of profit is central to capitalism and constantly reshapes the configurations of scarcity that this system generates, struggles over the profit rate are the logical place to begin. While the capitalist class benefits from a high profit rate, its pursuit of this objective often meets with resistance, especially from social groups that experience this pursuit as a threat to their conditions of life. The social struggles that result also affect the distribution of the burden of scarcity among the various groups within society.

Taking Bowles, Edwards, and Roosevelt's (2005: 251) useful

overview of some of the major determinants of the profit rate and the conflicts they generate as a starting point, the next few paragraphs illustrate some of the reasons profit-seeking companies may encounter popular resistance. Monopolistic companies that charge high prices can give rise to consumer movements that push government to enact and enforce stricter anti-trust legislation. When companies attempt to increase profit through production speed-ups and closer supervision that force workers to work harder, workers can resist by forming unions, going on strike, pushing for labor legislation that empowers them to resist capital's onslaught, and so on. When companies introduce labor-saving technology and dismiss workers, the latter can strike or put pressure on governments to increase unemployment benefits, to add to existing or develop new retraining programs, and/or to legislate a shorter working week so that more workers have a chance to find employment. Such policies may affect profits through their effect on the taxes that businesses have to pay. Similarly, these policies can affect the configurations of scarcity that workers face, since their adoption may also affect the taxes that employed workers pay, the length of their working week, and so on.

Companies can also try to raise profits by turning to suppliers abroad who are willing to sell at a lower price. In response, domestic suppliers may pressure governments to erect protectionist barriers. These struggles can be quite complex, affecting many competing social groups. On one side of the conflict will be the segments of the capitalist class seeking to reduce the cost of materials and machines, (possibly) their workers, domestic consumers, new suppliers and their workers. On the other side of the conflict will be the older suppliers and (possibly) their workers. Companies can also attempt to increase their profits by "support[ing] military intervention abroad to gain control of lower-cost raw materials" (Bowles et al. 2005: 251). They may receive support in this effort from corporations (and possibly even workers) implicated in the military–industrial complex and from some domestic consumers. Their attempt may spark resistance from citizens organizing themselves into a peace movement and from the capitalists and citizens of the foreign country under attack.

Companies can, of course, attempt to increase profits by reducing wages. They can pursue this objective by supporting immigration, moving their plants to low-wage countries, resisting unionization efforts, and engaging in union-busting campaigns of their own. Unions can respond by organizing immigrant workers, supporting unionization efforts in developing countries, and pressuring the government to strengthen labor rights. Some citizens may conceivably pressure the government to crack down on immigration. Finally, companies may attempt to increase their profits by employing production techniques that pollute the environment and reduce workplace safety. Such methods will likely spark resistance from environmental and community movements or by workers and labor unions.

CONFIGURATIONS OF SCARCITY AND CAPITALISM'S CROSS-CUTTING SOCIAL INEQUALITIES AND STRUGGLES

Another determinant of the configurations of scarcity in capitalist societies is the conflict of different groups of workers over coveted well-paid jobs. As Nancy Folbre (1993: 94) points out, the struggle for better wages has often led workers to organize themselves along gender or racial lines. Thus, for example, male workers and their trade unions have in the past excluded women from their ranks, and been complicit in gender and racial discrimination as well as in patterns of occupational segregation along gender and racial lines (Folbre 1993: 99, 102,172, 173, 178; Bowles et al, 2005: 335; Mies 1998: 106–7, 108–9; Nash 1988: 31; Federici 2009; Schor 1991: 95).

Employers themselves may find it in their interest to engage in racial and gender discrimination. To be sure, competition can undercut discrimination when employers who are only willing to hire higher-paid white/male workers are outcompeted by companies willing to hire women or minority workers who were equally or more qualified and productive. While this is the side of the relationship between profit-making and discrimination that neoclassical economists like to stress,[1] there is another side. After all, capitalists can also enhance profit by adopting discriminatory practices that divide the workers and reduce their ability to resist their employers' wishes. If the second tendency is stronger than the first, racial and gender discrimination in the workplace may not only persist but also in fact spread. Instead of non-discriminators outcompeting discriminators, it would be discriminators who would enjoy a profit advantage, thus exerting pressure on non-discriminating employers to follow their example (Bowles et al, 2005: 335). So contrary to the neoclassical assumption, capitalism does not so much eliminate racial and gender discrimination as select the degree and kind of discrimination that maximizes profits (Hahnel 2002: 252). In special cases when the optimal (for capitalist employers) level of racial and gender discrimination is zero, capitalist profit-making will tend to undermine discrimination. In all other cases, capitalist profit-making will perpetuate racial and gender discrimination alike.

There are, therefore, close interconnections and complex interactions between the different forms of social and economic inequality that characterize capitalist societies. The global dimension of the capitalist system adds a further layer of complexity. For example, in the same way that male white workers have often in the past increased their wages by supporting discrimination against women and racial and ethnic minorities, European workers in the past have supported colonialism, when the brutal exploitation of colonial populations made it easier to finance material concessions that employers might not have made otherwise (Mies 1998: 68, 200–1).

Such complex interactions between the different forms of social and economic inequality shape the prevailing configurations of scarcity. When capitalists adopt discriminatory practices to increase their profit, the burdens of scarcity will weigh more heavily on women, and racial and ethnic minorities, as well as on other relatively powerless social groups. Although the various forms of inequality and discrimination often lead to resistance and social struggles, the coexistence of multiple forms of social inequality can sometimes stabilize hierarchical social orders. Just as racial and gender divisions can reduce the ability of workers to challenge capitalism, so is it true that "[b]ecause they offer extra rewards not just to a certain gender, but also to a certain age group and a certain sexual preference, patriarchal societies are less vulnerable than they might otherwise be to feminist collective action" (Folbre 1993: 68). Similarly, racial divisions have often in the past prevented women from crossing racial lines and together engaging in feminist collective action (Folbre 1993: 167, 169, 173–4, 183, 221).

Thus, to account for the configurations of scarcity in any given society, we have to examine both the process through which individuals construct their identities and interests out of the multiplicity of their social positions, and the ability of different social groups to facilitate a social construction of identities that encourages their members to come together and fight for their common interests. By helping determine the lines along which collective action is likely to take place, these two aspects of social reality also contribute to the redistribution of the burdens of scarcity that collective action often brings about.

CAPITALISM, SCARCITY, AND HOUSEHOLDS

To adequately describe the configurations of scarcity facing people in their everyday lives we do not only have to look at the institutions, such as capitalist firms, that monopolize the interest of most economic analyses. Equally important is the institution of the family, which we do not always view as part of the economy. The importance of the family for our purposes stems from the fact that household labor absorbs a great deal of the total social labor expended in any society – up to 50 percent in the United States (Folbre 1993: 97, Bowles et al. 2005: 132). Indeed, as Nancy Folbre and other feminist scholars (Federici 2009: 50–4, O'Hara 2009: 182) rightly insist, "[t]he family cannot be conceptually segregated from 'the economy' – it is one of many sites where individuals pursue their diverse and sometimes contradictory interests" (Folbre 1993: 39). Moreover, as "men have collective interests as men that are at least partially opposed to the collective interests of women" (Folbre 1993: 5), this opposition has often given rise to collective action that has shaped family structures around the world as well as institutions, such as the state, that have an impact on the ability of families to meet their needs.[2] Meanwhile, Marxist feminists, such as Harriet Fraad, Stephen Resnick, and Richard Wolff (1994), stress the link between life within the household and the class struggles that take place in other economic and non-economic institutions.[3] For example, as the stagnation of real earnings since the 1970s has put an end to 150 years of uninterrupted growth in the standards of living of the US working class, Americans have sought to sustain rising consumption standards not only by working more hours and "sen[ding] more family members – and especially women – out to work," but also by borrowing more than "any working class in any country at any time" (Wolff 2008, 16).

These developments have had multiple effects. Exhaustion from overwork and the stress over mounting debt have predictably had devastating effects on many US families, contributing to deteriorating "statistics on divorce, abandonment, spousal abuse, neglect of children, and so on" (Resnick and Wolff 2003: 219–20). Meanwhile, women's increasing participation in the workforce[4] has challenged men's dominant position within the household by making women more economically independent, thus changing "[t]he relative bargaining power of family members, defined in terms of threat points (their fallback position, if they exit the relationship)" (Folbre 1993: 23). This development changes the configurations of scarcity confronting men and women today, since family members' relative bargaining power "affects the distribution of income, goods, and leisure time within the household. Inequality within the family reflects inequalities in individual power related to age and gender" (Folbre 1993: 23).

Social policy also affects both the opportunities available to women and the balance of power within households. Thus, for example, the availability (or not) of affordable child care inevitably affects women's ability to advance in their careers, achieve income equality, and not be dependent on the incomes of their husbands (Fraad et al. 1994: 17, 39–40). This means that societies in which the government provides affordable child care to all empower women more than those that leave child care to the forces of the market.

Conversely, in a society in which gender discrimination leads to lower pay for women, the absence of government-funded child care makes it more likely that it will be women who take time out of their jobs or interrupt their careers to take care of their children, and who, for that reason, will face even further discrimination in the workplace. Thus, a vicious circle may appear, as gender discrimination encourages a gender division of labor that confirms employer expectations, further encouraging discrimination against female workers. By discouraging women from placing as much emphasis on paid work as their male partners, this vicious circle undermines women's economic independence and bargaining power within the household, thus potentially confronting women with configurations of scarcity that are more adverse than those their male partners face (Folbre 1993: 21, 161).

ECONOMIC DEMOCRACY, HOUSEHOLDS, AND THE QUESTION OF TIME

For example, as their husbands or male partners often fail to make a sufficient contribution to housework, women who also work outside the home often find themselves working much longer hours while "enjoy[ing] less leisure" (Folbre 1993: 92). As a result, women in two-parent households are "likely to be 'time-poor,'" while single mothers are usually "both time- and money-poor" (Folbre 1993: 205). On the other hand, the fact that growing participation in paid work has increased women's economic independence and bargaining power is probably one of the reasons for the changing patterns of housework that economist Juliet Schor describes. While Schor (1991: 103–4) points out that more than two-thirds of employed wives still do either all or "the bulk" of housework, she also finds cause for optimism in studies that suggest both a change in people's values regarding the division of housework and an actual increase in men's contribution to housework.

While it is not clear how much this trend will reduce gender inequality within the household,[5] women's time poverty relates to the question of economic democracy in two ways. First, time poverty is an illustration of the more adverse configurations of scarcity that women have to navigate as a result of gender inequality. If, however, as Folbre and other feminists (e.g. Schor 1991: 84–5) have rightly pointed out, housework is an economic activity, the principle of economic democracy is as relevant to it as it is to economic activity carried out outside the home. In an economically democratic household all the adult members would democratically decide all questions regarding the household's economic goals, the amount and kinds of housework necessary for the household's reproduction, and the distribution of both household tasks and other economic burdens necessary to meet the household's needs. In this sense, the prominence of time poverty in the configurations of scarcity facing women around the world underlines the need for economically democratic households that divide paid and household work among their adult members equally. Time poverty is, however, as much an obstacle to economic democracy as it is a product of its absence. Indeed, economic democracy is inconceivable in the absence of enough time for all citizens, including women, to participate in the democratic deliberations determining their economic future. While lack of time is especially acute in the case of women, it is also a barrier to greater political participation for other social groups, including working-class men. It is therefore necessary to examine the connection between economic democracy and the time dimension of capitalism's configurations of scarcity a little more closely.

As Murray Bookchin has pointed out, capitalism's technological dynamism creates the possibility to drastically reduce the working day for the entire population. Without such a reduction, it is impossible to break with the political patterns of the past, when "[t]he 'masses' were always compelled to return to a lifetime of toil and rarely were they free to establish organs of self-management that could last beyond the revolution" (1986: 234).[6] Thus, Bookchin argues, the absence of an advanced technological basis contributed to the degeneration of social revolutions of the past into regimes reestablishing the rule of small economic and political elites.

However, both the drastic reduction of people's work time and

the use of some of the time freed to ensure broad popular participation in the democratic management of society's economic life
presuppose a radical break with the logic of profit. It is this logic
that accounts for the fact that, when productivity increases trickled
down to workers in the past, they usually took the form of higher
wages rather than of shorter work hours. As Juliet Schor has shown,
this preference follows from the search for profit, including the need
of employers to discipline workers.[7] An important implication of
Schor's argument is that the capitalist search for profit does not just
require that workers be exploited. It also favors those exploitative
economic outcomes that, by making it more likely that any concessions to workers will take the form of higher wages rather than an
increase in workers' free time, discourage workers from seeking to
understand and have a voice in the economic and political processes
that affect their lives.

CAPITAL AND THE VICIOUS CYCLES UNDERCUTTING ECONOMIC DEMOCRACY

As Schor and others have pointed out (Schor 1991: 70; Cross 1988a:
11), reductions in work hours under capitalism have always been
the result of working class and labor union struggles. Such struggles
had to overcome the opposition of capital, which has historically
deployed its economic power and resources as well as its access
to the media to promote a 'gospel of consumption' that sought
to channel worker gains towards higher consumption rather than
shorter work hours (Hunnicut 1988: 144–5; also see 42, 46–7).

Capital's partiality for long hours threatens a vicious cycle that
makes it hard to advance the conditions necessary for economic
democracy. Not only is the undemocratic nature of capitalism a
contributing factor to the persistence of long work hours, these long
hours themselves further undermine the conditions for economic
democracy because they deprive working people of the time necessary
both to understand the economic, political, and social forces affecting
their lives, and to engage in collective action capable of democratizing
social and economic institutions alike. This is why, in struggling for
shorter work hours, workers have in the past consciously fought to
loosen the grip of this vicious cycle on their lives. As a number of
labor historians point out, workers' struggles in the past have often
pursued shorter hours as a means to political participation and to
the ability of workers to exercise their rights as citizens. Indeed, just
as in nineteenth-century Britain Chartists supported a shorter work

day because it would "literally free the worker to participate capably in public and civic affairs" (Weaver 1988: 88), in the United States the American revolution had led "some workers ... to regard long hours as a roadblock to their full participation in political affairs and ... to make a distinction between working time and time for civic duty, even before they differentiated between labor and leisure" (Roediger and Foner 1989: 2).

In any case, the vicious cycle by which capitalism undermines the conditions for economic democracy has implications for the configurations of scarcity that this system generates. As Schor's analysis makes clear, capital's partiality for long hours contributes to "[o]ne of the great ironies of our present situation," namely the coexistence of "overwork for the majority ... [and] the growth of enforced idleness for the minority" (1991: 39). This partiality, along with the disciplining effects that unemployment has on the working class, accounts, moreover, for the fact that capital has used its considerable economic and political power to veto the more humane and rational alternative of reducing work hours as a means to reducing unemployment (Schor 1991: 75–6).

As if this was not enough, the situation facing women in contemporary capitalist society points to a second vicious circle obstructing economic democracy. Lack of economic democracy in broader society undermines the prospects of economic democracy within the household. And, as gender (but also class and racial) inequalities allow the strongest party to shift most of the work necessary to maintain the household to the weakest party, economic democracy in society as a whole suffers even further as members of oppressed groups become time- as well as money-poor. This time poverty makes it difficult for members of oppressed groups to influence economic and political processes and to engage in collective action, even though their need to do so may be especially great.

These two vicious cycles have important political implications. The latter one implies that struggles to democratize society as a whole complement struggles to democratize the household economy. If gender and other forms of social inequality outside the household can undercut democracy within it, successful struggles against the manifestations of gender and other forms of social inequality outside the household also inevitably weaken the imbalances of power within it. Conversely, struggles within households against the sexist ideologies and norms that have often in the past supported the undemocratic organization of households can, through the redistribution of household labor they produce, give women the time to contribute to struggles against social inequalities and for economic democracy outside the household. As work by Nalini Nayak and Andrea Moraes (2009) and Patricia E. Perkins (2009) suggests, lack of time is one of the main obstacles that women face in their pursuit of economic democracy through struggles for workplace rights and the democratic management of essential resources, such as water.

The more successful feminist struggles are, the more the pressure for economic democracy within the household will mount, and the less willing women will be to participate in non-democratic households. In fact, according to Harriet Fraad, women in the United States increasingly reject the overwork that traditional, undemocratic households impose on them by "rejecting marriage. For the first time in American history, the majority of women are single. Two thirds of divorces are now initiated by women" (2008: 27). In this respect, the fact that at least "[h]alf of first marriages and 60% of second marriages end in legal separation or divorce" (Fraad 2008: 27) bears witness to the serious crisis besetting the traditional undemocratic family model.

Households in the United States and elsewhere will, however, not become more democratic, without feminist struggles by women and men alike. While struggles against gender discrimination in the workplace and for the enforcement of child support payments by fathers "ha[ve] eroded the legal basis" (Fraad 2008: 27) of male-dominated households, feminism's impact on the general culture of household life is equally important because the conditions of economic democracy are not just legal or economic but also cultural.

In recognizing the cultural dimension of gender inequalities, the project of economic democracy challenges the neoclassical interpretation of a gender division of labor that often leads women to prioritize family over paid work. Ignoring the power implications of a division of labor that increases women's economic dependence on men, neoclassical economists often assume that "[w]omen simply have greater preferences for family life than men, and are therefore willing to sacrifice more for them" (Folbre 1993: 97). This acceptance of a socially constructed division of labor as purely a matter of individual preferences makes it possible to interpret women's predicament as unproblematic and consistent with economic efficiency. As Folbre (1993: 97) rightly points out, however, the cultural construction of women's (and men's) preferences often occurs through struggles that reshape culture and the gender order itself. In themselves, and in their implications for the cultural conditions for economic democracy, gender struggles are of crucial importance.

Indeed, the challenge of gender assumptions that encourage women to sacrifice career to their family and to accept a household division of labor which relies on and reproduces an imbalance of power within the household has to be an integral aspect of the struggle for economic democracy.

THE STRUGGLE OVER THE WORKING DAY AS A STRUGGLE FOR ECONOMIC DEMOCRACY

Just as the vicious circle of gender relations undercuts the conditions of economic democracy inside and outside the household, so does the vicious circle triggered by capital's power to impose long hours on working people. And just as the former vicious circle requires a simultaneous struggle for economic democracy within and outside the household, so does the latter vicious circle require a simultaneous struggle both against long hours at work and against the power of capital over social and economic life. Indeed, working people's struggle against capital can further their struggle for shorter hours, just as their struggle for shorter hours can further their struggle against capital's undemocratic economic power.

It is no accident, for example, that European workers won the eight-hour day immediately after the Bolshevik revolution, when a working-class "insurgency ... spread across Europe between 1917 and 1920" (Cross 1988b: 162–3). In view of its historic ability to bridge differences that separate workers, the struggle for shorter hours could once again make as significant a contribution to the struggle against capital's undemocratic economic power as it has in the past. Describing the ability of struggles for a shorter working day to unify workers with diverse backgrounds and ideological profiles, labor historian Gary Cross notes, for example, that

[i]n Britain in 1890, eight-hour demonstrations encompassed Tory-voting skilled artisans, the newly enfranchised unskilled docker, the voteless female matchmaker, as well as conservative trade union officials, young New Model Unionists, Marxists, and Fabians. The call for the eight-hour day ... provided a rallying cry that periodically united an otherwise dispersed and impotent working class movement.

(Cross 1988a: 13)

Similarly, in their study of the importance of struggles over time for the history of the American labor movement, David Roediger and Philip Foner also find that:

> The length of the workday ... has historically been the central issue raised by the American labor movement during its most dynamic periods of organization.
> ... In its tendency to foster unity, its capacity to evoke both political and trade union struggles, and its close relationship with the question of who would control workers' lives on and off the job, the shorter-hours movement stood apart.
> ... the shorter working day was an issue that could mitigate, though not completely overcome, the deep racial and ethnic divisions that complicated class organization in the U.S. ... Since the demand for shorter hours promised to spread employment, the jobless also had a stake in hours struggles.
>
> (Roediger and Foner 1989: vii–viii)

More recently, however, the US labor movement has abandoned this issue even as the hours Americans spend in the paid labor force have increased.[8] Meanwhile, its strength has been declining as union density has decreased to around 12 percent. Standing at 7.5 percent, union density in the private sector is, in fact, below even "what it was before the Great Depression" (Yates 2009: 21). This constitutes, as Michael Yates points out, "a tremendous loss for the working class: lost wages and benefits for all workers, still less response by the government to the needs of workers, and a smaller counterweight to the forces that have given rise to greater inequality" (2009: 19).

Weaker labor movements heighten the undemocratic nature of the capitalist system in the United States and around the world. In so doing, they also reshape the prevailing configurations of scarcity in ways that favor capital but harm the majority of the population. In the United States a weaker labor movement "has allowed a corporate-political alliance to sweep away most of the safety nets that protect us from the vagaries of the market and the inevitable occurrences of failing health, old age, and workplace injuries" (Yates 2009: 19).

Labor's weakness is especially serious, given the plunge of the global economy into the worst economic crisis since the Depression of the 1930s. As capital in the United States and around the world uses this crisis to attack even the most basic labor rights that workers won through lengthy and often bloody struggles, the need of the labor movement to take the offensive is as obvious as it is urgent.

Given the historic power of the short hours demand to advance this objective, Roediger and Foner's recommendation that this demand make a comeback may be an idea whose time has come. All the more so as "[s]cholarly researchers and labor organizers have agreed that women workers are most receptive to shorter-hour arguments" (Roediger and Foner 1989: 276). The appeal of organizing the rapidly growing numbers of women workers should be obvious, in view of the fact that deindustrialization continues to decimate the ranks of workers in the traditionally male manufacturing sector.

Organizing large numbers of female workers by reactivating the short hours demand would further the project of economic democracy in a number of ways. By strengthening the labor movement, the organization of female workers could limit capital's undemocratic economic and political power, and would do so precisely by challenging the vicious circle whereby capital's undemocratic power undercuts economic and political democracy even further by imposing long hours on workers. It would also advance economic democracy within the household by allowing more female workers to benefit from the significantly higher wages and benefits that unionized workers enjoy.[9] Such a development would in turn increase women's economic independence and bargaining power within the household, thus helping them to overcome men's continued resistance to a fair sharing of the burdens of household labor. Combined with the direct time benefits of the shorter hours demand for male and female workers alike, a shorter working day would provide women with additional time for collective action aimed at furthering economic democracy inside and outside the household. To be sure, a shorter working day would also have important implications for men's lives. In addition to increasing their ability to participate in the economic and political decisions affecting their lives, shorter working hours could also reduce their resistance to sharing household labor.

To the extent, moreover, that shorter hours facilitated increased rank and file participation within unions, they would revitalize labor movements everywhere, empowering workers to challenge both capital's power and the vicious circles undercutting economic democracy that this power entails. In doing so, shorter hours could lead to an alternative virtuous circle of economic democratization. Indeed, greater rank and file participation in union struggles would not only increase workers' democratic skills and strengthen the labor movement. As a stronger labor movement blocked even further capital's ability to impose long hours, workers could fight for even more free time and an even more ample opportunity to exercise their growing democratic skills. To the extent that they were successful, they would be contributing even further to the political and economic democratization of society as a whole. Last but not least, given the fact that the wage boost that unionized Black and Hispanic workers enjoy is especially high (Yates 2009: 18), increased unionization can also reduce racial inequalities and empower members of oppressed minority groups to increase their influence over political and economic outcomes, thus boosting economic democracy in yet another way.

THE CULTURAL DIMENSION OF THE STRUGGLE FOR ECONOMIC DEMOCRACY

Since class, racial, gender, and other forms of social and economic inequality have a cultural dimension, so will struggles against them. Thus, the concept of economic democracy I propose resists the temptation to treat concern with racism and sexism as issues of cultural identity that distract our attention from "the difference that a truly left politics would want to eliminate: class difference" (Michaels 2006: 199–200). According to Walter Ben Michaels (2006: 75), who has voiced this view, concern with racism, sexism, heterosexism, and discrimination amounts to little more than "the dream of a truly free and efficient market" which obscures the real source of injustice, namely class inequality. In Michaels's view, American society's interest in non-class forms of discrimination constitutes a capitulation to "the neoliberal consensus" that "[t]he only inequalities we're prepared to do anything about are the ones that interfere with the free market" (2006: 78).

Michaels's assumption that action against racial, gender, and other forms of discrimination simply furthers the free market project is false. Underlining the often-radical implications of anti-discrimination legislation, Nelson Lichtenstein reminds us that, far from idolizing free markets, such legislation means that

> [i]f you own a restaurant or a factory or a motel or run a college, you can't make use of your property as you wish. The state mandates you to hire, fire, promote, and otherwise deal with your employees or clients according to a set of rules laid down in Washington and refined by the EEOC and the courts. If litigated, the courts will force an employer to pay real money in compensation and hire or promote a worker if management is found to have transgressed this new kind of labor law.
>
> (Lichtenstein 2001: 2)

In this sense, Rand Paul, the Tea Party/Republican senator who believes that "a private business ha[s] the right to refuse to serve black people" understands better than Michaels what a truly free market might entail (Nagourney and Hulse 2010).

Michaels is also wrong to present the struggle against class exploitation as inconsistent with that against racism, sexism, and discrimination. In fact, his assumption that a world without sexist and racist discrimination is compatible with free market capitalism is closer to the view of neoclassical economics, with its denial of class exploitation, than to neo-Marxist approaches that recognize the ways in which capitalists can attempt to control workers by dividing them across racial and gender lines.[10] In other words, by dismissing the significance of continued gender and racial discrimination, Michaels unwittingly hampers the unification of working people into a movement that is strong enough to challenge economic exploitation. And, because of his apparent lack of interest in sexism and racism, Michaels is equally oblivious of the ecofeminist literature that has pointed out both the role that capitalism has historically played in the institutionalization of racism and sexism,[11] and the role that sexism plays in increasing economic exploitation by "bring[ing] down the general price of labour, since thanks to the sex/gender ideology that devalues women, their labour is cheaper than men's" (Nayak 2009: 109–10).

For all these reasons, the project of economic democracy cannot accept Michaels's false dichotomy between the struggle against class exploitation and that against racism and sexism. Michaels's protestations to the contrary, attention to non-class forms of oppression, as well as to the cultural dimensions of such oppression, is not a capitulation to neoliberal ideology. It is as essential a component of the struggle for economic democracy as the struggle against class exploitation.

6 CAPITALISM, SCARCITY, AND GLOBAL INEQUALITIES

One of the most surprising as well as hopeful products of the current economic crisis has been the inspiring revolutionary upsurge in the Arab world. Tracing the connections between this upsurge and the crisis, a number of commentators have shown how the dismal effects of neoliberal policies in many Arab countries have paved the road to the current explosions (Prins 2011; Amin 2011a, 2011b; Hanieh 2011; McNally 2011b; Marzouki 2011). These policies were adopted with the blessings of the International Monetary Fund (IMF) and the World Bank, two international institutions that have long contributed to the spread of the neoliberal gospel around the world. In fact, the IMF and the World Bank until recently touted Egypt and Tunisia as 'top reformers' and as models for other emerging countries (Marzouki 2011, Hanieh 2011). The cause for such lavish praise was rapid privatization and neoliberal reforms, which drastically increased inequality and unemployment, while also uprooting small farmers who sought to survive in the slums of large cities like Cairo (Amin 2011a, Kirkpatrick and El-Naggar 2011, Hanieh 2011). These changes met with popular resistance which led to the emergence of truly independent unions in Egypt, and that prepared the ground for the current upsurge (Human Experience 2011). The current crisis also fueled popular discontent through its negative effect on exports and remittances, as well as through its contribution to rising food prices (Hanieh 2011, McNally 2011b).

Highlighting people's will and capacity for self-organization (Amar 2011, McNally 2011a, Al-Atraqchi 2011), these movements have turned against undemocratic regimes, many of which have long enjoyed the support of the United States and the West. After their initial successes in Tunisia and Egypt, these movements have met with violent repression in a number of countries, including Bahrain, Iraq, Yemen, and Syria (Slackman 2011). While the United States and its allies in Europe and the Arab world have shown little concern for the repression of popular movements in Bahrain and Yemen by the friendly Saudi, Bahraini, and Yemenese governments, they have in a transparently cynical fashion appealed to humanitarian values to justify their military intervention against Libya's authoritarian ruler Colonel Gaddafi.

As Tariq Ali (2011a) has pointed out, this inconsistency reflects a fear, on the part of the United States and the West, of losing control of a region that is crucial to their economic and geopolitical interests. Far from siding with the democratic movements spreading throughout the Arab world, the intervention in Libya, Ali notes, seeks to establish a Western 'protectorate' and "to bring the Arab rebellions to an end by asserting western control, confiscating their impetus and spontaneity and trying to restore the status quo ante" (2011a). The United States and the West have reason to worry about the demands of these movements for an independent foreign policy that neither capitulates to US wishes nor refrains from challenging the unqualified support that the United States has long given to Israel (Ali 2011b, Eshragi 2011, Tarleton 2011, Abunimah 2011, Hanieh 2011). Central to the special interest of the United States and other Western countries in North Africa and the Middle East are the vast petroleum reserves that have long fueled the world capitalist system. This interest accounts for the successive wars in that region, as well as the vast amounts of money both the countries in the region and the United States spend on military expenditures.

These developments in the Arab world highlight the global dimension of the configurations of scarcity that people around the world have to navigate and struggle over. These developments emerge from a constellation of factors. Rooted in the legacy of Western colonialism and the resistance against it, these factors have so far resulted in a more or less continuous widening of the gap in economic and geopolitical power between the rich countries of the global North and those of the global South. The development of capitalism has affected the ability of different parts of the world to pursue economic development very differently. By making military conflict and war a means that the more powerful actors use to pursue their interests, this division also shapes the quality of the material output that capitalism produces. As my discussion of Baran and Sweezy's work in an earlier chapter made clear, the prominence of military expenditure in contemporary capitalist societies shows that, in studying the configurations of scarcity that these societies create, it is as necessary to examine what kind of economic output these societies produce as it is to measure its quantity.

To understand the configurations of scarcity facing people around the planet, we need a sense of the history of the world capitalist system, from the time of European colonialism to the recent spread of neoliberal policies around the world. This is a history of social struggle and popular resistance, and that is why this chapter covers recent struggles against neoliberalism as well as the long-term historical processes that have led to the division of the world into an affluent global North and a less affluent global South.

GLOBAL INEQUALITIES AS A DIMENSION OF CAPITALISM'S CONFIGURATIONS OF SCARCITY

While, in the few centuries it has existed, capitalism has often led to rapid rates of productivity and output growth, this growth has always been uneven. This unevenness does not just reflect the cyclical nature of capitalist development, with its periodic tendency to produce serious economic crises, like the current one. Also reflecting this unevenness are the great inequalities between the affluent countries of the global North and the often-poor countries of the global South. These inequalities form part of the very adverse configurations of scarcity that billions of people in the global South live under and struggle against, and this is why this section, and chapter, are devoted to a description of their extent, as well as a discussion of both the long history that produced them and the social struggles that they in turn have given rise to.

These configurations are of course not the sole product of the relations between North and South. They are also shaped by class, gender, racial, and other social inequalities within the countries of the South, as well as by the struggles that these inequalities give rise to. In turn, these struggles affect the state policy of governments in the global South, with respect to both the domestic economy and the historically more powerful governments in the global North. The policies that result from this process of domestic and inter-national pressures and counter pressures have historically affected the ability of the countries in the global South (and today's global North) to experience the kind of dynamic capitalist development capable of ameliorating the configurations of scarcity facing their populations.[1] In short, the configurations of scarcity facing people in the global North and South are the compound product of the forms of inequality and struggles I discussed in Chapter 5 and the global dimension of the capitalist system, which is the focus of this chapter. And it is because of this complex interaction of domestic and global dynamics that some countries (for example, the United States, Germany, and Japan) have historically been more successful than others in industrializing and becoming major economic powerhouses.

While these successes, as well as more recent ones, such as those of the Asian 'tigers' and the BRIC (Brazil, Russia, India, China) countries, are important to recognize, at least as important is the tendency of many other parts of the global South to fall further and further behind the affluent countries of the global North. In fact, Branko Milanovic has gone as far as to describe this tendency as "the 'Great Divergence'": "[a]s in a kind of Big Bang, to which the industrial revolution can be likened, parts of the world that used to be similar in income levels have steadily diverged, and continue to do so" (2005: 140).

In documenting in great statistical detail this process of divergence, Milanovic questions the view among economists that:

> through either international trade or movement of factors of production (migration of labor from poor to rich countries, and capital flows from rich to poor countries), and/or the spread of technology that allows the poor to catch up with the rich, poor countries [will] grow faster than the rich.
>
> (Milanovic 2005: 45)

Hardly unique to economists, this belief was at the basis of the post-war 'development age' launched by President Truman's 1949 inaugural address (Rist 1997). In an international context of decolonization, the cold war, and US hegemony over the capitalist world, development discourses set up Western industrialized countries as models that 'underdeveloped' countries were supposed to emulate (Sachs 1999). By bringing their social, political, and economic life in line with the Western model, underdeveloped countries could expect to go through "the stages of economic growth" outlined in W. W. Rostow's (1990) influential statement of the supposed conditions of development, and to eventually partake in the 'mass consumption' lifestyle pioneered by Western industrial societies. In President Truman's words, greater production and "democracy" would conquer "hunger, misery and despair" and usher in an age of "personal freedom and happiness for all mankind" (Rist 1997: 249–50). This developmentalist vision was "the promise of the twentieth century" (Milanovic 2005: 1).

While seeing some progress in the economically more dynamic parts of the global South, the twentieth century was clearly not able to fulfill this promise, thus also revealing the perpetuation of capitalism's global inequalities as one of the ideological functions of the influential approaches to development advanced both by Rostow himself and by 'modernization' theorists more generally.[2] Despite

the economic growth in the 60 years since the inauguration of the
development era, hunger and misery are sadly still with us. According
to the World Bank 1.4 billion people live on less than $1.25 per
day, the World Bank's updated poverty line, while the international
humanitarian agency Oxfam expected this number to increase by
100 million people as a result of rising food prices (Schifferes 2008).
Even before the current economic crisis and the global food crisis
immediately preceding it, there were, according to United Nations
estimates, "close to 1 billion [people] suffer[ing] from chronic
hunger," while "[t]he total number of food insecure people who are
malnourished or lacking critical nutrients [wa]s probably closer to
3 billion – about half of humanity"(Magdoff 2008: 1).[3] Thus, even
before the current crises, 'routine hunger' and malnutrition claimed
the lives of 18,000 children a day (Magdoff 2008: 1).

This sad reality is not due to insufficient production of food,[4]
but to the fact that, under capitalism, food is a commodity like
any other, available only to those who can pay for it (Robbins
2005: 179). This means that large numbers of people even in rich
countries, such as the United States, become vulnerable to hunger
when economic crises, such as the current one, increase unemployment, or when food prices spike, as they have been doing in
recent years (Bosman 2009, Robbins 2005: 184). Furthermore, as
Milanovic reminds us,

> [w]hile a part of the rich world was discussing techniques that
> would prolong the human life-span to over 100 years, millions
> were dying from easily preventable diseases, lack of safe water, or
> infections. Tuberculosis, syphilis, and other diseases that seemed
> to be a thing of the past returned on the heels of economic crises
> and social anomies. Scholars were seriously debating to what
> extent poverty and deprivation were behind the many civil wars
> that erupted after the end of the Cold War, as well as behind
> terrorist acts.
>
> (Milanovic 2005: 2)

All in all, the human toll that hunger and global poverty exact is so
large that in the 15 years since the end of Cold War:

> some 18 million human beings have died prematurely each year
> from poverty-related causes, accounting for fully one-third of
> all human deaths. This fifteen-year death toll of 270 million is
> considerably larger than the 200-million death toll from all the

wars, civil wars, genocides and other government repressions of the entire 20th century combined.[5]

(Pogge 2002: 2)

While they are only one facet of the variable and complex configurations of scarcity that people in the global South are faced with, these realities are especially shocking in view of the fact that humanity already has at its disposal the material means necessary to eradicate them. The estimated cost of ending the global poverty at the root of all this unnecessary human suffering is US$312 billion per year, or "a mere one percent of the total global annual income" (Schweickart 2008: 472). As Richard Layard reminds us,

> extra income increases happiness less and less as people get richer. This was the traditional argument for redistributive taxation, and modern happiness research confirms it. The argument applies both within countries and across countries. In poor countries extra income increases happiness much more than in rich countries, and that is why helping the Third World should be one of the major ethical goals for Western society.[6]

(Layard 2005: 230)

As Layard recognizes, and as I discussed in the chapter on consumption, the toxic consumerist culture that capitalism generates stands in the way of substantial increases in the level of happiness of people living in the affluent global North. This means that a redistribution of 1 percent of the world's output towards the poorest of the poor need not represent a major sacrifice even for the people living in the affluent global North.[7] In fact, the inequalities that capitalism generates are so great that the super-rich of the world could more than cover the needed amount and still enjoy a very affluent lifestyle (Singer 2006).

Global inequalities and the poverty they produce present capitalism's configurations of scarcity in all their starkness. The real problem of scarcity facing humanity today is not the one that neoclassical economics worries about, namely the gap between the infinity of human wants and the finite productive potential at our disposal. The real problem lies in capitalism's inability to allocate resources where they are most needed, and in its propensity to concentrate resources in the hands of those least likely to need or derive much satisfaction from them. In other words, the fact that resources are scarce relative to conceivable human wants is much less significant than the way capitalist societies waste and misuse available resources. This means, however, that the main obstacle to human well-being is not the existence of scarcity in the abstract, but the specific configurations of scarcity that contemporary capitalist societies generate. As previous chapters have shown, shaping these configurations are the logic of profit, the various forms of social inequality traversing capitalist societies, and the cross-cutting social and political struggles that these forms of inequality inevitably produce. This chapter goes further by indicating how the stark inequalities and configurations of scarcity with which this chapter opens are the product of the long history through which capitalism has become a global socio-economic system.

The purpose of this brief account is to show the link between global inequalities and the development of the world capitalist system. While the development of this system generates enough material wealth to eradicate the extreme misery prevailing in many parts of the world, it has proven unable to turn this potential into reality. Because of this inability, people in the global South have long fought against both the domestic political and economic elites exploiting them and the major powers in the global North that have often exercised their economic, political, and military power in ways that are as harmful to the majority of the population in the global South as they are beneficial to themselves.

THE GROWTH OF GLOBAL INEQUALITIES: A BRIEF HISTORICAL OVERVIEW

In his history of the capitalist system, Michel Beaud notes, "[f]rom its beginnings, capitalism has been national and global, competitive and monopolistic, liberal and state-connected" (2001, 42). As world systems theorists also note, capital accumulation has historically taken place not just through market competition. Capitalists have always sought to increase their profits by securing monopolistic positions that insulate them from unwelcome competitive pressures. They have also benefited from state interventions that have facilitated capital accumulation both through domestic legislation and through (often military) interventions in territories far beyond the boundaries of their own nation state (Wallerstein 1999: 25; Robbins 2005: 84; Shannon 1996: 40–2; Bagchi 2005).

Recently described as 'globalization,' capitalism's world-girding tendencies were vividly described in Marx and Engels's (1978: 476) *Communist Manifesto*: "The need of a constantly expanding market for its products chases the bourgeoisie over the whole surface of the globe. It must nestle everywhere, settle everywhere, establish connections everywhere." Thus, the global economic links that capital forges lend production and consumption "a cosmopolitan character" (Marx and Engels 1978: 476). By advancing the means of production and communication, capital is able to reduce costs and achieve competitive advantages that allow it to "batter down all Chinese walls," thus bringing more societies, along with their populations and territories, under its orbit. In doing so, capital "creates a world after its own image" (Marx and Engels 1978: 477).

While some scholars have been skeptical of the concept of 'globalization,' others have noted the uneven history of the process this concept describes, and underlined the extent to which globalization represents a political project, both the initiation and staying power of which depend on "[n]ational policies and relations among national governments" (Frieden 2006: xvii).[8] In this view, globalization is not an irreversible development, since the lack of policies and governance structures that take into consideration the legitimate concerns of those globalization hurts could produce a popular backlash against globalization that may prove strong enough to reverse it.[9]

A comprehensive account of the debate on the concept and history of globalization lies beyond the scope of this chapter. What is certain is that the history of capitalism is one in which economic and political means were deployed in the worldwide spread of capitalism. The very emergence of industrial capitalism in England was crucially dependent on the natural resources of the New World, as well as the enslavement and transplantation of millions of Africans to the Americas (Pomeranz 2000). Thus, the rise of industrial capitalism in England, Europe, and North America was inseparable from colonialism, the brutal exploitation of people around the world, and the plundering of the natural wealth of the territories of today's global South (Tucker 2002: 177, 179–80; Dowd 2000: 51–2). It was also inseparable from the extermination and dispossession of indigenous peoples around the world (Steinberg 1989: 13–21, Robbins 2005: 267–74). In Karl Polanyi's words, it was through such processes that:

> [t]he mobilization of the produce of the land was extended from the neighboring countryside [in England] to tropical and subtropical regions – the industrial-agricultural division of labor was applied to the planet. As a result, peoples of distant zones

were drawn into the vortex of change the origins of which were obscure to them.

(Polanyi 2001: 190)

And as Polanyi (2001: 188, 223) also recognizes, "th[is] subjection of the surface of the planet to the needs of an industrial society" imposed "unspeakable suffering" on the populations living in those areas.

Amiya Kumar Bagchi (2005) has described in some detail how far-reaching and devastating the impact of colonialism and of the geographic expansion of capitalist powers has been historically. Contributing to the outbreak of famines that claimed the lives of tens of millions of people in India and China, and using the economic surplus from the colonies for the development of the colonizing powers rather than of the colonies themselves, colonialism and capitalist expansionism did as much to destroy indigenous economic structures and ways of life as they did to facilitate the industrialization of the colonizers. In addition, part of the surplus from the non-European colonies was used to populate and build up North America and other parts of the global North that lie outside Europe. In so doing, the surplus extracted by colonial powers, such as England, also made possible the improvement of the social and economic conditions of the population in both Europe and North America.

In this respect, the flow and use of the colonial surplus, in combination with the enslavement of millions of Africans and the extermination and dispossession of indigenous people around the world, changed the prevailing configurations of scarcity in a number of ways. One of these ways was the use of the spoils from the exploitation of non-Western people to alleviate and make more bearable the exploitation of workers in today's global North. Intense as the exploitation of industrial workers in England and other early industrializing countries undoubtedly was, it usually paled in comparison with the exploitation of African slaves and colonial populations (Wallerstein 1979: 289, 293; Shannon 1996: 37–9, 66). African slaves, in particular, did not just lack the most basic freedoms, but often performed the most backbreaking labor that free wage workers were not willing to do (Steinberg 1989: 27). Insofar as they picked the cotton used by the textile industry in the nineteenth century, slaves from Africa played a crucial role in the rise of industrial capitalism and the accumulation of capital in both Europe and North America (Steinberg 1989: 27–9, Aronowitz 1992: 145).

In addition to increasing the production of wealth and creating new configurations of scarcity that imposed most of the burden of scarcity on both Western and especially non-Western workers, these developments expanded the reach of the capitalist mode of production. As Dowd (2000), Bagchi (2005) and others have pointed out, this expansion was dependent as much on the use of force as it was on the impact of market competition emphasized in Marx and Engels's *Manifesto*. In fact, the benefits that major capitalist powers have reaped in the past (and continue to reap in the present) from colonialism and from their use of military power to control foreign lands and to subjugate the people living on those lands have meant that "arms and conquest at the service of capitalists, and states controlled by them, have destroyed human lives in their millions down to the present" (Bagchi 2005: 48).

In short, capital has always tried to bring non-Western populations and territories into its orbit in ways that bolstered the pursuit of profit and capital expansion in the industrial capitalist centers (Hunt 2002: 348–9). Originating in an international division of labor that gave rise to "a racialized process of colonial 'underdevelopment'" (McMichael 2004: 12), and using the racist belief in the 'civilizing mission' of the colonizers (Bagchi 2005: 48), the pursuit of capital accumulation over the last few centuries generated the growing gap between the global haves and the much more numerous have-nots I described at the beginning of this chapter.

The rise and consolidation of these global economic inequalities did not occur without resistance. In fact, it was precisely such resistance to the British economic hegemony that allowed a number of countries to emerge as leaders within the global economic order. By "hasten[ing] the completion of their national states – the victory of the industrial North in the US Civil War; the unification of Germany; and the Meiji restoration in Japan" and ignoring "the ruling free trade ideology," some of the world's economic backwaters managed to rise to an economic prominence that they still enjoy (Desai 2009: 49). While the United States, Germany, and Japan industrialized by breaking with the free trade orthodoxy, the Soviet Union did so by bringing resistance to a whole different level when it attempted to break with capitalism altogether. Relying on the directive powers of the state even more than the United States, Germany, and Japan, the Soviet Union's industrialization effort seemed so successful that

[b]izarre as it may seem today, between 1930 and 1960 level-headed observers assumed that the state-commanded economic system of

the USSR under the Five-Year Plans, primitive and inefficient as even the most sympathetic visitors could see it was, represented a global alternative to western 'free enterprise'.... Level-headed observers considered it might actually outproduce it.

(Hobsbawm 2003: 414)

Also present in other parts of the world, popular resistance brought old-style European colonialism and imperialism to an end in the decades after the Second World War. This end was the joint product of anti-colonial independence movements in Asia, Africa, and the Caribbean, and of the restructuring of the global capitalist economy under the aegis of a new hegemonic power, the United States. Although it was not averse to using military force when its ruling political and economic elites deemed it necessary, this new hegemonic power often preferred to advance its interests by installing and supporting repressive and undemocratic regimes and dictators (Harvey 2005: 27). In so doing, the United States also defended the grotesquely inegalitarian configurations of scarcity that prevailed in various parts of the world against popular movements seeking progressive social and economic reforms. As David Harvey has pointed out, "whenever there was a conflict between democracy, on the one hand, and order and stability built upon propertied interests, on the other, the US always opted for the latter" (2003: 59).

The realities of the cold war did, however, at times moderate the usually implacable opposition of the United States to any progressive shifts in the configurations of scarcity prevailing in post-war capitalist societies around the world. The need to contain communism, as well as the reality of working-class struggles, made capitalist elites in rich industrialized countries more amenable to both the expansion of social programs and the establishment of welfare states, which for a time reduced the inhumanity of the configurations of scarcity prevailing in those countries (Aronowitz 2006: 188, Panitch and Miliband 1992: 4). Supporting these developments was the Bretton Woods system regulating the international capitalist economy in the period after the Second World War. Shielding the economic and social policy of national governments from the pressures of the world economy, even as it boosted international trade, the Bretton Woods system combined with Keynesian economic policies, state-centered industrial policies, and the expansion of the welfare state to produce unprecedented rates of economic growth (Steger 2003: 37–9, Rupert and Solomon 2005: 39–40, Cox 1997). It was this impressive economic performance that led some scholars to describe the immediate post war period as "the golden age of capitalism" (Marglin and Schor 1990).

This golden age had come to an end by the 1970s as the post-war boom gave way to economic crisis and stagnation. A constellation of factors, including the rise of popular movements around the world, in combination with the intensification of capitalist competition that resulted from European reconstruction and the rise of Japan and the newly industrialized countries in Asia and in other parts of the world, undercut capitalist profitability and triggered a crisis (Brenner 1998, Beaud 2001: 223–34, Bowles and Edwards 1993: 454–61, Hardt and Negri 2000: 262). The replacement of this model by neoliberal regimes that restructured national economies while also integrating them into an increasingly global economy was a response to this crisis. Neoliberalism thus became a 'global hegemonic project' that sought to restore the power of the capitalist class and to increase its share of the economic pie at the expense of working people in both the global North and the global South (Rupert and Solomon 2005: 57, Harvey 2005, Silver and Arrighi 2000: 61, Perelman 2008).

Thanks to their control of the economic surplus that the workers produced, the functionaries of capital were able to both advance the neoliberal ideological project and take advantage of the globalization-friendly policies that the success of this project produced (Harvey 2005: 43-55, George 2001: 18-19). As neoliberal economic globalization, in the form of free trade, capital market liberalization, privatization, and so on, increased the mobility of capital, it also increased capital's power over labor (Milani 2000: 48, Hardt and Negri 2000: 296, Sklair 2002, 278, Rupert and Solomon 2005: 41).

The result was an aggravation of economic inequalities and an increased ability of capitalist elites to 'invest' in politicians willing to implement and further the neoliberal consensus. While complicit in the consolidation of the neoliberal project, with all the devastating impacts that this project entailed for the majority of the population in rich and poor countries alike, political elites often found it expedient to absolve themselves of all responsibility, claiming that the constraints of already existing 'globalization' tied their hands and left them no alternative but to adopt policies that advanced the neoliberal project even further (Sklair 2002: 6, Panitch 2000: 374, Rodrik 1997: 79).

The neoliberal model also spread around the world as a result of the growing indebtedness of developing countries. By the 1980s, the international debt crisis not only bore witness to the exhaustion of the post-war model of development, it also served as a vehicle for the imposition of the neoliberal model on developing countries. This imposition was exemplified by the structural adjustment programs forced upon developing countries by international institutions, such as the World Bank and the IMF, which were now assigned the task of "displac[ing] the effects of capitalist crisis onto the world's poor" (Bond 2000: 133).

Although these programs, and neoliberal globalization more generally, have usually been devastating for working people, the poor, women, and the environment in developing countries, their imposition represented not a mistake, but an attempt to ensure that developing countries would repay their mounting debts, no matter how steep the social and environmental costs of repayment might turn out to be (Amin 1996; Charkiewicz et al. 2001: 35; McMichael 2004: 128–9, 133–5; Dickerson 1997: 100–1; Marchand and Runyan 2001: 144; Egan and Robidoux 2001: 83–7; Fisher 2001: 204; Ashman 2001: 235–6). Under neoliberalism, David Harvey points out, it is no longer the case that:

> lenders take the losses that arise from bad investment decisions ... [instead,] the borrowers are forced by state and international powers to take on board the cost of debt repayment no matter what the consequences for the livelihood and well-being of the local population.[10]
>
> (Harvey 2005: 29)

The nature and impact of these structural adjustment programs help to explain why many scholars analyze contemporary global capitalism as a continuation of colonialism by other means (Cato 2009: 2, 161; Sachs 1996: 261–2; McMichael 2004: 292). In fact, as the exploitation of the global South can for the most part continue even in the absence of military intervention and overtly colonial relationships, some scholars have argued that contemporary global capitalism may actually represent not just a continuation but also a rationalization of this exploitation (Meszaros 1995: 452, George 2001: 15).

While the rise of the neoliberal economic model shifted the prevailing configurations of scarcity at the expense of working people and the poor, the effects of this shift were especially dramatic in low-income countries. In a context where social safety nets had never been strong, the drastic cuts in education, health care, and other public services that structural adjustment programs often required could not but inflict irreparable harm on these countries' social fabric. To the extent that the under-provision of education and health care affected the productivity of present and future workers, such programs also damaged these countries' productive capacities. As a number of scholars point out, the social destabilization that neoliberal globalization and structural adjustment programs often bring about in developing countries has also contributed to the proliferation of ethnic conflict and civil war (McMichael 2004: 227–8, Stiglitz 2003: 8, Grimes 1999: 36–7, Lappe 1998: 21–3).

Successful as it has been in restoring the power of capitalist elites and increasing economic inequalities, neoliberalism has failed to match the economic performance of the Bretton Woods era (Hahnel 2002: 196–7, Sackrey et al. 2002: 101, Skidelsky 2008). While neoliberals and conservatives often defend growing inequalities by arguing that it is better, even for the poor, to grow the economic pie than to fight over its distribution, the fact is that "[t]he main substantive achievement of neoliberalization ... has been to redistribute, rather than to generate, wealth and income" (Harvey 2005: 159).[11]

Interestingly, this redistribution from the poor and the working people to capitalist elites, and from the South to the North, may have contributed to neoliberalism's unimpressive economic performance in general, and its present crisis in particular (Bello 2008a, Kotz 2007). As the growth of inequalities undercuts aggregate demand and leads to low capacity utilization, the ironic result of growing inequalities may have been to undercut not just wages but also capitalist profits (Hahnel 2002: 241). By making opportunities of profitable productive investment harder to come by, low capacity utilization and economic stagnation predictably encouraged the pursuit of profit through financial speculation (Bello 2008a, Wallerstein 2008, Tabb 2008a: 45–6). With economic inequality having increased to levels comparable to those prior to the Great Depression (Harvey 2005: 188–9), the bursting of successive financial bubbles has produced the most serious and painful economic crisis since the 1930s.

As the response to the crisis has, in the United States and elsewhere, primarily served the interests of the banks that helped to bring this crisis about, the growing inequalities underlying economic stagnation persist. Although massive government intervention in the economy has led some to announce the death of neoliberalism (e.g. Foster 2009a: 20), these interventions have been consistent with neoliberalism's regressive redistribution of wealth.

All in all, the configurations of scarcity that neoliberalism generates are devastating for working people in high- and low-income countries alike. While the configurations confronting working people in low-income countries are especially grim, the advent of neoliberalism has confronted even working people in the global North with stagnant wages, greater economic insecurity, deepening debt, longer and more flexible work hours, and a rollback of the welfare state and public services at a time when working people are required to pay a growing share of the taxes collected by governments (Cato 2009: 161, Bourdieu 1998: 127–8, Barnet and Cavanagh 1994: 344, Beck 2000: 1–8).

Even the recent economic success of some parts of the developing world does not contradict the general picture of neoliberal failure. In particular, the impressive rise of East Asian countries became possible through policies that defied free-market neoliberalism. Indeed, beginning with Japan, a number of these countries managed, by virtue of interventionist developmental states and a cold war context that led the United States to tolerate the existence of such states, to achieve rapid industrialization and economic growth, which, in turn, made possible dramatic increases in the material standard of living of their populations (Amin 1994: 109; Hahnel 2002: 184, 268–9; Tabb 2001: 64; Peet and Hartwick 2009: 63–4). More recently, China has experienced more than a quarter-century of economic growth rates above 9 percent, making it the only large country to have grown "so rapidly for so long in the economic history of the world" (Wen, Dale, and Minqi Li 2006: 130).

China's record is especially important given the fact that it is the most populous country in the world. Its rapid economic growth has permitted impressive increases in per capita income, and contributed to a reduction of extreme poverty by "some 400 million since 1981" (Schweickart 2006c: 173). As David Harvey (2005: 148) points out, however, underlying this performance have been wages and working conditions that are comparable to the realities of English factories during the Industrial Revolution.[12] Inequalities within China have been increasing, while "corruption is rampant" (Schweickart 2006c: 162). In fact, China's growing inequalities have shut out large numbers of people from access to education and health care, while, as the distribution of the fruits of economic growth is highly unequal, social unrest inevitably spreads (Wen et al 2006: 133, Tabuchi 2010). The Chinese leadership's anxiety of the possibility of such unrest is evident in its recent attempts to prevent any spread into China of the revolutionary upsurge throughout the Arab world (Chang 2011).

In any case, while the intensity of China's social problems partly reflects the fact that it is still a much poorer country than Japan or South Korea, one of the things that all these countries have in common is the ecological unsustainability of their respective models of economic development. Indeed, the rapid economic rise of the East Asian 'Tigers' has been as devastating to the environment as that of older industrial powers in Europe and North America (McCormack 1999, Lee 1999). As Gowan McCormack (1999: 149–50) points out, while Japan may have in the past seemed an attractive model for other countries in the region, the intense consumption of natural resources that the Japanese model presupposes makes its universal adoption impossible. In fact, McCormack suggests, the long-term maintenance of this model even in Japan may prove impossible "without some mechanism of coercion" (1999: 150). Most recently, of course, the nuclear catastrophe at the Fukushima nuclear reactors has highlighted the dangers of an ecologically unsustainable model of economic development which is hardly unique to Japan.

Meanwhile, China's own economic expansion has required it to engage in economic diplomacy around the world, including in areas, such as the Middle East, Africa, and Latin America, which are rich in resources that the United States considers to be essential to its 'national security' (Foster 2009: 18). Thus, the economic expansion of China and other countries in the world raises the prospect of geopolitical tensions, regional arms races, and continuing wars over resources (Klare 2001). The prospect of such wars can only strengthen the long-standing connection between capitalism and the spread of vast military–industrial complexes which use scarce resources in ways that threaten the ecological integrity of the planet and the very survival of the human species.[13]

In addition to the global scramble for resources that it has triggered, the economic expansion of China (as well as other large countries, such as India) inevitably magnifies the environmental challenges that the world will face in the twenty-first century. Having doubled its greenhouse emissions in the course of the last 20 years, China now emits more greenhouse gases than any other country in the world, including the United States (Li 2008).[14] Economic expansion has taken its toll on China's own physical environment and natural resources, leading China's deputy minister of environmental protection to predict that environmental degradation would likely derail the impressive rates of economic growth that China has experienced in the last 30 years (Wen et al 2006: 133–4). In fact, in an admission of how ecologically unsustainable China's economic model has been, by early 2011 even the Chinese prime minister Wen Jiabao was "suggest[ing] that China would reconfigure the emphasis that places economic growth above all else" (Jacobs 2011).

It is worth noting, however, a component of China's economic success that is consistent with the pursuit of ecological sustainability. Reflecting the experience of previous industrializers, China has recently come to "control almost half of the $45 billion global market for wind turbines" by flouting the simple free trade orthodoxy that has become a mark of global neoliberalism. Against this orthodoxy, China was able to benefit from attracting foreign capital, which it then subjected to rules that encouraged the rapid rise of an indigenous windmill turbine industry. As Keith Bradsher notes, China's success story in that industry "follows an industrial arc traced in other businesses, like desktop computers and solar panels. Chinese companies acquire the latest Western technology by various means and then take advantage of government policies to become the world's dominant, low-cost suppliers" (2010).

THE STRUGGLE(S) AGAINST NEOLIBERALISM AND THE LOGIC OF PROFIT

The dramatic shifts in the configurations of scarcity that the neoliberal model and now its crisis produced have predictably given rise to much social and class struggle. In fact, the rise of neoliberalism has signaled a systematic offensive on the part of capital against working people and against any social or environmental restrictions to the logic of profit (Foster and Magdoff 2008: 17, Aronowitz 2006: 40, Budd 2001: 174–5). The advance of the neoliberal agenda around the world has, however, been uneven because of the different levels of power that the working class and social movements still enjoy in different parts of the world (Harvey 2005: 13). Nonetheless, the attempt to restructure national capitalisms in accordance with neoliberal precepts has been general, thus giving rise to struggles against neoliberalism in all parts of the world (Budd 2001, Shooter 2001: 233, Fisher 2001: 204–10, Charlton 2001). These struggles are becoming increasingly global, as growing economic integration inevitably leads to the realization that fighting against the global dimensions of the neoliberal project also requires the globalization of resistance to both the project itself and to the logic of profit that it seeks to advance.

An interesting development in recent years that has come to complement the ongoing national struggles against neoliberal capitalism has been the emergence of a global justice movement. Rallying around the affirmation that 'another world is possible,' a multiplicity of groups including labor activists, feminists, environmentalists, anti-war activists, and indigenous rights activists, among others, has not only opposed the harmful effects of a generation of neoliberal policies but also sought to formulate alternatives through the formation of the World Social Forum. The World Social Forum is a space that understands itself as both an alternative to the World Economic Forum in which the world's economic and political elite meets every year and as a site of interaction and intellectual exchange between the various movements struggling against the injustices and social and environmental problems that global capitalism inevitably engenders (Leite 2005).

The lineage of the evolving global justice movement can be traced at least as far back as the 1999 protests against the World Trade Organization (WTO) in Seattle, and the Zapatista rebellion in Mexico, which intentionally coincided with the inauguration of the North American Free Trade Agreement on January 1, 1994 (Negri 2008, Leite 2005, Charlton 2001). At a time when capitalist globalization, with the aid of the deregulated financial and capital markets that it helped to engineer, has allowed Wall Street's toxic financial assets to threaten with bankruptcy entire countries (such as Iceland, Greece, Ireland, and counting) and with unemployment or poverty affecting an additional 100 million people worldwide, the objections of global justice activists to the injustices and the negative impact of capitalist globalization seem prophetic indeed (Zizek 2009: 9, La Botz 2008).

Needless to say, most politicians, bureaucrats, and journalists dismissed the validity of these criticisms. Accepting the precepts of neoclassical economic theory, politicians and opinion-makers simply assumed that, to the extent that capitalist globalization promoted free markets, it had to lead to greater economic efficiency and stability as well as to general prosperity (Keen 2001: 2). The fact that mainstream opinion makers accept at face value a theory that has long failed the test of reality is not just a sign of dogmatism (Keen 2001: 158). It also explains why it has taken a cataclysmic near-collapse of the global economic system to force even conservative Republicans like then-President George W. Bush (2008) to admit that "[t]he market is not functioning properly." Unfortunately, however, the lesson that politicians and policy makers, like Bush and Alan Greenspan, seemed to have learned as a result of the crisis has not taken that long to be unlearned, as the current crisis is now being used to entrench even further the failing neoliberal model.

Although it may seem ancient history by now, George W. Bush's admission, three years ago, of the limitations of the market was also an implicit admission of the bankruptcy of the economic and political elite that has long managed the capitalist globalization process. Despite the fact that the restructuring of the global economy along free market lines has reduced economic growth even as it increased inequalities and environmental degradation (Sackrey et al, 2002: 101, Hahnel 2002: 197, Skidelsky 2008), this elite has heaped scorn on the citizens and movements around the world fighting against the impact of capitalist globalization.[15] As far as this elite is concerned, participants in the global justice movement are either dangerous troublemakers deserving of political repression, pre-emptive arrests, and tear gas (Starr and Fernandez 2007); or naïve, if well-intentioned, fools who are too ignorant to understand that the goals they stand for in fact require the policies they object to (Bhagwati 2005).

The 1999 protests in Seattle offer a good example of how these two attitudes have complemented each other. While the Seattle police were doing their utmost to suspend basic democratic rights for the duration of the WTO meeting (Cockburn and St. Clair 2000), *New York Times* columnist Thomas Friedman graciously offered to disabuse the Seattle protesters of their silly ideas. Suggesting that they were relics of the past, Friedman dismissed the protesters as "a Noah's ark of flat-earth advocates, protectionist trade unions and yuppies looking for their 1960's fix" (1999). What the protesters did not understand, Friedman explained, is that globalization had a way of policing itself. The concern of transnational corporations with their image, Friedman assured us, led to garment factories in poor countries that "I would let my own daughters work in" (1999).

Ten years later, in addition to threatening to sink the global economy, the economic integration that Friedman was celebrating in his tirade against the Seattle protests has, as Stephen Castle (2009) recognizes, generated "a bull market for protesters." As a result, news stories on reported industrial unrest throughout Europe have mushroomed (BBC News 2009, Pan 2009). A major and long-lasting general strike also erupted in the French Caribbean, major strikes have taken place in China and Bangladesh, authoritarian regimes in the Arab world are starting to crumble under the pressure of citizens tired of unemployment, corruption, and high food prices, young people are revolting in Europe, while in Latin America the backlash against the failures of neoliberalism had begun even before the current crisis (Lamy 2009, Wong 2010, Panayotakis 2011a, Ahmed 2010). As Joshua Holland's "The whole world is rioting as the economic crisis worsens – Why aren't we?" (2009) makes clear, with demonstrations, riots, and general strikes becoming the new norm, the United States stood out until recently as an exception.

But even in the United States things are starting to change. The frontal attack on the labor rights of public-sector workers in Wisconsin, Indiana and other states around the country has recently led to a resurgence of labor struggle in that country (La Botz 2011, Aronowitz 2011). Workers and sympathizers have turned out for massive rallies, the largest since the Vietnam war era (Kelleher 2011). Many of the unionized workers in the private sector have shown their support, as they understand that the attack on public-sector workers is an attack on the last bastion of labor unionism in the United States. With a union density of 36.2 percent, as against the measly 6.9 percent union density in the private sector (La Botz 2011), public-sector unions are the last obstacle that capitalist elites face in their bid to intensify their exploitation of American workers even further, and to continue shifting the cost of a crisis they themselves caused on to those least responsible for it.

Thus, from the Arab world to the United States popular resistance is on the rise. What fuels this resistance is the manifest bankruptcy of political and economic elites that are responsible for the disastrous socio-economic conditions facing ordinary people around the world. As their responsibility for the current state of affairs continues to discredit them, the need for self-management and a democratization of economic and social life will continue to play an important role in the various struggles unfolding across the planet. In Argentina, where the crisis of neoliberalism had already sparked a massive economic crisis in 2001, the workers in hundreds of companies that went out of business have successfully reclaimed these companies and begun to collectively run them in a democratic and egalitarian fashion.[16] As the oral accounts of the participants in this movement suggest, this has been a life-changing experience for workers who had never imagined that they would themselves run the companies instead of simply acquiescing with company hierarchies that only sought to maximize the profit going to the company's often corrupt owners (Lavaca Collective 2007).

In Greece, the aspiration for self-management was a component in the massive youth uprising that erupted in December 2008 after a police officer shot and killed an unarmed teenager. This aspiration found an expression in the occupation of public buildings, with an intention to transform many of them into self-managed cultural spaces that could function as social and political meeting points and as a counterpoint to both capitalism's alienating urban landscape and the sterility of its consumerist culture (Panayotakis 2009a). About a year after this uprising Greece became the epicenter of the global capitalist crisis, and faced with an unmanageable foreign debt, acceded to a brutal 'rescue' package by the European Union and the IMF. Involving salary cuts for state workers and wage freezes for private-sector workers, reduced pensions, the abrogation of basic and hard-won labor rights, measures that make it easier to fire workers, while reducing their severance pay, this package has been a gift to Greek employers, while also functioning as an indirect bailout for the European banks holding Greece's sovereign debt.

While the aspirations for self-management and economic democracy animated Greece's 2008 uprising, the EU/IMF package serves as a reminder of the deeply undemocratic nature of the capitalist system. Indeed, the government adopting this program is a socialist government that ran in late 2009 on a platform that explicitly repudiated austerity. The turnabout of the Greek socialists has contributed to the discrediting of the Greek political system, confirmed by most recent polls as well as by the dramatically lower turnout in the local elections held in the fall of 2010 (Panayotakis 2011b).

The austerity policies imposed on Greece are now spreading around Europe and the world. Just as in Greece, resistance is spreading.[17] There have already been a number of general strikes in Greece, and workers in other parts of Europe are getting in on the action (BBC News 2010, Okello 2010). Underlying these struggles is a growing recognition that the dynamics of global capitalism create bleak configurations of scarcity, not just for workers and ordinary people in the global South. Instead, the current crisis underlines the fact that a global economy driven by the pursuit of profit is one that endangers the living conditions of ordinary people even in the global North, even as it bestows fabulous rewards to the privileged few whose decisions wreak havoc on humanity and the planet.[18] In so doing, it also suggests that the project of economic democracy may be our best hope to reduce human suffering, enrich human life, and protect the ecological integrity of the planet.

7 SCARCITY AND THE DEEPENING ECOLOGICAL CRISIS

I began writing this chapter soon after the April 2010 explosion on BP's 'Deepwater Horizon' oil rig.[1] Having claimed the lives of 11 oil workers and spilled 5 million barrels of oil into the Gulf of Mexico (*New York Times* 2010, Stolberg 2010), this explosion, caused by BP's "money-saving shortcuts and blunders" (Daly and Henry 2010), "ha[d] led to the largest oil spill in American history" and in the history of the Gulf (*New York Times* 2010, CBS News 2010). Far from an isolated phenomenon, this ecological disaster is merely one example of the ecological devastation that forms part of capitalism's normal operation. In fact, while the world watched in shock as the BP disaster continued to unfold over the next two months, Adam Nossiter was reporting that:

> [b]ig oil spills are no longer news in … [t]he Niger Delta … [which] has endured the equivalent of the Exxon Valdez spill every year for 50 years by some estimates. The oil pours out nearly every week, and some swamps are long since lifeless.
>
> (Nossiter 2010)

If the water pollution caused by BP is only one example of the water pollution caused by the extraction and transportation of oil, water pollution is itself only one of the manifestations of the deepening ecological crisis confronting humanity. In fact, oil contributes to this crisis even when its extraction and transportation do not involve major accidents. As it leads to the accumulation of greenhouse gases in the atmosphere, burning oil and other fossil fuels contributes to climate change and to the devastating impact of this phenomenon on people and ecosystems around the world. And beyond water pollution and climate change lie other ecological problems – deforestation, loss of biodiversity and high species extinction rates, depletion of fish stocks and acidification of the oceans, desertification and soil depletion, and the list goes on.

All these problems have serious implications for the configurations of scarcity people face worldwide. As they affect people's housing, health, and access to food and water, these problems create new needs while also affecting the means to the satisfaction of these needs that people have at their disposal. Environmental refugees uprooted by the ever more frequent extreme weather phenomena find themselves in need of a new home, while not having the job or material means to procure one. Children or adults whose health suffers as rising temperatures now allow mosquitoes and other disease vectors to thrive where they live will now be in need of drugs and find their performance in school or productivity at work suffering. As their needs increase, their ability to meet them declines.

While its implications for the configurations of scarcity confronting people will vary widely from one part of the world and from one social group to another, the deepening ecological crisis does aggravate the challenges and suffering facing billions of people worldwide. This chapter links the ecological crisis and the changed configurations of scarcity that it brings about to the operating logic of the capitalist system, thus suggesting that protecting the ecological integrity of the planet is inconceivable within the framework of that system.

THE DEEPENING ECOLOGICAL CRISIS

Commenting on the wide range of ecological problems facing humanity, Joel Kovel (2002: 20–1) has pointed out that, while each of them is enormously significant in its own right, it is their coincidence that makes them part of a broader, all-encompassing ecological crisis. Tracing the root of this crisis to the logic of profit and the growth of economic output this logic entails, Kovel points out that, just in the last 30 years of the twentieth century, the extraction and consumption of fossil fuels increased dramatically (by 59 percent in the case of oil, 72 percent in the case of coal, and 180 percent in the case of natural gas), the rate of transformation of trees into paper doubled, "the global motor vehicle population almost tripled," while "air traffic had increased by a factor of six" (2002: 3).

As these statistics make clear, the exponential increase, under capitalism, of economic output and the standards of living of some has drastically increased pollution as well as the depletion of natural resources. In fact since the 1980s humanity has been using up the planet's resources faster than they can be regenerated through natural processes, and by 2007 people consumed 50 percent more renewable resources than the planet could regenerate within a year (World Wildlife Fund 2010: 6). This state of ecological overshoot is likely to grow worse, since "even with modest UN projections for population growth, consumption and climate change, by 2030 humanity will need the capacity of two Earths to absorb CO_2 waste and keep up with natural resource consumption" (World Wildlife Fund 2010: 9).[2] The consumption of the affluent countries of the global North, and of the consumerist upper class whose numbers and wealth swelled in the neoliberal decades of widening domestic and international inequality, is mainly responsible for this 'ecological debt'.[3] In addition to the suffering that these developments cause in their own right, they have also been instrumental in pushing humanity ever closer to a number of ecological tipping points. Crossing those tipping points would inflict irreversible damage to the planet (Agence France-Presse 2010).

Neoliberal globalization has over the past 30 years seriously aggravated ecological degradation, while the volume of still-outstanding developing world debt often forces low- and middle-income countries to lift environmental protections and pillage their resources in a bid to increase exports and repay their debts (Cato 2009: 76, Schaeffer 1999: 200–1, Charkiewicz et al. 2001: 190–1, Sachs 1999: 143). Meanwhile, as the media sector comes to be dominated by large transnational corporations that broadcast the resource-intensive lifestyles of the upper classes of the global North to every corner of the globe, consumerist aspirations spread (Robertson 1990: 2, Sklair 2002: 166, 171, Waters 2001: 203, Barnet and Cavanagh 1994: 15–16).

In a world that is no longer "living within its ecological means" (Barber 2007: 148–9), the likelihood of conflict and 'resource wars' increases as developing countries seek greater access to the planet's resources and, in the process, put the disproportionate use of resources by the affluent countries of the global North into question.[4] This means that, in addition to its inability to translate its great technological achievements into a richer, more satisfying life for all human beings, and to manage scarcity efficiently, capitalism threatens to misuse these achievements in ways that pose grave threats to humanity and the planet. As nuclear weapons and problems such as global warming illustrate, capitalism increases the destructive as well as the productive capacities of humanity. In view of this fact, economic democracy is as necessary for the prevention of an unbearably dystopian future as it is for the achievement of a future of ecological sustainability and a richer, more fulfilling life for all.[5]

The problem of climate change illustrates how capitalism's ecological destructiveness affects the configurations of scarcity confronting people around the world. While the wealth and consumerist lifestyles of the global North rely on the abundant use of fossil fuel-based energy (Altvater 2006), the climate change that results from such use imposes risks on people worldwide, including the populations in the global South who benefit the least from the burning of fossil fuels. In particular, the coastal flooding that global warming can induce could turn large numbers of people around the world into environmental refugees. As rising temperatures change the locations mosquitoes and tsetse flies can thrive in, such disease vectors "introduce[e] ... malaria, dengue and yellow fever to new populations." Such health impacts are already operative, since according to UN-sponsored research, "global warming was responsible for 150,000 extra deaths in the year 2000." As dry areas become even drier, people in areas like Africa are more likely to experience hunger, while drought is likely to "[push] people to drink from ever more unsafe water sources" (Simms 2005: 67). As warmer temperature contributes to storms and extreme weather phenomena, "the mortality figures could become truly staggering as well as the cost of repair" (Grimes 1999: 31).

Most of the burden of these adverse changes is likely to be borne by the poorest people in the world: the people, in other words, who are both least responsible for the accumulation of greenhouse gases in the atmosphere and least able to "adapt to unanticipated environmental impacts" (Spitzner 2009: 223).[6] Women, especially racialized women living in the global South, are likely to be hit especially hard as they comprise "70 per cent of the world's poor" (Spitzner 2009: 223).[7] In any case, the fact that the high levels of output and consumption in the affluent countries of the global North are based on the disproportionate burden that these countries place on the planet's ecological sinks has led some scholars to suggest that the global North owes an ecological debt to the global South (Salleh 2009: 2, Simms 2005, Alier 2006: 285). In fact, estimates suggest that just the part of the debt that relates to the North's disproportionately high carbon emissions could be as high as US$13 trillion per year (Foster 2004: 195–6). Bolivia has sought to insert this question of climate debt into the international negotiations over climate change, but the countries of the global North have not only refused to address this issue in a meaningful way but have in fact tried to bully countries of the global South into submission by threatening "to cut vital aid to the developing nations" critical of the inadequate "deal agreed at the UN climate summit in Copenhagen" (Vidal 2010).

As this discussion makes clear, an adequate understanding of the deepening ecological crisis is inseparable from the analysis of the structural inequalities that capitalist political economies have long generated. Indeed, the Brundtland Report's classic definition of sustainability, which requires that the needs of present generations be met "without compromising the ability of future generations to meet their own needs" (World Commission on Environment and Development 1987: 8) can only lead us to the conclusion that capitalism is inherently unsustainable. After all, this is a system that has always been characterized not only by ecologically destructive practices that undermine the prospects of future generations, but also by extreme inequalities, poverty, and hunger that make it impossible to meet even the most elementary needs of large segments of the present generation.

ECOLOGICAL PROBLEMS AS ECONOMIC EXTERNALITIES?

Such a conclusion is, however, shunned by the neoclassical approach, which is almost as hegemonic in environmental policy circles as it is among economists. In the neoclassical view, problems like pollution are the product of economic 'externalities' that compromise the efficiency of capitalist markets whenever a discrepancy exists between the benefits or costs of a transaction to the actors immediately involved and the total social benefits or costs of the transaction, including those on third parties. In other words, the presence of externalities implies that the prices that economic actors respond to fail to reflect the full social costs and benefits of the good or service being exchanged. When this is the case, neoclassical economics argues, the economic actors' self-interested action will misallocate resources. In the case of goods and services that entail negative externalities (that is, costs imposed on third parties), this misallocation will lead to greater production of these goods than warranted by considerations of efficiency, while in the case of goods and services that entail positive externalities, the opposite will be the case.

Two examples will clarify this line of reasoning. Immunization that protects an individual from infectious disease involves positive externalities. Immunized individuals confer benefits not just on themselves but also on everybody else around them, because they reduce everybody else's risk of getting infected. If immunization is left completely up to the market, individuals' decisions whether to get immunized will take into account only the private benefit to themselves. Because of this discrepancy between private and social benefit, leaving immunization completely to the market would result in a lower number of immunized individuals than would be optimal for society.

Pollution resulting from the production of a good, on the other hand, illustrates the concept of negative externalities. Such pollution has a negative impact on parties other than the buyer and the seller of the good in question. To the extent that the price of the good reflects the cost of labor, land, and raw materials but ignores the cost of pollution to third parties, the producer will be faced with a deceptively low private cost, while the consumer will be faced with a deceptively low price. The discrepancy between the real social cost of the good in question and the cost/price faced by the producer and consumer respectively will lead to a level of production and consumption of that good that is higher than is optimal for society.

Thus, for example, motorists who buy gasoline will not take into account most of the externalities associated with the production and extraction of oil. The price they are called upon to pay may reflect the cost to the oil company of extracting and transporting oil, but it will probably not include the financial cost that the recurrent oil spills in the Niger Delta impose on local fishing communities, or the health costs inflicted on local children who have to swim in contaminated waters. It will also not include the external costs that result from climate change. Such costs include the cost imposed on displaced people because of rising sea levels, the health costs imposed on people living in areas that will become vulnerable to diseases like malaria as the temperature rises, the cost of drought on farmers, the cost of wars over water on the people caught up in the middle, and so on. Because of all these externalities, a neoclassical economist would argue, more scarce resources will be diverted to the production of oil than warranted by efficiency considerations.[8]

One of the ways in which externalities can be addressed, according to neoclassical economists, is by subsidizing goods involving positive externalities, and taxing goods involving negative externalities. In other words, government action can seek to correct the market failures generated by the existence of externalities by, for example, subsidizing vaccination and taxing goods the production of which leads to pollution. One application of this idea has been the pursuit of ecological tax reform in a number of European countries, including Germany under the coalition government of Social Democrats and Greens. The objective of ecological tax reform is to shift the tax burden from socially useful activities, such as work, to pollution-generating activities, such as resource-intensive production and consumption (Cato 2009: 164–5).

An alternative way of removing externality problems is suggested by the Coase theorem, named after economist and Nobel laureate Ronald Coase, who considered the assignment of relevant property rights as a substitute for the use of taxation and subsidies. For example, Coase suggests, it may be possible to address the external effects of a polluting plant on its neighbors by assigning property rights over clean air. If the rights are assigned to the community, the plant could pay the community for the right to pollute and would only do so as long as the benefits of pollution to itself outweighed the costs to the local community. If the rights are assigned to the plant, it would be the community that would have to pay the plant not to pollute beyond the point where the cost of pollution to the community outweighed the benefit of pollution to the plant. The necessary conditions for such an alternative strategy to work are usually not present, however, because externalities that affect a large group of people involve high transaction costs, including the cost of bringing together all the individuals affected by the externality so that they can negotiate with the party producing the externality. The fact that the Coase theorem assumes no transaction costs significantly limits its practical usefulness.[9] It also limits the plausibility of 'free market environmentalist' arguments that government intervention is not necessary since the perpetrators and victims of externalities could, in theory, negotiate directly. As Robin Hahnel notes:

> the realm of real-world situations where voluntary negotiations could be reasonably expected to provide efficient solutions to environmental problems is so small that free-market environmentalism no more deserves a seat at the policy table than miracles deserve a role in the operating room.
>
> (Hahnel 2011: 124–5)

Yet another strategy of addressing negative environmental externalities is what neoclassical economists pejoratively describe as 'command and control' regulations. By specifying the level of pollution that all the different actors are allowed to produce, neoclassical economists argue, rigid bureaucratic regulations do not differentiate between economic actors who can reduce pollution at a low cost to society and economic actors who cannot, do not give companies an incentive to reduce pollution any more than is required by law, and thus do not minimize the economic cost to society of reducing pollution to the desired level (Frank 1999: 208–10).

This critique of 'command and control' regulation has gained strength in the neoliberal era. While dominating environmental policy in the 1970s, command and control regulation has increasingly been replaced by more market-friendly approaches, such as the trading of pollution permits (Bond et al, 2007: 14). Supporters of this approach argue that it avoids the pitfalls of command and control regulation because it gives companies the incentive to reduce pollution as cheaply as possible (Frank 1999: 208–10; Hahnel (2011, esp. chs 7, 9, 10; Stavins 2003). Cap and trade, as this approach is also known, sets a maximum level of emissions and then either auctions off a number of pollution permits corresponding to that level, or sets acceptable levels of emissions for industries and/or countries and allows industries and countries to trade emissions if they exceed or fall short of the required pollution reductions. Since they can sell any extra pollution rights in the cap and trade market, companies that can easily reduce pollution have an incentive to do so as well as to pursue innovations that reduce pollution even further.

This approach was incorporated into the Kyoto agreement to reduce greenhouse gases. One problem with the Kyoto agreement was the provision regarding carbon offsets, which allowed companies and countries to forgo the necessary carbon reductions by funding projects around the world that would reduce carbon emissions to a level lower than would have prevailed in the absence of these projects. Lax enforcement of the agreement, as well as the ambiguity inherent in any comparison to a counterfactual scenario (what would have happened in the absence of the project) have led to carbon fraud and an abuse of the system by corporations claiming credit for projects they would have pursued anyway (Bond et al. 2007).

More generally, the Kyoto accord was too weak to address the scale of the problem. Its goal of reducing emissions by 5 percent compared with the 1990 level was hopelessly modest in view of the risks that climate change involves (Longfellow 2006: 2–3, Foster 2002: 19–20). To add insult to injury, carbon emissions in the early 2000s were actually rising faster than even the predictions of "the most fossil-fuel intensive of the Intergovernmental Panel on Climate Change emissions scenarios developed in the late 1990s" (Foster 2008a: 5). As a result, the planet "is changing faster than even pessimists expected" and is poised to reach a tipping point, with respect to greenhouse emissions, that could trigger catastrophic results (Krugman 2009a, 2009c; Foster 2009a; Clark and York 2008: 13; Wallis 2008: 25). Thus, timid as the Kyoto goals were, even they were not fully met (*New York Times* 2009). Furthermore, the attempt to agree on a follow-up treaty at the 2009 conference in Copenhagen has proven a disappointment, with results that "fell short of even the modest expectations for the summit" (*New York Times* 2009). Meanwhile, even the great ecological catastrophe in the Gulf has not shaken the US political establishment from its complacency. In fact, even market-friendly responses to environmental problems, such as cap and trade, are becoming politically untenable in the United States (Broder 2010).

Although the prospects for a market-based response to climate change seemed to brighten somewhat after the 2010 climate conference in Cancun, Mexico, this conference too produced modest results that "fell well short of the broad changes scientists say are needed to avoid dangerous climate change in coming decades" (*New York Times* 2011). The global inequalities that capitalism creates are clearly an obstacle to a meaningful response to climate change, as countries of the global North, including the United Kingdom, France, and the United States, use their economic power to penalize countries of the South, such as Bolivia, that oppose the pseudo-solutions the North favors, and to bribe other countries, such as the Maldives, that had in the past led "the campaign against low emissions targets" (Bond 2010).[10]

In any case market-friendly solutions, such as cap and trade, cannot address global warming for two main reasons. First, such solutions do not break with the logic that led Adam Smith to claim that the invisible hand of the market could make self-seeking behavior unwittingly serve the common good. In the case of cap and trade this logic suggests that, once the system is set up, even narrowly self-interested actors with no interest in the ecological integrity of the planet will, in their pursuit of profit, come up with and implement new methods of production, which reduce pollution and allow them to either sell the pollution permits they no longer need or to reduce costs by having to buy fewer permits.

This argument ignores the implications of the role that markets have in the constitution of human agents.[11] Markets both require and encourage human agents to act and view themselves as self-interested individuals. Simultaneously, the Smithian ideology of the invisible hand legitimizes self-interested action in the market by presenting it as a commendable way to serve your fellow human beings. The problem with market solutions to problems such as global warming is that this logic breaks down in the case of externalities. In such cases, the pursuit of self-interest does not lead to socially optimal outcomes, and the Smithian ideology, with the complacent faith in the benign nature of markets that it instills, inevitably becomes an obstacle to the realization of this basic fact.

The supporters of market-friendly solutions fail to recognize that the narrowly self-interested economic agents that capitalist markets and pro-market ideologies help to create are as likely to pursue profit by gaming whatever cap and trade system is set up, as to respond in the benign way that their models project.[12] This gaming becomes all the more likely given the fact that the resources that corporate capitalist interests can devote to that end usually far outweigh the resources devoted to strict enforcement by international organizations laboring under and hampered by pro-market ideologies suspicious of any restrictions of 'free enterprise.' In this respect, the fraudulent use of the carbon offset proposals in the Kyoto protocol is not accidental, but a predictable product of the type of human subject created by capitalism and the pro-market ideologies dominating the economic and environmental policy debates.

The narrowly self-interested subject that capitalist markets and ideologies promote will likely compromise not just the implementation of cap and trade systems but their ability to adopt caps that are restrictive enough to prevent grave consequences for future generations. As William Ophuls (1976) has pointed out, the narrowly self-interested actors created by capitalist markets are unlikely to curb polluting activities today in order to prevent ecological consequences that may be catastrophic for future generations, but are not grave enough during their lifetime to outweigh the benefits these activities confer upon them. In this respect, both the timidity of the Kyoto goals and the failure of their implementation confirm the ideological nature of market-friendly solutions, which do more to lull the general public into a sense of complacency regarding the ability of capitalism to address the deepening ecological crisis than to protect the ecological integrity of the planet.

The second shortcoming of market-friendly solutions, such as cap and trade, stems from the power relations inherent in the capitalist socio-economic system. Faced with the grave risks that global warming generates, a neoclassical economist can at most say that, if governments decided to take aggressive action and drastically reduce the amount of greenhouse emissions by 60 to 70 percent as suggested by scientists (Bond et al. 2007), then a market-friendly cap and trade system would allow them to pursue this goal in an economically efficient fashion.[13] In so doing, however, the neoclassical economist would skirt the real question, namely the power of capitalist interests to block the government action necessary to correct negative externalities that pose a grave threat to humanity and the planet. It is to this question that we now turn.

POLITICAL ECONOMY, EXTERNALITIES, AND
THE ROLE OF THE STATE

Far from skirting that question, Marxist and neo-Marxist political economists have no trouble answering it. In their view, addressing the negative externalities plaguing capitalist economies is a political rather than a technical question. Declaring that cap and trade or some other market-friendly measure could in theory address the problem of negative externalities is meaningless, if the power balance implicit in capitalism's class relations makes it unlikely that governments will intervene to do so. This is why Marxists and neo-Marxists analyze capitalism from the standpoint of political economy. Even a seemingly technocratic objective like economic efficiency cannot be studied in abstraction from politics, since its attainment is as dependent on political conditions as it is on the economic conditions that neoclassical economists have always recognized.

James Boyce (2002: 7), whose work exemplifies this insight, has described this difference between neoclassical economics, on the one hand, and critical political economy, on the other, in a way that foregrounds the difference between their respective approaches to the question of scarcity. While neoclassical economics primarily focuses on "the allocation of scarce resources among competing ends," political economy is concerned with "the allocation of scarce resources not only among competing ends, but also among competing people," including competing social groups and classes.

This difference in emphasis translates into contrasting understandings of the nature of 'market failures,' such as environmental degradation. Neoclassical economics is inclined to see environmental degradation as the result of specific failures, on the part of the impersonal mechanism of the market, to aggregate the self-interested action of individuals into outcomes that reflect the interest of society as a whole. This means that neoclassical economics organizes its approach to the question of scarcity around the relationship between individuals, on one side, and society as a whole, on the other. Capitalist governments and the market are then assumed to mediate this relationship in a way that allows the pursuit of individual self-interest to be reconciled with the interest of society as a whole. In the normal run of events capitalist markets can be trusted to produce this outcome. When market failures prevent markets from performing this function effectively, it is up to governments to shift the incentives facing individuals in ways that reconcile the pursuit of self-interest with the general interest in using scarce resources efficiently.

Political economy, by contrast, questions the neoclassical presumption of "a non-partisan, efficiency-maximizing state" and focuses on "the distribution of wealth and power" (Boyce 2002: 118, 7). From political economy's more critical standpoint, negative environmental externalities emerge not as a failure of the impersonal market mechanism to reconcile the pursuit of individual self-interest with the interest of society as a whole, but rather as the creation by powerful groups of externalities that are beneficial to themselves even as they harm the rest of society. As political ecologist Joan Martinez-Alier notes, "[e]xternalities are not so much market failures as cost-shifting successes" (2006: 282).

Having removed the presumption that, faced with market failures, governments can be trusted to intervene in a way that restores efficiency, Boyce (2002: 36) sees such efficiency-maximizing intervention as one special case within a large spectrum of possible government responses. Such an efficiency-maximizing intervention "corresponds to an equal distribution of power between winners and losers," while at the other end of the spectrum is the laissez-faire scenario, in which the government fails to do anything to address externalities. The latter scenario is likely to prevail when "the losers exercise no power whatsoever."

In other words, where in this spectrum the response of governments to negative economic externalities lies will obviously depend on the "relative power of the winners and losers" (Boyce 2002: 35). In highly unequal societies the powerful groups will be better positioned to impose negative environmental externalities on the poor because the latter will be less capable of resisting. Reflecting this balance of forces, governments will be more likely to tolerate and/or support the imposition of such externalities on the poor, thus placing highly unequal societies closer to the laissez-faire side of the spectrum. By contrast, the limiting case of a government consistently intervening in a way that maximizes efficiency presupposes the absence of systemic wealth and power inequalities that allow some powerful groups to impose negative environmental externalities on others. In the terms of the present work, it presupposes a non-capitalist socio-economic system consistent with the principle of economic democracy. Indeed, the link between democratization and environmental protection is a recurrent theme in Boyce's work ((2002: 11, 44, 83, 125, 128). In this sense, addressing market failures requires more than striking the right balance between states and markets. At least as important is the achievement of a society that is egalitarian enough to ensure that the government will be inclined to intervene in a way that seeks to maximize efficiency rather than simply furthering the interests of powerful minorities (Boyce 2002: 128).

By contrast, the deep class and economic inequalities that capitalism generates mean that the wealthy will not only be able to impose negative environmental externalities on the poor, but will also be willing to do so. Indeed, the wealthy derive more benefits from the generation of pollution thanks to their ownership of productive assets and their higher levels of consumption. As all production entails some degree of pollution, the producers and consumers of any given good exert, through their production/consumption, a negative environmental impact on everybody else. This means that the producers and consumers of any given good benefit whenever governments stick to laissez-faire policies that do not address the negative externalities inherent in the production and consumption of that good. The alternative to such policies, such as a tax commensurate to the pollution that the product in question generates, would, by contrast, be good for society as a whole but costly to the producers and consumers of the product in question (Boyce 2002: 25, 50). In other words, capitalist inequalities inevitably produce a powerful economic elite with both the incentive and the power to impose negative environmental externalities that systematically destroy the planet. In view of this connection between inequality and environmental degradation, it is hardly surprising that:

> [i]nternationally, countries with a more equal income distribution, greater political rights and civil liberties, and higher rates of adult literacy – indicators of a more equitable distribution of power – tend to have less air pollution, less water pollution, and wider access to clean drinking water and sanitation facilities .... Within the United States, states with a more equal distribution of power (as measured by ... voter participation, tax fairness, Medicaid access, and educational attainment) tend to have stronger environmental policies, less environmental stress, and better public health outcomes.
>
> (Boyce 2002: 5)

The connection between capitalist inequalities and environmental degradation is further aggravated by the deep poverty that these inequalities tend to generate. Poverty does not just make it harder to resist both the degradation, by the economically powerful, of the environment poor people live in, and the depletion of the natural resources poor people depend on for their survival. It also makes it more likely that poor people will be trapped in a vicious circle of poverty and environmental degradation that will make it harder for them to ever improve their plight. As the priority of the very poorest people on the planet is to secure immediate survival, they are often forced to engage in environmentally unsustainable practices that allow them to survive now even as they degrade the environment on which their long-term survival depends (Boyce 2002: 25–6).

Capitalist societies' traditional response to questions of poverty has been to pursue economic growth as a substitute for economic redistribution (O'Connor 1998: 10, Ophuls 1976: 185–7). Postulating the existence of an 'environmental Kuznets curve,' some authors have recently argued that pollution rises with income up to a certain level of industrialization and starts to decline beyond it (Boyce 2002, ch. 5). According to Boyce, however, "[a]n examination of international variations in income distribution, literacy, and political rights and civil liberties suggests that these may be more important than average income per se in determining environmental outcomes" (2002: 10).

This means that investing in people can be a means to environmental protection. "Improvements in nutrition, health, and education of the poor," for example, could make it easier for poor people worldwide to break through the vicious circle of degrading the physical environment they depend on in a desperate bid to secure immediate survival (Boyce 2002: 25–6). While it is true that capitalism creates powerful economic elites with the motivation and the ability to impose negative externalities on others, a strategy of reducing inequalities, enhancing the rights of the poor, and investing in nutrition, health, and education will increase the motivation and the ability of the poor to resist such imposition. Improved education, in particular, can increase poor people's understanding of the costs imposed on them by the environmentally destructive activities of the economically powerful. Thus, improved education will increase the motivation of the poor to struggle against the environmental degradation caused by the economically powerful, even as the reduction of economic and political inequalities will increase the effectiveness of such struggles (Boyce 2002: 27).

EXTERNALITIES, EFFICIENCY, AND THE CONFLICT APPROACH TO SCARCITY

Boyce exemplifies what could be described as the 'conflict' approach to the question of scarcity. This approach questions the neoclassical claim that market capitalism, with a little help from the government when market failures require it, can be trusted to manage scarce resources efficiently. Instead, it lays emphasis on the implications of structured class and social inequalities for the strategies that different groups deploy in negotiating the configurations of scarcity that such inequalities create. Class and social inequalities do not just represent an unjust distribution of the burdens of scarcity. They also mean that governments in capitalist societies cannot be trusted to correct market failures and pursue economic efficiency. Instead, they are likely to tolerate and support market failures, when these serve the interests of powerful classes and social groups. As far as the conflict theorists of scarcity are concerned, the distribution of the burdens of scarcity that capitalism effects is both unjust and inefficient.

In repressing these truths, conflict theorists argue, neoclassical economics "attempts to provide both an obscurantist veil and an ideological defense" of capitalist economic realities (Hunt 2002: 390). The ability of neoclassical economics to perform this function has been enhanced by the move of economic theory away from political economy that neoclassical economics has, since its inception, carried out so effectively. Unlike neoclassical economics, political economy has always been cognizant of the need to study economic life in its connections with society's other institutional spheres.[14] By abstracting from these connections, neoclassical economics makes it easier to assume that market failures could in principle be addressed by appropriate government action, and that market capitalism, with a little help from the government, can assure economic efficiency.

This conclusion is, of course, unwarranted, if the balance of class forces within capitalism, as well as the impact of this balance on the political system, makes it unlikely that the government will indeed seek to address market failures. It is because it ignores the socio-political conditions for such action that neoclassical economics makes it easier to mistake the theoretical possibility of government action restoring the conditions of efficiency for an accurate description of capitalist reality. This mistaken conclusion is all the more likely to be drawn if, as is usually the case, the discussion of the conditions for economic efficiency is seen as the exclusive province of (neoclassical) economists.

In this respect, E. K. Hunt (2002: 381) is right to charge that neoclassical economics easily lends itself to the role of an apologist of the capitalist status quo. What Hunt fails to acknowledge, however, is that the neoclassical admission of the dependence of economic efficiency on the removal of externalities still leaves an opening for a critique of the capitalist status quo. Indeed, the fact that such removal depends on government action implies that economic efficiency is inconceivable in the absence of some broader social and political conditions.

If, for example, the class inequalities generated by capitalist society undercut the democratic character of the political system, one conclusion that follows is that even the neoclassical economists' narrow definition of economic efficiency as Pareto optimality requires, as one of its conditions, a non-capitalist economic system consistent with the principle of economic democracy. This latter principle requires that all citizens have an equal say over the priorities and goals that the economy serves. Only a socio-economic system conducive to economic democracy could plausibly claim to generate economic and political outcomes that promote Pareto optimality by addressing market failures instead of serving the interests of powerful minorities by perpetuating these market failures.[15] Luckily for neoclassical economists, their move away from political economy, with its emphasis on the interaction between economic and non-economic aspects of social life, minimizes the risk that such 'dangerous' thoughts will interfere with their construction of abstract models that are as mathematically elegant as they are oblivious of the brutal realities of actually existing capitalism.[16]

Failing to acknowledge that its own conception of economic efficiency may point in the direction of a socio-economic system beyond capitalism is not, however, the only problem with neoclassical economics. The very concept of economic efficiency it employs is problematic. The concept of efficiency normally used by non-economists refers to the ability to achieve a given goal as fully as possible given the scarce resources at one's disposal (or alternatively, to fully achieve one's goal with as little expenditure of scarce resources as possible).[17] When neoclassical economists describe negative externalities, such as pollution, as a source of inefficiency, the goal they attribute to the capitalist market economy is the satisfaction of the wants of the sovereign consumer. As discussed in Chapter 3, the neoclassical assumption that the capitalist economy is there to serve the consumer refuses to acknowledge the contribution that the logic of capital accumulation makes to the construction of a consumerist culture that shapes consumer preferences. Thus, from the point of view of this book, the true goal of capitalist economies is not to satisfy the wants of consumers, but to pursue profit and a never-ending accumulation of capital.

As soon as we recognize this, our view of externalities has to be turned upside down. Far from representing an exceptional example of inefficiency, externalities emerge as efficient methods of pursuing the true goal of the capitalist economic system, namely profit and capital accumulation. After all, externalizing environmental costs on the rest of society has long boosted capitalist profitability and the rate of capital accumulation (Milani 2000, Wallerstein 2009: 4). It is therefore very misleading to interpret the deepening ecological crisis as the product of externalities that compromise the system's economic efficiency. Such an interpretation implicitly affirms that the most fundamental goal served by the capitalist system is to serve consumers – that is, all of us – and that the deepening ecological crisis is the product of a dysfunction that runs counter to the fundamental logic driving the system.

Thus, the neoclassical interpretation of externalities represses the fact that the deepening ecological crisis does not run counter to the logic of the capitalist system, but on the contrary, represents a logical corollary of the most fundamental principle driving this system, namely the never-ending pursuit of profit and capital accumulation. In so doing, neoclassical economics breeds complacency, even as the prospect of soon-to-be-crossed ecological tipping points threatens the planet with irreversible damage and the poorest of the poor in this world with even greater suffering. Neoclassical economics has this effect by creating the illusion that the ecological crisis runs counter to the fundamental commitments of market capitalism, and that it can therefore be resolved within the framework of this system. In other words, neoclassical economics enables the deepening of the ecological crisis by assuring the general public that the resolution of this crisis does not require the attainment of a fundamentally different, non-capitalist, socio-economic system.

THE LINK BETWEEN CROSS-CUTTING INEQUALITIES AND ECOLOGICAL PROBLEMS

The alternative socio-economic system required to resolve the ecological crisis has to be consistent with the principle of economic democracy. This conclusion follows from the ways in which capitalism's ecological outrages are linked to its exploitation of class and other social inequalities. To begin with, the functionaries of capital derive their ability to continue externalizing costs on society and future generations and to resist a meaningful response to urgent environmental problems, such as global warming, from their control of the economic surplus produced by workers.

Indeed, capital's ability to externalize costs and receive subsidies for environmentally destructive economic activities stems from the use of corporate profits to lobby politicians, make campaign contributions, and launch public relations campaigns that greenwash polluting industries.[18] This ability is also enhanced by the influence over the media that corporate interests enjoy thanks to their channeling of a significant portion of the economic surplus into advertising (Charkiewicz et al. 2001: 60).

In this respect, capital's externalization of environmental costs is one more way the undemocratic nature of the capitalist economic system worsens the configurations of scarcity confronting present and future generations alike. Although environmental movements often struggle against the ecological havoc wrought by capital, the undemocratic nature of the capitalist economic system makes it much harder for such struggles to succeed. As Eva Charkiewicz, Sander van Bennekom, and Alex Young point out, "[c]ivic organizations cannot match the funds which corporations provide for promotional activities" (2001: 60).

Capital's ability to externalize the environmental costs of its activity on society and future generations is strengthened by the very adversity of the configurations of scarcity that it generates. The poverty, unemployment, and misery to which the undemocratic nature of the capitalist system consigns large segments of the population even in the global North make people vulnerable to "environmental job blackmail" (Bullard 1994: 260). The desperate need for jobs puts pressure on communities and even labor unions to support environmentally harmful industries and oppose environmental regulations that are thought to "lead to job loss" (Bullard 1994: 261). This problem is especially acute for minority communities in the United States and around the world, which often suffer from both limited economic opportunity and increased exposure to environmental risk.

In this context, it becomes easier for capital to exploit potential divisions between environmentalists and low-income communities, just as it exploits racial, ethnic, gender, and other divisions between workers. The very companies responsible for the environmental job blackmail of low-income communities adopt a populist posture that accuses environmental movements of an elitist disregard of "the needs of 'workers and the poor'" (Schnaiberg 2005: 712). In view of these challenges, Robert Bullard is right to emphasize the environmental movement's need to:

> [address] the fact that social inequality and imbalances of social power are at the heart of environmental degradation, resource depletion, pollution, and even overpopulation. The environmental crisis can simply not be solved effectively without social justice.
>
> (Bullard 1994: 261)

A project for economic democracy based on the recognition of the connection between the undemocratic logic of capital and the adverse configurations of scarcity confronting people around the world can address the challenge outlined by Bullard. Indeed, the defining characteristic of economic democracy is a challenge of all the economic, racial, gender, and other social inequalities that obstruct the democratic determination of the goals and priorities that the economic system serves. As it also demonstrates the connections between capital's undemocratic economic power, and the human misery and ecological degradation that characterize the configurations of scarcity that capitalism generates, this book's conception of economic democracy can help bring together the popular movements that capital has always sought to divide.

A society consistent with economic democracy would do much to remove the forces that, under capitalism, have led to a deepening ecological crisis. At the same time, however, the resolution of this crisis also presupposes an abandonment of the consumerist lifestyles that capitalism promotes. An economically democratic society could contribute to such a development by abolishing capital and its use of the economic surplus to create a culture that equates success with and promises fulfillment through rising levels of material consumption. Instead of this culture, ecological sustainability requires a new social system that allows us to live within our ecological means.

In one sense, this may seem like a formidable task, especially for the consumerist societies of the affluent global North. However, the limited ability of ever-rising standards of living to enrich human life and increase people's happiness suggests that the task may not be quite as daunting as it seems. Abandoning consumerism is not a regrettable but necessary sacrifice. It is an opportunity to redefine the 'good life' by shifting emphasis from material possessions to the cultivation of human relationships that, as the literature on happiness confirms, is the true key to human happiness.[19]

There may in this sense be a silver lining to the deepening

ecological crisis that capitalism generates. Much as this crisis may aggravate the configurations of scarcity facing humanity and people "in poorer societies," who are disproportionately hurt by the ecological crisis (Cato 2009: 178), the sheer magnitude of the threat that the ecological crisis poses for the human species and the planet increases the likelihood that people around the world will finally recognize the futility of the consumerist lifestyles that capitalism promotes. As discussed in Chapter 4, even in the absence of the ecological crisis, capitalism could be condemned for its inability to translate the growing technological potential at our disposal into a correspondingly richer life for all human beings. As recognition of this basic fact increasingly becomes a condition for the prevention of irreparable harm to humanity and the planet, the growing salience of new forms of ecological scarcity may at long last catalyze a broad recognition of capitalism's long-standing inability to manage scarcity in accordance with the common good.

8 IMAGINING ECONOMIC DEMOCRACY: TWO MODELS

Up to this point, this book has focused on capitalism's irrational, inhumane, and ecologically destructive management of scarcity. Instead of using technological advances to promote human well-being and protect the ecological integrity of the planet, capitalism creates configurations of scarcity that inflict a lot of unnecessary suffering on people worldwide, lead to an increasingly serious ecological crisis, and do little to enrich even the lives of the minority of the world's population that lives in the affluent societies of the global North.

I have also shown the link between capitalism's failings, in all these respects, and its undemocratic nature. Capitalism precludes a democratic determination of society's economic goals and priorities, instead subordinating all economic actors to the logic of profit. As a counterpoint to the logic of profit, I have offered economic democracy, the principle that all citizens should have equal voice over the goals and the operation of the economic system. In this respect, in using the term economic democracy, I am not referring to a specific blueprint of what a non-capitalist socio-economic system might look like, but to a yardstick by which all socio-economic systems, including capitalism and any conceivable alternatives to it, could be measured.

This chapter and the next attempt to make the principle of economic democracy more concrete by exploring two questions: how it can help us evaluate proposals of alternative socio-economic systems that capitalism's critics have advanced, and what political strategy might help people work towards a new, non-capitalist and economically democratic, society. This chapter takes up the first question by examining recent debates between supporters of market socialism and those of marketless, democratic planning. It does not do so with the intention of presenting an exhaustive treatment and evaluation of the arguments on either side of the debate. Instead, it seeks to illustrate how the concept of economic democracy I propose can provide another angle from which to evaluate the strengths and weaknesses of the alternative economic systems that capitalism's critics propose. Chapter 9, by contrast, will examine how the concept of economic democracy can guide the struggle for a humane and ecologically sustainable non-capitalist society.

POST-CAPITALIST ALTERNATIVES: MARKET SOCIALISM VERSUS DEMOCRATIC PLANNING

Haunting the current debate on alternatives to the capitalist socio-economic system is the failure of the Soviet-style regimes that first appeared on the scene with the Russian revolution. In fact, competing interpretations of the reasons for the failure of these regimes are often at the center of the debate regarding the nature of a desirable post-capitalist alternative. Supporters of market socialism usually attribute this failure to the excessive dependence of Soviet-style regimes on central planning. For market socialists such excessive dependence cannot but lead to bureaucratic inefficiency and political authoritarianism.[1]

At the same time, market socialists reject the claim that the failure of Soviet-style regimes signals the bankruptcy of the socialist aspiration for a more democratic and just alternative to capitalism. As John Roemer has pointed out:

> The failed 'communist' experiment was characterized by the following three features:
> 1   public or state ownership of the means of production,
> 2. noncompetitive (that is, single-party) politics, and
> 3. command/administrative allocation of resources and commodities.
>
> (Roemer 1994a: 269)

According to Roemer, the failure of this experiment discredits the combination of these three features but does not preclude the possibility of a desirable alternative to capitalism that rejects undemocratic politics and a command economy, even as it retains "public ownership of the principal means of production" (Roemer 1994a: 270).

Supporters of marketless alternatives to the capitalist system, on the other hand, locate the weakness of Soviet-style regimes in their institutionalization of a top-down undemocratic form of planning. Hillel Ticktin, for example, contrasts the Marxist understanding of planning as a social relation involving "the control over the surplus product ... [by] the majority of the population through a reso-lutely democratic process" to the Stalinist and orthodox reduction of planning into a "technicality" involving nothing but "a form of a priori coordination of producers intentions" (1998: 58–9). Similarly, Michael Albert and Robin Hahnel have contrasted the central planning practiced in Soviet-style regimes with an alternative form of participatory planning that would draw on the input of all producers and consumers, respect people's aspirations for self-management, and prevent the formation of a Soviet-style class rule of technocratic 'coordinators'.[2]

Obviously, both sides in the debate regarding post-capitalist alternatives view the socio-economic models they favor as more economically democratic than the capitalist system they oppose. In this respect, this is also a debate on the meaning and practical implementation of the principle of economic democracy. In using this principle to evaluate the different alternatives to capitalism that are currently under debate, this chapter is also an evaluation of the strengths and weaknesses of the conceptions of economic democracy implicit in each of these models. While there are numerous models of what a post-capitalist socio-economic system might look like,[3] in this chapter David Schweickart's work on 'economic democracy' will represent those arguing that any viable and desirable alternative to capitalism has to make use of markets, while Michael Albert and Robin Hahnel's work will represent the proponents of a market-less non-capitalist economic system. I will begin by sketching the main components of Schweickart's and Albert and Hahnel's models, and then discuss, in both this chapter and the next, the extent to which they are consistent with the concept of economic democracy I propose.

DAVID SCHWEICKART'S 'ECONOMIC DEMOCRACY'

Schweickart calls his model 'economic democracy' because he views it as an "extension of the democratic impulse ... into ... the workplace and investment decisions" (Albert and Schweickart 2008: 48–9). At the same time, however, he insists on the need for markets even in a post-capitalist society because of a fear that over-reliance on democracy as a method of organizing an alternative economic system could undercut this system's viability and desirability. A truly viable and desirable alternative to capitalism requires, in Schweickart's view, a judicious balance between democracy, planning, and markets.[4]

To achieve this balance Schweickart proposes the introduction of democratic workers' control within companies, the retention of markets in which companies compete for customers, and 'social control of investment,' which allows people to democratically determine their society's long-term economic development (Schweickart 1993: 67–77; 2008: 49–52); 1992: 30–4). In Schweickart's (1993: 69) model the means of production would be "the collective property of the society," but workers would control the company in which they worked subject to certain restrictions, including minimum wage laws and a legal requirement to protect the value of the company's capital stock. The worker-controlled companies would still have authority over what they produced, how much they produced, and what they charged for their products. Workers themselves would both decide how to distribute among themselves the company's income and elect the worker council that selected and monitored the company's managers.

Companies would continue to buy capital goods and sell their goods and services in markets (Schweickart 1993: 70). Although the government could intervene in cases of market failure, the existence of market competition would encourage companies to operate effi- ciently. As their income depended on the surplus of revenues over non-labor costs, workers would have a greater "incentive to work hard, and to see to it that [their] cohorts do likewise" than is the case "under traditional capitalism or traditional socialism" (Schweickart 1992: 31).

Schweickart's call for a democratic control of investment is in line with the argument by other market socialists that because of the existence of a variety of market failures, long-term social planning of investment must complement market forces (Roemer 1992: 460–2; 1994; Estrin and Winter 1989). In defending this claim, market socialists also point to the crucial role that government intervention in the process of investment has historically played in the industri- alization of countries around the world (Peet and Hartwick 2009: 63–4, Stiglitz 2001: xiii–xv, Erber 1994: 354–5, Roemer 1994: 106–7).

In Schweickart's model, the necessary funds for investment would come not from a rich capitalist elite but from the taxation of the capital assets used by the different enterprises. The capital raised in this way would be available for further investment, and be distributed to different regions in accordance with their population size. Whereas, under capitalism, people have to follow the flows of capital, in Schweickart's model capital would "[flow] to where the people are" (Albert and Schweickart 2008: 49). By providing enterprises with an incentive to economize on the capital assets they used to produce, this way of raising capital would also ensure that companies used capital assets efficiently (Schweickart 1993: 70–1; 1992: 32–3; Albert and Schweickart 2008: 49–50).

According to Schweickart, the institutional pillars of his model are "instantiations of three forms of democracy" (1992: 33). To begin with, markets would subordinate the economic system to the needs of consumers by allowing them to "vote their preferences with their purchases" (Schweickart 1993: 33–4). Schweickart recognizes, of course, that markets also generate inequalities that do not distribute these 'votes' equally, but that does not prevent him from concluding that, all in all, markets do give consumers "real influence over the (production) decisions that affect them" (Schweickart 1992: 34). Second, democratic workplaces would allow individual workers to have an impact on the conditions of their work and, given their often small size, provide them with an opportunity to engage in the practice of direct democracy. Finally, because of the population sizes involved, social control of investment would take the form of "a mediated, representative democracy" (Schweickart 1992: 34). Nonetheless, even the planning of investment could take into account popular input, and its subordination to the principle of democracy, rather than profitability, would make possible "rational development that accords with the real needs of the population" (Albert and Schweickart 2008: 51).

Although he views his model as "something very different" from capitalism, "a democratic order genuinely responsive to human needs" (Albert and Schweickart 2008: 53), Schweickart also insists that his model is not a utopian scheme "spring[ing] out of thin air" (Albert and Schweickart 2008: 50) because it seeks to build on existing historical trends. In particular, it preserves the beneficial aspects of capitalist dynamism even as it "eliminat[es] [capitalism's] destructive effects" (Albert and Schweickart 2008: 50). Schweickart defends this claim by noting the long history of producer cooperatives in Europe and North America, as well as the fact that such cooperatives are "as efficient as their capitalist counterparts, and often more so" (Albert and Schweickart 2008: 50). Similarly, he points out that the growing government role in capitalist societies has been the product of the havoc wrought by laissez-faire capitalism and of the need to use tax revenues to finance public investment in "infrastructure, education, basic research, social security, environmental protection, etc." (Albert and Schweickart 2008: 50).

In addition to being "vastly more democratic than capitalism," his model of economic democracy, Schweickart argues, manages to be more egalitarian and ecologically sustainable than capitalism without falling short when it comes to efficiency (Albert and Schweickart 2008: 52). Schweickart develops this argument in great detail in *Against Capitalism* (1993). He does so by comparing his model of economic democracy both with the laissez-faire type of capitalism that conservatives favor and with more liberal models of 'fair capitalism' that respond to the excesses of free market with some government intervention in the economy.

With respect to efficiency, Schweickart argues that his model has a number of advantages over capitalism. To begin with, Schweickart examines and rejects neoclassical claims that worker self-management is likely to reduce the economic system's allocative efficiency. On the contrary, he suggests that his model would be less likely to lead to the formation of monopolies, as companies would not feel the pressure for perpetual expansion that haunts companies that operate within a capitalist context (Schweickart 1993: 96–8, 122; Albert and Schweickart 2008: 53). Economic democracy would do away with mass unemployment, since it would not be a class society in which economically and politically powerful employers valued some degree of unemployment for the discipline it imposed on workers (Schweickart 1993: 112, 253).

Finally, Schweickart argues that economic democracy will reduce 'X-inefficiencies' by helping companies use the resources at their disposal more efficiently. Workers will have a greater incentive to work hard and to ensure that their coworkers do the same, if their income depends on the company's performance. This will boost democratic companies' productivity and reduce their surveillance costs. Finally, because workers can usually recognize managerial incompetence much earlier than 'distant owners,' economic democracy will facilitate the replacement of incompetent managers "before things spiral out of control." (Albert and Schweickart 2008: 50; also see Schweickart 1993: 81, 102–3).

By decoupling investment from private property, Schweickart argues, his model will do away with a major source of "the grotesque inequalities characteristic of capitalism" (1992: 32–3). In addition to reducing the inequalities between employers and workers, economic democracy will also reduce the inequalities between managers and workers.[5] As managers will no longer be accountable to boards of directors made up of affluent individuals but to workers themselves, they will find it difficult to get away with grossly inflated pay packages (Schweickart 1993: 198–9).[6]

With respect to ecological sustainability, Schweickart argues that his model will not share capitalism's dependence on economic expansion. Unlike his model, capitalism requires economic growth on both the micro- and the macro-economic level. Individual companies that do not continue to grow risk losing their competitive edge and going out of business, while macroeconomic growth is necessary to legitimize the great economic inequalities at the basis of the capitalist system. As it places a burden on the environment, this compulsion to grow has turned capitalism into a grave threat to the ecological integrity of the planet (Schweickart 1993: 122, 154–5, 158–9, 168–9, 260–1; Albert and Schweickart 2008: 53).

ALBERT AND HAHNEL'S MODEL OF A PARTICIPATORY ECONOMY

Michael Albert and Robin Hahnel have long advocated a marketless, non-capitalist economic system that, in their view, best serves the values of "equity, solidarity, diversity, self-management, ecological balance, and efficiency" (Albert 2008a: 398; also see Albert 2003, Albert and Hahnel 1991, Hahnel 2002). An equitable distribution of the fruits of social labor should, according to Hahnel and Albert, reflect the sacrifice individuals make for the production of useful goods and services. In their view, this distributive principle is not consistent with either capitalism or market socialism.[7]

According to Hahnel and Albert, capitalism rewards individuals according to the contribution that these individuals' talents, skills, and productive assets make to production. Market socialism, on the other hand, only rewards individuals in accordance with their skills and talents. Capitalism makes it possible for individuals who have never sacrificed for the sake of social production, but who have inherited highly valued productive assets, to earn rewards that are much higher than those of people sacrificing most of their lives to the production of useful goods and services. Similarly, market socialism would reward individuals at least partly on the basis of talents that individuals have been born with. As Hahnel and Albert point out, rewarding individuals for a talent they were lucky to be born with is no more defensible than rewarding them for being born into a wealthy family.

In embracing solidarity as a value, Hahnel and Albert argue that a desirable economic system should encourage people to take the interests of others into account rather than simply pursuing their selfish individual interests even at the expense of others. Their affirmation of diversity reflects their conviction that the existence of multiple ways of life within a society can enrich every individual's life experience, while, in affirming the value of self-management, Hahnel and Albert argue that how much say individuals have over a given decision that affects their lives should reflect the magnitude of this effect.

In affirming ecological balance, Hahnel and Albert affirm an economic system that allows people to recognize the true environmental costs of their economic activity so that the right balance can be struck between production to meet people's material needs and the ecological integrity of the planet. Finally, in affirming economic efficiency, Hahnel and Albert want to avoid:

> wast[ing] our energy and resources by producing output that fails to meet needs and develop potentials, or by producing harmful byproducts that offset the benefits of intended products, or by splurging what is valuable in inefficient methods and as a result wasting assets needlessly.
>
> (Albert 2008a: 399)

For Hahnel and Albert, market socialism, market capitalism, and centrally planned socialism are not consistent with these values. While market socialism is preferable to market capitalism because it is less unequal than the latter, it is, as I noted earlier, inconsistent with Hahnel and Albert's conception of justice. Market socialism and capitalism alike violate many of the values that Hahnel and Albert affirm because of these systems' reliance on markets.[8]

Markets undercut solidarity by encouraging individuals to violate the golden rule of treating others the way they would want others to treat them. In particular, markets lead to cutthroat competition that encourages people to manipulate and exploit others. Markets also undercut solidarity by virtue of their opacity, which often hides from individuals the effects of their economic decisions on other people worldwide.[9] In this respect, markets do not just encourage individuals to act in ways contrary to the value of solidarity. By keeping from them information regarding the effects of their choices, they prevent even those willing to take into account the interests of others from doing so.

Markets are also inconsistent with self-management, since they encourage hierarchical divisions of labor like those prevailing in capitalist corporations. These concentrate power in the hands of managers, while denying workers any say over the decisions regarding the productive process that affect them (Albert and Hahnel 1991: 13–14). Albert and Hahnel also challenge the ideological view of markets as paragons of economic efficiency. As they point out, externalities are the rule rather than the exception in all market economies. This leads not just to misallocation of economic resources but to a distortion of individual preferences which compounds economic inefficiencies even further (Hahnel and Albert 1990). Since these externalities also include the negative impact of production and consumption decisions on the environment, Albert and Hahnel also argue that both market capitalism and market socialism are inconsistent with the value of ecological balance.

Central planning is also not desirable, according to Hahnel and Albert, because of its top-down nature. Even under the most favorable assumptions, central planning is not consistent with the principle of self-management. To secure implementation of their directives, central planners will favor hierarchically organized workplaces that increase their ability to "[hold] subordinates accountable" (Albert and Hahnel 1991: 16). Apart from denying workers a say over the productive decisions affecting them, central planning is inconsistent with another condition of self-management, namely the general availability of information regarding the relationships between the different parts of the social productive process as well as the impact that each of these parts has on the others. Furthermore, because of its bias against self-management, central planning is likely to distort individual preferences by steering them away from a desire for self-management, thus also leading to worker apathy and growing economic inefficiencies.

It is to these weaknesses of central planning that Hahnel and Albert attribute the class nature of Soviet-style regimes. Ruling these regimes, Hahnel and Albert argue, was a class of 'coordinators' who derived their power from the crucial organizational functions that they alone were responsible for.[10] This class of 'coordinators' is not unique to Soviet-style regimes, but is also present in capitalist societies. In contrast with Soviet-style regimes, however, the institutional basis of coordinators in capitalist societies is not central planning but the corporate division of labor that assigns organizational and decision-making power to a minority at the top, while consigning everybody else to a life of taking orders and implementing other people's decisions. In this respect, Hahnel and Albert view capitalism as a three class system, with coordinators being as integral a part of the system as the capitalists and the working class that have often monopolized the attention of Marxist theorists.

The practical political implication that Hahnel and Albert, as well as their followers, draw from this insight is that the struggle for an alternative to the present socio-economic order has to be not only anti-capitalist but also 'pro-classlessness' (Albert 2008a: 398). For Albert and Hahnel and their followers, the experience of Soviet-style regimes makes clear that the expropriation of capitalists will not lead to a classless society unless, in the new social order that results from this expropriation, it is not a small class of co-coordinators but "people themselves who 'take power'" (Wetzel 2008: 192).

The first characteristic of Hahnel and Albert's model is the absence of private property in the means of production, which allows control over the economic process to pass from a minority of owners to self-managed workers' and consumers' councils.[11] Every worker is a member of the workers' council at their workplace, and every citizen is a member of the consumers' council in their neighborhood. The self-managed nature of these councils means that their members can have a voice in different decisions in proportion to the impact that these decisions have on them. These local councils are part of broader federations of workers' and consumers' councils with which they interact throughout the process of formulating the plans guiding economic activity.

A second characteristic of Hahnel and Albert's model is the existence of 'balanced job complexes' which seek to preserve technical specialization even as they challenge the division of the population between a minority of coordinators who focus exclusively on decision making and empowering organizational tasks, and a majority of working people who implement the decisions that coordinators make. Every worker in a participatory economy will have to carry out some empowering organizational tasks and some less challenging, executive tasks.

Hahnel and Albert's insistence on the need for balanced job complexes reflects their conviction that economic activity has a constitutive effect on human beings. In other words, the nature of the work people spend much of their lives on has a big impact on who people are, and what skills and preferences they have. Balanced job complexes will ensure that every individual has a meaningful opportunity to participate in the self-managed councils on an equal basis. A participatory economy that tried to institute workers' and consumers' councils without challenging the social division between coordinators and workers would make it possible for coordinators to use the skills, knowledge, and experience they derived from their monopolization of empowering organizational tasks to dominate the councils' decision-making processes.

Workers' and consumers' councils will be instrumental in

implementing the two other features of a participatory economy, namely compensation in accordance with sacrifice for the sake of production, and participatory planning. The planning process will begin at local workers' and consumers' councils. Taking into account the input of individual workers, local workers' councils will formulate an initial proposal regarding the output they will produce in the coming year, the inputs they will require, and the number of hours their members will spend working. This proposal will have to be approved by the broader regional or industry-wide workers' councils of which local workers' councils are a part. Approval will depend on whether the expected social benefits from the production a workers' council proposes justify the expected social costs.

Similarly, individuals will submit consumption proposals for the coming year to their local consumers' council. To be approved, proposals will have to be justified by the work effort individuals plan to contribute to the production of goods and services. Workers' and consumers' councils at each level will aggregate the production and consumption proposals/requests of all their members. Throughout this process individuals and councils will use indicative prices to reflect the relative social benefits and costs of the different goods and services. Facilitating boards will adjust these prices in order to balance the proposed supply and demand of goods and services. These boards will not act as central planners, but rather simulate the coordinating function of markets, while keeping the process consistent with the self-managed council structure. Each time the indicative prices are adjusted, local and regional councils will have to update their production and consumption proposals. After a few iterations, either a plan that balances the proposed supply and demand of goods and services emerges, or people choose, through popular vote, from a menu of plans that are consistent with the data that the multiple iterations of the participatory planning process produce.

Although, for Albert and Hahnel, this model embodies the values of equity, diversity, self-management, ecological balance, and efficiency, it is possible that this model will give rise to a number of tradeoffs between these values (Panayotakis 2009b). Nonetheless, as the discussion above makes clear, Albert and Hahnel's model does attempt to address some of the shortcomings of capitalism and market socialism that they criticize.

In addition to showing that their model is more consistent with the values they espouse than either capitalism, market socialism or centrally planned socialist economies, Hahnel and Albert have also analyzed and compared their model's welfare properties with those of the other three systems (Hahnel and Albert 1990, Albert and Hahnel 1991). More than confirming the superiority of their model of participatory economy to the formal models of the other three systems, this analysis indicates that:

> [r]ealistic capitalist and coordinator economies differ from their formal representations in ways that magnify their failings, while realistic participatory economies differ from their formal representation in ways that enhance their capacity to attain desirable results in fewer steps and at reduced cost.
>
> (Albert and Hahnel 1991: 106)

ECONOMIC DEMOCRACY AND THE DEBATE ON POST-CAPITALIST ALTERNATIVES

However carefully post-capitalist economic models may be thought through, it is of course impossible to know in advance how well they will work in practice. Albert (2006) admits as much with respect to participatory economy, and so has John Roemer (1992: 452) with respect to the model of market socialism that he favors. Given the uncertainties involved, it is hardly surprising, therefore, that a common criticism of such models is that they simply will not work. Schweickart (2006) levels this charge against Hahnel and Albert's model, as do Pat Devine (1992) and Hillel Ticktin (1998) against market socialism.

Schweickart and market socialists tend to dismiss as utopian and dangerous any attempts to revive the socialist ideal by holding up the promise of an economic system that would coordinate economic activity without making use of markets. For market socialists, markets can be transformed from a 'meat grinder' to a 'can opener' that serves people's needs and socialism's "non-market purposes" (Harrington 1994: 108, Lawler 1998: 140, Weisskopf 1992: 23, Bowles 1991: 16, Le Grand and Estrin 1989). Far from being antithetical to socialism and planning, markets need 'socialism and democratic planning,' if they are "to serve the common good as Adam Smith thought they did under capitalism" (Harrington 1994: 84). This relationship cuts both ways, however, as "the most effective planning requires the use of markets" (Roemer 1992: 456). The issue for market socialists, then, is not to choose either markets or planning, but to replace the undemocratic 'planning within a market framework' characteristic of contemporary capitalist corporations with a democratic socialist economy composed of 'markets within a planning framework' (Belkin 1994: 34).

Just as market socialists believe that planning without markets is neither desirable nor economically viable, critics of markets reject the notion that a desirable post-capitalist society is compatible with markets (Ollman 1998b). Presenting market socialism as a futile "attempt to square the circle," such critics point out that the market's alleged contributions to economic efficiency are inseparable from the inhumane and destructive aspects of capitalism itself (Devine 1992: 76). Thus, for example, while some market socialists would preserve labor markets for the sake of efficiency (Roemer 1994b: 120), critics of market socialism point out that the ability of labor markets in capitalist society to motivate workers crucially depends on the stick of chronic unemployment. To the extent that market socialists humanized markets by reducing unemployment, they would also reduce the benefits that markets are supposed to deliver (Ticktin 1998: 60–1).

Although it cannot be settled on the basis of theoretical argument alone, this debate between market socialists and their critics does make an important contribution to the project of economic democracy. To begin with, as both Albert and Schweickart (2008) point out, the development of models that provide a plausible and detailed description of what a desirable post-capitalist economic system might look like does add credibility to the affirmation, by the global justice movement and social movements around the world, that 'another world is possible.'

At the same time, it is also true that even the most convincing elaboration of non-capitalist economic models is not always sufficient to dispel the cynicism that prevails in large segments of the population. As both Albert (2003: 292) and Hahnel (2005: 383) recognize, this cynicism is at least in part a reaction to the failures of Soviet-style regimes. Despite Albert and Hahnel's effort to distinguish their model from central planning, their proposal to abolish markets is probably not reassuring to those whose skepticism regarding the possibility of a society beyond capitalism stems from the failure of Soviet-style regimes. To the extent that such skeptics join the project of economic democracy, they are more likely to seek inspiration in a model such as Schweickart's.

On the other hand, Hahnel and Albert and the other critics of markets do make a contribution to the project of economic democracy by undermining belief in the 'invisible hand' ideology that sees in markets the means through which capitalism reconciles the pursuit of private interest with the interests of society as a whole. In this respect, market socialists and those favoring non-market alternatives to capitalism can serve complementary functions within the project of economic democracy. While critiques of the market undermine the ideological supports of the undemocratic capitalist system, models of market socialism can potentially recruit into the project of economic democracy people who might otherwise respond to those critiques with a cynical acceptance of a system seeming to them as immutable as it is flawed.

While in one sense complementary to each other, the models that Schweickart, and Albert and Hahnel, advocate do represent two different views regarding the conditions for economic democracy. Schweickart understands economic democracy as a matter of introducing democratic institutional mechanisms into the workplace and the social process of investment. In so doing, he tends to underestimate the subjective conditions of economic democracy, which derive from the fact that economic institutions are not simply instrumental but also constitutive of human beings.[12] In other words, economic institutions do not just mediate the production and distribution of the goods and services that individuals desire. They also help to produce those individuals themselves, including their skills and preferences (Bowles and Gintis 1986, Bowles 1991).

In this respect, Albert and Hahnel's emphasis on 'balanced job complexes' and the need for a socio-economic system that is 'pro-classlessness' as well as anti-capitalist is consistent with the principle of economic democracy, as I define it in this book. The concept of balanced job complexes recognizes what Schweickart's model does not, namely that economic democracy requires not just democratic mechanisms that register people's individual preferences, but also a division of labor that makes it possible for all people to make a meaningful contribution to the deliberative process that determines society's economic goals and priorities.

True economic democracy does not therefore simply seek to keep economic and political elites accountable by ensuring that their actions conform to the wishes of the workers or citizens who elected them. True economic democracy empowers workers and citizens to challenge the division of the population into directive elites and obedient masses. Challenging this division is inconceivable in a society in which decision-making and empowering organizational tasks continue to be in the hands of relatively small elites.

All in all, Albert and Hahnel are more cognizant than Schweickart of the implications of the constitutive nature of economic institutions for economic democracy. The closest the latter comes to recognizing the subjective conditions for economic democracy (in the sense that this book, rather than Schweickart himself, uses the term) is when, in discussing his own model of economic democracy, he argues that:

> [w]hen I talk about the structure of Economic Democracy, I am fully aware that economic structure is not the whole story. The quality of a democracy depends on the consciousness of the people, on their values, on what they see as priorities. That's why social movements focusing on such things as racism or sexism or homophobia or ecology are so important. Economic democracy makes it possible to have a society without racism, but democracy itself does not eliminate racism.
>
> (Albert and Schweickart 2008: 70)

Here Schweickart acknowledges the importance of people's consciousness, values, and priorities, but views these cultural traits as largely external to the economic structure his model proposes. This structure "makes it possible to have a society without racism," sexism, and so on, but it is up to social movements to change the culture that makes such phenomena possible.

Schweickart's claim illustrates a major difference between his understanding of economic democracy as an institutional structure, and my analysis of economic democracy as the principle that people should democratically control their society's economic goals and priorities. My analysis makes the elimination of sexism, racism, homophobia, and so on, a precondition of economic democracy, since all these forms of oppression make it impossible for all members of society to contribute on an equal basis to the process that would determine these economic goals and priorities. In this sense, economic democracy in this work is not the name of an economic structure but a 'yardstick' by which concrete economic structures can be measured.

This means that some economic structures will do better by this yardstick than others. For example, one advantage of Albert and Hahnel's model is that, by calling for balanced job complexes, it is likely to challenge racism, sexism, homophobia, and so on, much more effectively than Schweickart's model. Indeed, a post-capitalist society that preserves a social division of labor between those who carry out empowering organizational tasks that involve a greater degree of decision-making and those who primarily follow orders is likely to sort workers by their gender, race, and other ascribed social statuses. Though an improvement over capitalism, such a society may therefore still not provide members of historically oppressed groups with an equal opportunity to develop the skills they need to participate, on an equal basis, in the process of determining society's economic goals and priorities.[13]

9 THE WAY FORWARD: ECONOMIC DEMOCRATIZATION AS A STRATEGY OF REFORMS AND FUNDAMENTAL SOCIAL CHANGE

While, as I discussed in Chapter 8, some scholars question the viability of post-capitalist economic models, others have questioned the existence of a plausible path from the capitalist present to such non-capitalist futures.[1] This chapter tackles the question of transition by proposing a strategy of economic democratization that will simultaneously democratize existing economic, political, and social institutions, while also creating the space for alternative economic institutions, such as democratically run worker cooperatives, which challenge the logic of capital and build the democratic skills of ordinary workers and citizens. This strategy can articulate with various struggles for progressive reform and build bridges between the various strands of the left, including social democrats, Marxists, anarchists, feminists, environmentalists, and anti-racist and global justice activists. It can therefore make a positive contribution to the reconstitution of the Left that is so urgently needed at a time when capitalism's most severe crisis in many decades is leading in many parts of the world to the deepening of the neoliberal project that has created the current crisis and devastated ordinary people and natural eco-systems worldwide.

As political and economic elites use the crisis to attack the living conditions as well as the social and economic rights of ordinary people, economic democrats have to fight back. They have to defend ordinary people's social and economic rights, while also advancing progressive alternatives. But they also have to experiment with new institutions that empower ordinary people to collectively take control of their economic lives. Thus, the purpose of this chapter is to lay out a two-pronged political strategy that seeks to democratize the state and affect its policies, while building alternative economic spaces that hone people's democratic and self-management skills. Taken together, the two prongs of this strategy of economic democratization can not only reduce the inhumane and ecologically destructive qualities of capitalism's configurations of scarcity. They

129

can also initiate a process of transition towards an economically democratic society that manages scarce resources in accordance with ordinary people's aspirations and needs.

The strategy of economic democratization I propose seeks to synthesize two opposing impulses that have often dominated the political imagination of capitalism's critics. One impulse is to put one's hopes for fundamental change on the state, while the second impulse is to ignore the state and build alternative institutions without the state's permission. Discussing these two approaches and their weaknesses, this chapter also offers economic democratization as a more viable alternative.

In a debate with Michael Albert during the 2007 US Social Forum, this is how David Schweickart addressed the question of transition to the model of economic democracy that he favors:

> it's not so difficult to imagine a transition from what we have now to Economic Democracy – at least not in theory… not all that much need[s] to change-in order for everything to change…
>
> Suppose we had a stock market collapse. There would be an enormous clamor from below for the government to do something – for the pensions of millions are at stake. Suppose a progressive government is swept into office. It then buys up the stock of the publicly traded companies for almost nothing and turns these companies over to the workers, to be run democratically. (Notice, the capitalist class has been mostly eliminated, since their paper assets have become nearly worthless. The expropriators have been expropriated, not by an angry proletariat but by the irrationality of their own financial markets.) The government then institutes a capital-assets tax. It then nationalizes the banks –which are also in deep trouble – and apportions the capital-asset tax to them.
>
> There you have it – Economic Democracy. For most people, at first, very little would have changed. And yet, soon enough it would become apparent – a capitalist economy had been replaced by something very different – a democratic order genuinely responsive to human needs.
>
> (Albert and Schweickart 2008: 53)

Although Schweickart added at the time that this scenario was not meant as a prediction, it is remarkable how events in late 2008 and early 2009 matched its premises. The stock market did collapse, the pension funds of millions of Americans were wiped out, and a new progressive-sounding president was swept into office by campaigning against the failed philosophy of trickle-down economics. The paper assets of most banks had become worthless as a result of the irrationality of financial markets, and the government could have indeed bought them for next to nothing. Similarly, the giants of the US auto industry, an industry at the very heart of the manufacturing sector, were only saved from bankruptcy by government intervention. In other words, the conditions were as close as they will ever be to the scenario outlined by Schweickart.

However, the transition to economic democracy never took place. President Obama promptly surrounded himself by people, such as Larry Summers and Timothy Geithner, who had played an active role in the deregulation of financial markets that set the stage for this crisis and who were partly responsible for the havoc that neoliberal globalization had wrought all over the world.[2] Thus, instead of expropriating the expropriators, the Obama administration pumped into zombie banks much more money than would have been necessary to buy them altogether. The candidate who interpreted the crisis as a manifestation of the bankruptcy of trickle-down economics quickly made the transition into a president who could think of no better response to the crisis than massive Wall Street bailouts.

Clearly the transition to an economically democratic society is not going to be as simple and short as Schweickart's scenario would suggest. It is simply not true that "not all that much need[s] to change – in order for everything to change." Schweickart's scenario glosses over the fact, recognized even by scholars sympathetic to the vision of market socialism, that economic democracy is as much a cultural project as it is a matter of changing the institutional structures of the economy (Lawler 1998: 46, Bowles and Gintis 1986: 89). As Antonio Gramsci warned more than 70 years ago, capitalist economic crises cannot be expected swiftly and automatically to lead beyond capitalism. This is not only because of the political and ideological resilience of ruling classes, which usually helps them to weather the original shock of the crisis and swiftly regroup. It is also because of the ideological power of the institutions of civil society, such as the media, which promote interpretations of social and economic phenomena that facilitate the capitalist system's survival, while at the same time disorienting working people and obstructing their organization into a force capable of swiftly turning economic crises into an opportunity to replace capitalism with a more democratic socio-economic order (Gramsci 1971: 210–11, 233–8).

More generally, however, the project of economic democracy

also has to recognize the full implications of the fact that capitalism reduces the great majority of working people into the subordinate position of implementing orders from above. As Gramsci also points out, this subordination tends to reduce workers into passive objects of the production process (1977: 333, 340, 345; 1978: 419). Thus emancipatory politics, in Gramsci's view, has to consciously struggle against capitalism's disempowering effects and to cultivate the skills that working people need in order to become subjects capable of assuming collective control over their economic and social lives.

In other words, the ability of Schweickart's model to lead to "a democratic order genuinely responsive to human needs" crucially depends on the qualities of the 'workers/citizens' who bring this model to life, as well as on the further impact that this model has on these qualities. Economic democracy depends as much on people's democratic skills, values, and needs as it does on the reshaping of economic institutions. Thus, although the presence of workplace democracy is a welcome feature in Schweickart's model, it is not by itself a guarantee of an economy that is genuinely democratic. Just as the passive role of workers in the capitalist division of labor increases their passivity in leisure as well as in politics (Bowles 1998: 99), so might an uncritical acceptance of this division of labor drain the institutional structure in Schweickart's model of its democratic content. Indeed, an important theme in the literature on worker cooperatives is the ever-present danger of a "democratic cooling off"[3] that leaves the old hierarchical structure in place and minimizes the participation of workers, as the latter opt "to work from 'nine-to-five' and not have to stay behind to take part in management meetings" (Gall 2010: 127).

This point can be amplified by looking at a criticism that Schweickart has leveled against Hahnel and Albert's model of a participatory economy. According to Schweickart, one of the weaknesses of this model is its failure to recognize the 'inequality of democracy':

> All participants in the various assemblies (and in society at large) face each other as equals in Parecon [parecon, which is short for participatory economics, is the shorthand term used by Hahnel and Albert to describe their post-capitalist economic blueprint]. But as anyone who has participated in a democratic assembly knows, all are not in fact equal. Some are quicker on their feet than others, some have more rhetorical skill, some are better adept at the formal rules of the game ... some are more at home in the dominant culture of the assembly, etc ...

... these inequalities exist quite apart from the power-inequalities that so corrupt our present political system. Albert is sensitive to the latter inequalities, but he seems blind to the other kinds of inequalities that exist among human beings.

(Schweickart 2006b)

Although the premise of Schweickart's argument is undoubtedly correct, the conclusion he draws from this premise is rather surprising. Schweickart's response to the fact that some individuals are better positioned to play the 'game' of democracy is not to devise institutional mechanisms that would reduce democracy's inequalities but "to caution against over-reliance on [the] important yet delicate tool" of democracy. In effect, Schweickart is here not only throwing out the baby (democracy) with the bathwater (the advantages that some individuals may enjoy in the democratic game), but also criticizing Albert and Hahnel for not doing the same.

Indeed, Schweickart's criticism applies even more to his own model than it does to Hahnel and Albert's. A model, like Schweickart's, that did not make a conscious effort to rethink the division of labor in ways that equalized the empowering traits of different jobs would, as Hahnel and Albert recognize, make it more likely that those with the empowering jobs benefit from the 'inequality of democracy' that Schweickart worries about. This is especially the case as many of the reasons for this inequality that Schweickart cites are the result of the kind of experience and learning that people in empowering jobs are more likely to acquire and cultivate. People with natural talents that make it easier for them to excel in the game of democracy would, of course, be the other group to carry a political advantage in Schweickart's model.

As these two groups came to dominate the democratic game, the stage would be set for a vicious circle that could potentially drain the institutions Schweickart proposes of their democratic content. Individuals with political talent and/or empowering jobs that gave them an advantage in the democratic game would not just be more likely to be elected to the democratic institutions within the workplace. In fulfilling the duties attached to their elected positions, they would also cultivate their political and organizational skills even further, thus further increasing the gap between their skills and those of their fellow workers. Hahnel and Albert's idea of balanced job complexes, on the other hand, would eliminate the monopolization of empowering tasks by some workers, cultivate the political and organizational skills of all workers, and, in so doing, reduce the advantages that even the 'naturally' talented enjoyed in the democratic game.

If it is true that economic democracy cannot be instituted overnight as a result of an economic crisis and the election of a progressive government, it is also true that the outbreak of serious economic crises, such as the present one, does have important implications for the project of economic democracy. To begin with, the current crisis has revealed both the bankruptcy of our economic and political elites and the contribution of their actions and inaction to the conditions that gave rise to this crisis.[4] Thus, although the current crisis may not have produced the dramatic outcomes envisaged in Schweickart's scenario, it did discredit economic and political elites enough to make possible what would have been unimaginable just a few years ago, namely the election of an African-American to the presidency of the United States. This discrediting of political and economic elites has been recognized by a number of commentators (Ehrenreich and Fletcher 2009, Landy 2009), and has manifested itself in other ways as well, including both the popular fury over corporate bailouts and AIG bonuses, and the framing of the crisis in terms of the Wall Street/Main Street polarity.[5]

In recent years, and especially since the outbreak of the crisis, resistance to the inhumanity and irrationality of capitalist society has taken a number of different forms, including the election of left-wing governments throughout Latin America, general strikes in Guadeloupe and Martinique, a wave of strikes in China, popular uprisings, such as the Greek uprising of 2008 and the Tunisian uprising in early 2011, general strikes in Greece and Europe, and student and labor protests in North America and (especially) Europe (Foster 2009b). In Argentina, where the neoliberal model had plunged the country into a serious crisis by the early 2000s, workers have responded to the closing of factories by taking them over and operating them as worker-controlled cooperatives (Howarth 2007 esp. ch. 1 and pp. 39–40, Ranis 2010). The severity of the current crisis has accelerated the spread of this movement in Argentina, "with more takeovers in the [first] four months [of 2009] than in the previous four years" (Klein and Lewis 2009). Meanwhile, the movement in Argentina has become an inspiration for workers around the world responding to plant shutdowns and demands for wage concessions with "a new wave of direct action" (Klein and Lewis 2009).

Apart from inspiring militant workers' action in other countries, the movement in Argentina has important implications for the project of creating the conditions for an economically democratic society.

The experience of the movement in Argentina can shed light, for example, on the debate regarding the attitude that a movement for economic democracy should adopt towards the state. In contrast to the scenario of instituting economic democracy through the election of a progressive government, the anarchist and autonomist strands of the anti-capitalist movement often argue that the focus should not be on capturing the state. Instead, it should be on creating liberated spaces and parallel institutions based on direct democracy and the rejection of both consumerism and the colonization of people's everyday life by the logic of capital (Katsiaficas 2006). In this view, "[t]he revolution has already occurred," and animates local social experiments around the world, including the Zapatista revolution in Mexico, workers' cooperatives in South Africa and Argentina, utopian communities in Europe, and "gardens and childcare co-ops and bicycle lanes and farmers' markets" in the United States (Solnit 2009).

Doug Henwood (2009) has attacked the autonomous strategy for allegedly "drawing heavily on an ancient American fantasy of self-reliance and back-to-the-land escapism." The autonomist critique of contemporary capitalism is not so easy to dismiss, however, because it points to real problems, including the weakening of community ties and social solidarity; the commercialization of culture, and the futility and environmental destructiveness of consumerism; capitalism's complicity in the reproduction of racism and patriarchy; and the subordination, more generally, of everyday life and the structure of human needs to the logic of capital accumulation. These problems exemplify the irrationality of the configurations of scarcity that capitalism generates, since they contribute, as I noted earlier in this work, to capitalism's manifest inability to use the growing technological potential at its disposal to drastically reduce human suffering, enrich human life, and protect the planet.

It is, however, true that the autonomist movement lacks a compelling strategy of fundamental and comprehensive social transformation. This lack does create the risk of escapism that Henwood alludes to, or the risk of integration into the system that Katsiaficas (2006: 164) has discussed. On the one hand, alternative institutions and the formation of alternative subcultures can to some extent help people meet the real need for identity, community, and conviviality that, as Gary Cross (2000) points out, capitalism has used in the past to fuel consumerism. On the other hand, in performing this function, the autonomist movement always runs the risk of helping reproduce the existing system by providing an oasis that alleviates popular discontent with the social and cultural wasteland surrounding it. Moreover, as Stanley Aronowitz (2006: 117–18) reminds us, even such alternative oases often tend to be short-lived within capitalism, as they often trigger commercialization and urban gentrification processes that undermine their economic conditions of existence.

For guidance on how to preserve the valid insights of the autonomist strategy, while avoiding its pitfalls, a good place to start is the occupied factory movement in Argentina.[6] One of the lessons of this movement is that the project of economic democracy makes it necessary to combine the autonomist pursuit for alternative institutions and an alternative culture with the pursuit of a more democratic state.

Indeed, Rebecca Solnit sets up a false dilemma when she cites the Argentine movement as one of the revolutions that "have been less interested in seizing and becoming the state than circumventing it to go straight to becoming other people doing other things without state permission" (2009). On the one hand, Argentine workers' accounts of their experience in the factory occupation movement undoubtedly confirm that, to the extent that their efforts to reclaim their factories have been successful, they have indeed become "other people doing other things."[7] On the other hand, their relationship to the state is much more complicated than Solnit's contrast suggests. To begin with, the workers in the occupied factory movement did not just 'circumvent' the state, but have fought long and hard to win legislative changes that recognized the conversion of the occupied factories into worker-controlled cooperatives. The difficulty of this struggle stemmed from the fact that capitalist employers and the state recognized that worker-controlled factories were a living refutation of the claim that, in view of the workers' supposed inability to take collective control over production, capitalist property relations and the undemocratic economic system they give rise to were simply indispensable.

Thus, Argentine workers have faced the hostility of the media, the judicial system, and a government that often seemed to prefer paying unemployment benefits over the creation of jobs through the conversion of abandoned factories into democratically run cooperatives (Lavaca Collective 2007: 178). Despite the great obstacles, however, the movement has had some success pushing for expropriation laws that allow the formation of such cooperatives (Lavaca Collective 2007: 211–12, Trigona 2008, Ranis 2010). The struggles, moreover, of workers throughout Argentina to reclaim their workplaces have been integral to the process through which workers become "different people." The lengthier and more hard-fought the struggle to reclaim a given workplace has been, the stronger the solidarity between the workers is, and the more likely it becomes that the new cooperative will be run according to egalitarian principles that challenge the organizational model of traditional capitalist enterprises (Lavaca Collective 2007: 220).

The experience of Argentina's cooperative movement suggests, therefore, that even the project of building alternative institutions and an alternative culture at the interstices of contemporary capitalist societies is not necessarily best advanced through a strategy of circumventing the state, but through a strategy of challenging the grip of political and economic elites on the state: that is, a strategy of democratizing the state. This experience also suggests that the struggle to democratize the state and create the space for alternative institutions can help forge new people capable of ensuring that these institutions will indeed be animated by an egalitarian spirit, by the principle of self-management, and by a logic that does not subordinate humanity and the planet to the imperatives of capital accumulation.

In other words, the project of economic democracy stands to benefit from the pursuit of a dialectic between economic democratization initiatives achieved through the application of pressure on the state, and the building of alternative institutions which both cultivate people's self-management skills and allow the construction of an alternative culture that reduces the grip of capital on the structure of people's needs as well as on the texture of their everyday life. Thus, the project of economic democracy requires a two-pronged strategy that includes both a state-oriented and an autonomist component. The interaction between these components can propel the project forward by giving rise to a virtuous circle. In particular, state-oriented democratization initiatives can make it easier for an autonomous sector to survive and flourish, while the development of this sector can in turn build people's democratic and self-management skills, facilitate their liberation from the impact of capitalism's consumerist culture, and increase support for further policy changes aimed at democratizing the economy and further encouraging the development of the autonomous sector.

This strategy is more viable than both the expectation that economic democracy can be instituted overnight through the election of a progressive government, and the belief that revolution will occur through alternative institutions that circumvent the state. In their one-sidedness these two views are mirror images of each other. The first ignores the importance of supplementing changes introduced by a progressive government with a concurrent cultural project through which people develop "the skills, attitudes, and values consistent with a [more democratic] economic system" (Bowles and Gintis 1986: 89). The second, in contrast, underestimates the contribution that progressive policies and the democratization of the state can make both to the building of autonomous institutions and to the project of economic democracy more generally.

There is a wide range of policies that could advance the project of economic democracy. One of the manifestations of the Argentine state's hostility to the cooperative movement is its willingness to subsidize large capitalist enterprises even as it has failed to make sufficient loans available to worker-run enterprises (Lavaca Collective 2007: 181). The opposite should in fact be the case. To the extent that capitalist enterprises, with their hierarchical divisions of labor, undercut political participation and the quality of democracy within the political system (Bowles 1991: 15–16), their operation clearly involves negative externalities. The hierarchical division of labor in these enterprises, in other words, does not only affect the owners, managers, and workers of these enterprises. All other citizens are also affected, as the weakening of democratic skills that the capitalist organization of production promotes is likely to undermine the soundness of the choices that a democratic political system is capable of. By increasing people's democratic skills and strengthening local communities, on the other hand, cooperatives involve positive externalities.[8] Thus government support for cooperatives and higher tax rates for capitalist enterprises can be defended not only on the grounds of economic democracy, but also on the grounds of efficiency.

The cooperative movement could also benefit from the fact that the problem of insufficient credit, which has hampered the survival of worker cooperatives in the past, becomes easier to address once the cooperative movement reaches a critical mass, which facilitates relations of mutual support between cooperative enterprises (Gall 2010: 126–7). Central to the longevity and expansion of the Mondragon cooperatives in Spain,[9] for example, have been both the use of company surpluses to create new cooperatives and the establishment of a savings bank that services the members of the cooperative while also "encourag[ing] the creation of new cooperatives through its business division ... [and making] possible the growth of each cooperative, which would be impossible with their internal resources alone" (Azevedo and Gitahy 2010: 11).

Since the principle of economic democracy touches on all aspects of social and economic life, it can provide a principle that guides a wide range of struggles for social and economic change. Economic democracy, as well as capitalism's manifest inability to translate its growing technological potential into a richer and happier life for all, requires, for example, a rethinking of the role of education. Instead of subordinating education to the logic of capital by treating it as the vehicle for reproducing the skilled labor power that capitalism needs, an economically democratic society would emphasize preparation not just for production but also for consumption, as well as for self-management (Robertson 1990: 148, Wolff 2010b: 12). A greater emphasis on the development of cultural skills would also allow people to derive the enjoyment from leisure that sterile consumerism often fails to provide (Sciotvsky 1992), while economic democracy would also require a more egalitarian educational system that would cultivate the critical thinking and democratic skills of all students. Adopting such a goal would of course have wide-ranging implications for social and urban policy, and would require a concerted effort to address inner-city poverty and unemployment, racial discrimination and segregation, as well as institutional racism in all its forms.

As households are a major site of labor, the project of economic democracy points in the direction of policies that reduce gender inequalities, while increasing educational and occupational opportunities for women. It also presupposes greater support for families in the form of more generous parental leave policies, adequate provision of affordable childcare, and so on. While such policies are, as Richard Layard (2005) reminds us, conducive to human happiness, they would, when combined with expanded opportunities for women, also reduce the imbalance of power within households that gender inequalities outside the household tend to create. Since homophobia plays a major role in the reproduction of oppressive gender relations and ideologies, the project of economic democracy also points in the direction of social policies that promote equal rights for lesbian, gay, bisexual, and transgender people.

Also consistent with the principle of economic democracy are the practices of participatory budgeting that have been tried in developing countries, such as India and Brazil. These practices attempt to increase the participation of citizens in the formulation of budgets and in the determination of the ways in which public money is spent. This is usually done by allowing a portion of a city's or regional government's budget to be allocated not by politicians and state bureaucrats, but by citizens participating in democratic assemblies.

In addition to participating in such assemblies, citizens often receive "technical education and training in public speaking," which make such participation meaningful even for poorer and less educated citizens (Menser and Robinson 2008: 296). As Michael Menser and Juscha Robinson point out:

> [v]arious studies have suggested that participatory budgeting can lead to more equitable public spending, higher quality of life, increased satisfaction of basic needs, greater government transparency and accountability, increased levels of public participation (especially by marginalized residents), and democratic and citizenship learning.
>
> (Menser and Robinson 2008: 294)

Similarly, Richard Franke reports that the introduction of participatory budgeting in the Indian state of Kerala:

> radically improved delivery of public services, brought about greater caste and ethnic equality, facilitated the entry of women into public life at a much greater pace, and enhanced democratic practice. By the third year the Campaign [that introduced participatory budgeting] began to generate local employment utilizing and improving upon the famous Grameen Bank micro credit idea to bring households above the poverty level.
>
> (Franke 2008: 130)

The benefits of participatory budgeting illustrate the validity of the idea, advanced by green economists and ecofeminist theorists, that the definitions of 'welfare' and 'development' guiding public policy have to be reached through participatory democratic processes rather than remaining "the prerogative of credentialed experts" and the flawed measures, such as gross domestic product, that these experts often use (O'Hara (2009: 186).[10] These benefits also demonstrate that the neoliberal agenda of privatization and a 'small' government is not the only response to the bureaucratic dysfunctions and inefficiencies of the capitalist state. This is an important contribution, since the private sector touted by the neoliberal model is hardly devoid of bureaucratic inefficiencies. In fact, as the health care system of the United States makes abundantly clear, the bureaucratic inefficiencies of private corporations can sometimes be much greater than those of any government-run program.

The benefits of participatory budgeting would be amplified by the spread of democratically run, worker-controlled cooperatives. Indeed, the combination of participatory budgeting and the cooperative production model can generate a synergistic effect that will allow the experience people gain in each of these two spheres of the socioeconomic system to be carried over to and enhance the operation of the other (Pineiro Harnecker 2010). The knowledge and democratic skills built through the process of participatory budgeting can enhance workers' ability to contribute to the democratic process within their workplace, increase the quality of their decisions, and keep elected managers or worker councils accountable. Conversely, the self-confidence, technical knowledge, and democratic skills honed in cooperative workplaces can further enhance the operation of the participatory budgeting process, thus further increasing both the effectiveness with which this process is carried out and the benefits resulting from it.

This possibility of a virtuous circle between participatory budgeting and cooperatives once again demonstrates the pitfalls of circumventing the state and setting up an opposition between the building of alternative institutions and the effort to democratize the state. Putting pressure on the state can not only contribute to the building of alternative institutions directly, by forcing the state to tolerate, or even positively support, existing alternative institutions, such as cooperatives, occupied residential buildings, and community centers. The democratization of the state, through participatory budgeting and other measures, such as a reorientation of the educational system towards the cultivation of critical thinking and democratic skills, can also enhance the operation of alternative institutions by helping people develop technical knowledge and democratic skills that will increase alternative institutions' democratic self-management capacities.

Their prefigurative function notwithstanding, experiments such as the cooperative movement in Argentina are often motivated by the failures of the contemporary capitalist system and the harsh configurations of scarcity it confronts people with.[11] As the current crisis makes clear, these configurations result from the undemocratic nature of the economic system. Thus, the immense and unnecessary human suffering facing billions of people worldwide cannot but be one of the driving motivations of the project of economic democracy. In this respect, the project of economic democracy requires a simultaneous struggle to render capitalism's configurations of scarcity less inhumane and ecologically destructive and to create the conditions for an alternative social and economic order that is more genuinely democratic than the existing capitalist system.

This simultaneous struggle to win reforms within capitalism as well as to build alternative institutions and create the conditions for replacing capitalism with a more economically democratic social order can be thought of as a strategy of economic democratization. Such a strategy should ensure that the principle of economic democracy informs both struggles to mitigate the human suffering and environmental destruction wrought by the capitalist system, and struggles for cultural and institutional transformations that advance the project of replacing capitalism with an economically democratic social order. In this respect, the strategy of economic democratization represents an alternative to the two strategies of transforming capitalism that dominated the twentieth century, namely social democracy and Soviet-style communism.

As we saw in Chapter 3, while Soviet-style communism facilitated the industrialization of Russia and a number of other countries, especially in Eastern Europe, it was fundamentally flawed because of its lack of economic, as well as political, democracy. In addition to being problematic in itself, this lack of democracy also contributed to the horrendous environmental record that may have in fact contributed to that system's demise (Altvater 1993: 34–5, O'Connor 1998: 264–5, Kovel 2002: 203–6, Sarkar 1999). One unintended consequence of the Soviet experiment, however, was the space it created for state-based development models that allowed the industrialization of some developing countries in the capitalist world, especially in Asia. The political pressure that the existence of the Soviet bloc exerted on rich capitalist countries encouraged these countries to build more or less extensive welfare states, and to adopt more or less comprehensive social policies aimed at protecting the general population from the vagaries of the market, and at mitigating the inhumanity of the configurations of scarcity ordinary workers and citizens had been confronted with up to that point (Panitch and Miliband 1992: 4, Bagchi 2005: 322, Stiglitz 2001: xv).

While the existence of the Soviet Union made the political and economic elites of rich capitalist countries more amenable to progressive reforms, social democratic movements often played a leading role in the adoption of the reforms and policies that went into the building of their countries' welfare states. As the recent spread of brutal austerity policies across Europe reminds us, however, all such gains remain precarious under capitalism. The precarious nature of reforms mitigating the inhumanity of the configurations of scarcity that capitalism creates is directly connected to the undemocratic nature of this system. Indeed, capitalism's undemocratic nature makes it possible for capitalist elites to use their structural power and the resources at their disposal to reverse popular gains as soon as changing circumstances make concessions to workers and ordinary citizens seem unnecessary. It is also this structural power of capital that partly accounts for the gradual drift of European social democratic parties from a position that envisaged replacing capitalism with an alternative socio-economic system to one that accepts the existence of mass unemployment, as well as the use of the European Union as a vehicle for eroding European welfare states and restructuring European societies along neoliberal lines.[12]

As historian of European social democracy Donald Sassoon (1996) has pointed out, the viability of European welfare states largely depended on nationally based models of economic development that insulated social policy from the competitive pressures of the international market.[13] The neoliberal project of creating an integrated global economy with minimal barriers to the flow of capital – a project that, as Kim Moody (2001: 299) notes, social democrats have more often than not supported – has undermined such nationally based models, however. Combined with a communications revolution that has greatly increased the mobility of capital, capitalist globalization has shifted the balance of power in favor of capital, increased economic inequality, and undermined the premises upon which welfare states were historically built (Beck 2000:1).

The fact that these growing inequalities have contributed to economic stagnation and the most serious economic crisis since the Great Depression has led some scholars to suggest that capitalist elites might favor a shift from neoliberalism to a model of 'global social democracy' as a way of getting out of the crisis. According to Walden Bello (2008b), a number of establishment figures, including former UK prime minister Gordon Brown and former UN secretary-general Kofi Annan, businesspeople such as Bill Gates and George Soros, and a number of economists and social scientists, such as Jeffrey Sachs, David Held, and Joseph Stiglitz, have articulated views that are consistent with such a shift. Global social democracy would recalibrate the process of capitalist globalization, avoiding the excesses of neoliberalism, and placing somewhat greater emphasis on equity, environmental sustainability, global justice, and multilateral diplomacy. As Bello points out, a response to the current economic crisis that ran along those lines would not represent a shift to an economically democratic social order. If it emerges as a response to the crisis, global social democracy is likely to be a technocratic project of top-down reforms aimed not at challenging the undemocratic logic of capital, but at managing more effectively the social, economic, and ecological contradictions that this logic inevitably generates.

Nonetheless, it is probably true that a turn to global social democracy and economic policies informed by a progressive Keynesian outlook might render the configurations of scarcity confronting people around the world less inhumane and environmentally destructive. The same can be said about the 'full Keynesian program' that Hahnel (2002: 274) endorses as a step in the direction of the participatory economic system that he and Albert support. Such a program, Hahnel argues, should seek to:

> [s]ubordinat[e] finance to the real economy rather than the reverse, pursu[e] full employment fiscal and monetary policies and intelligent industrial policies, embrac[e] a wage-led rather than profit-led growth strategy, [reform] the tax system to be more efficient and more equitable, and [accept] public ownership where practical.
>
> (Hahnel 2002: 273–4)

Such policies are consistent with the struggle for economic democracy. Full employment policies would not just reduce human suffering, but also increase the ability of working people to resist capital.[14] Furthermore, as William Dugger and James Peach (2009: 189–91) have pointed out, full employment could encourage the spread of democratically run cooperatives by improving their competitive position in relation to capitalist corporations, while also helping to democratize households by reducing female unemployment and increasing the leverage of women within the household.

A wage-led growth strategy would also increase equity and render capitalism's configurations of scarcity less inhumane by recognizing the potential contribution of higher wages to aggregate demand and the revitalization of an economy mired in crisis. As far as the tax system is concerned, just as reforms making the system more progressive would increase equity and render capitalism's configurations of scarcity less inhumane, a greater emphasis on taxing bads, such as pollution, would also be a first step towards addressing the deepening ecological crisis. As discussed in Chapter 6, the economic inequalities at the basis of capitalism make it difficult to resist the pursuit of profitability through externalization of the environmental costs of economic activity. In this respect, a progressive economic policy that reduced poverty and inequality could make it easier both to internalize the environmental costs of economic activity, and to reduce the economic desperation of poor communities faced with the choice between jobs and the presence in their midst of polluting industries. The revenues from environmental taxes could be used in ways that both reduced inequality and took measures against the ongoing destruction of the planet. Part of the revenue could be returned to citizens (especially low-income ones), while another part could be used to fund research in green technologies as well as environmental restoration projects. The contribution of economic inequality to the ecological crisis facing us means that a full response to the latter presupposes an economically democratic post-capitalist society. In the meantime, however, the connection of this crisis to social and economic inequality creates a synergistic link between ecological and social justice struggles.

Finally, a reinvention of domestic and global financial systems, as well as of the institutions of global economic governance, is necessary. Neoliberal policies of financial deregulation have to be revised since they carry great risks and are as likely to reduce economic efficiency as they are to increase it (Hahnel 2002: 208–12). There is no better proof of this basic fact than the devastation wrought by the current economic crisis. A move away from the 'Washington consensus,' which, with the help of the 'unholy trinity' of the International Monetary Fund, the World Bank, and the World Trade Organization, requires an uncritical adoption of free market policies, will prevent a further aggravation of the configurations of scarcity facing human beings and the planet alike.[15] It will also prevent these organizations from continuing to act as a roadblock to the pursuit by developing countries of strategies of independent development (Vasudevan 2009: 26). Indeed, recent history suggests that economic success for developing countries requires not an uncritical adoption of free markets, but a willingness of the state to play a strategic role within the economy through the implementation of a carefully crafted industrial policy (Peet and Hartwick 2009: 63–4, Stiglitz 2001: xiii–xv, Erber 1994: 354–5, Roemer 1994: 106–7).

Last but not least, a reinvented global economic and financial system has to include capital controls that reduce capital's ability to wield the threat of investment strikes as a club against national governments willing to adopt policies that promote economic democracy (Block 1994). This is an important point, because it also has implications for the quality of political democracy. Indeed, neoliberalism's conversion of "[t]he state into an agency for adjusting national economic practices and policies to the perceived exigencies of the global economy ... where heretofore it had acted as the bulwark defending domestic welfare from external disturbances" cannot but erode political participation (Cox 1992: 30–2). As the political system loses credibility as an instrument for implementing people's priorities and defending their welfare, "[c]ynicism, depoliticisation, and a sense of the inefficacy of political action, and a disdain for the political class" proliferate (Cox 1992: 33). The increasing transformation of political debate into a special branch of marketing both reflects and further fuels this sad state of affairs. As Stuart Ewen points out, "[d]emocratic choice, like grocery shopping, has become a question of which product is most attractively packaged, which product is most imaginatively merchandised" (2000: 53).

Nobody understands this better than Barack Obama. So impressed was the public relations industry by his campaign that it "named Obama '*Advertising Age*'s marketer of the year for 2008,' easily beating out Apple" (Chomsky 2009: 19). Obama's pre-election rhetoric about Main Street and the failure of trickle-down economics may have been the reason that Bello (2008b) identified him as a potential carrier of the project of global social democracy. Obama's actions as president of the United States, however, sharply contrast with his pre-election rhetoric. As his policies have been kinder to Wall Street than to Main Street, it is doubtful that global social democracy is on the agenda. This is all the more the case as the traditional center of social democracy, Europe, is even more committed to brutal austerity measures. In this context, the role of economic democrats is to resist the drift towards a conservative response to the crisis, and to struggle both for policies that reduce inequalities and increase labor and democratic rights, and for more fundamental institutional and cultural changes that do not just ameliorate capitalism's inhumane and environmentally destructive configurations of scarcity, but also seek to increase the space for economic practices consistent with the principle of economic democracy.

Traditional social democracy has historically focused on progressive reforms, while ignoring the need for autonomous spaces that point beyond the logic of capital. Even when industries were nationalized, for example, capitalism's hierarchical organizational structures were not replaced by new, more democratic ways of organizing production.[16] Thus, although some social democratic movements, such as the one in Sweden, have been able to have a lasting effect on the political culture and values of their societies (Vartiainen 2001), the relative neglect of reforms consistent with economic democracy has prevented social democracy from making a greater contribution to people's democratic skills and taste for economic democracy. As a result, social democracy has evolved from a political force aspiring to replace capitalism, to one seeking to make capitalism a little more cognizant of equity, social solidarity, and environmental sustainability.

The recent history of European social democracy makes clear, however, that leaving the structural power of capital largely intact inevitably turns any attempt to ameliorate capitalism's configurations of scarcity into a Sisyphean task that is vulnerable to reversal as soon as changing circumstances allow capital to retract the concessions it makes in periods of intense political pressure. In this sense, just as progressive reforms can serve to advance the project of economic democracy, so can the struggle for economic democracy serve to promote and defend any progressive reforms achieved through state action. As Richard Wolff (2010a, 2010b) has rightly pointed out, as long as workers are denied the surplus they produce, part of this surplus will be used to resist any progressive changes that the left may fight for.

Traditional social democratic and progressive politics is clearly devoid of any vision or strategy capable of dealing with these basic realities. There may, for example, be no better manifestation of the exhaustion of European social democracy than its relative inability to benefit from an economic crisis that has exposed the bankruptcy of the neoliberal cult of the free market.[17] Worse still, even the social democratic parties that have recently held power, notably in Greece, Portugal, and Spain, are adopting austerity measures of unprecedented brutality, which intensify these countries' commitment to the neoliberal policies that produced the crisis in the first place. Similarly, in the United States the hope that the election of Barack Obama represented for many progressive Americans is rapidly turning into disappointment with his "go-easy approach on Wall Street, ineffectual efforts to reduce high unemployment, watered-down healthcare and financial regulation reforms and escalation of the Afghanistan war" (Whitesides 2010).

In the meantime the Right is on the rise. While the Tea Party movement in the United States has helped Republicans make a comeback in the 2010 midterm elections, the ability of the Right to prevail in the 2009 European elections, along with the disturbing electoral growth of the neofascist and anti-immigrant streams of the extreme Right, make it clear that a new vision is required, if the immense technological potential at the disposal of contemporary society is to be used for the benefit of humanity and the planet.[18] It is one of the contentions of this book that economic democracy may be just that vision. By synthesizing the most vital concerns and insights of the various fragments of the left today, from social democracy and left liberalism to Marxism, anarchism, feminism, anti-racism, global justice activism, and ecology, economic democracy can become the rallying cry for the majoritarian and inclusive social movement necessary to prove that another, non-capitalist, world is indeed possible.

CONCLUSION

We have reached the end of our exploration of the relationship between capitalism, scarcity, and economic democracy. What follows therefore reviews and at times builds on this book's main themes and conclusions. To begin with, this book identifies economic democracy as the condition for a use of scarce resources that is consistent with ecological sustainability, the elimination of unnecessary human suffering, and a richer life for all human beings on this planet. The undemocratic nature of the capitalist economic system, by contrast, accounts for its inability to make a more rational use of the immense technological potential that its dynamism generates. Although this dynamism has vastly increased economic output and wealth, the pattern of economic development it has unleashed is geographically uneven, socially unjust, and ecologically dangerous.

Because of this, technological development is currently as much a development of capital's forces of destruction as it is a development of technologies that could promote human well-being and ecological sustainability. Capitalism's record of nuclear proliferation, two world wars that have claimed millions of human lives, global warming, and ecological devastation demonstrates that this system is not just wasteful, it is downright dangerous, since it turns the very technological potential that could increase human well-being and enrich human life into a series of grave threats to humanity and the planet alike.

While serving as a counterpoint to capitalism, economic democracy in this book does not refer to a detailed blueprint of what a non-capitalist socio-economic system might look like. Instead, it refers to the principle that all citizens should democratically determine their society's economic goals and priorities. This principle, I argue, can guide the struggle for reforms within capitalism and serve as a criterion for evaluating and comparing the different blueprints for a non-capitalist society that are on offer.

This principle also suggests a political strategy of economic democratization that can push the struggle for reforms beyond the alleviation of capitalism's disastrous consequences. Important as the alleviation of capitalism's inhumane and environmentally destructive configurations of scarcity remains, economic democratization can also trigger a dynamic whereby the creation of alternative institutions within the existing society will cultivate people's democratic skills and appetite for economic democracy. Such a dynamic can drive the process of reforms further, even as it makes it more likely that this process will eventually lead to an alternative socio-economic order that, unlike capitalism, will be genuinely democratic.

A process of economic democratization can bring about an alternative and more democratic socio-economic order by also bringing about subjective changes that will undermine the continued viability of capitalism as a system. There has been a tendency within Marxism and the Left to predicate fundamental social change on economic crises and the objective breakdown of capitalism as a system. Alec Nove, whose vision of what a 'feasible socialism' would look like was otherwise critical of Marx and Marxism (1983), has, for example, argued that:

> in the end much will depend on the ability of contemporary capitalism to surmount its many problems, not least that of mass unemployment and ecological decline (acid rain, deforestation, over-fishing, etc.). The masses will not opt for a different system unless faced with the bankruptcy of the existing one. To repeat, it was Marx who wrote that no mode of production passes from the scene unless and until its productive potential is exhausted.
>
> (Nove 1990: 248)

The problem with this point of view is that both the mass unemployment and ecological decline that Nove mentions are intimately connected to capitalism's continued ability to increase its productive potential. Indeed, Johannes Berger (1994: 777) has gone as far as to suggest that, as far as ecological degradation is concerned, the problem with capitalism may not be its weakness but its strength.

There is arguably no better proof of capitalism's fundamental irrationality than the dialectical irony by which that system's economic strength becomes a source of serious problems for humanity and the planet. Capitalism's irrationality stems from its undemocratic nature and its subordination of humanity to an abstract logic of profit and capital expansion that escapes human control. It is because of this logic that capitalism's regular development of its productive potential is inseparable from its threat to inflict unprecedented levels of harm on human beings and the planet.

In this respect, the bankruptcy of the capitalist system does not contradict its economic strength, but is this economic strength's mirror image. As a number of authors going back to Marx (1964: 69) have recognized, capitalism is a disaster for the majority of humanity even in its periods of economic prosperity.[1] Since economic crises accentuate the inhumanity and irrationalities of the capitalist system, it is tempting to envisage the transition to another socio-economic order as the result of an irrevocable capitalist breakdown.[2]

In contrast with such approaches, the strategy of economic democratization proposed in this book points in the direction of a social constructionist conception of capitalist crises. In other words, capitalist crises are not purely economic facts that derive from "the material transformation of the economic conditions of production, which can be determined with the precision of natural science" (Marx 1970: 21).[3] A system-transcending crisis is as likely to result from a struggle over subjectivity that leads to a redefinition even of times of capitalist 'prosperity' as a state of unacceptable economic and ecological crisis, as it is to result from a spectacular and massive collapse of the capitalist system. In other words, we must recognize the possibility of a dialectic between the objective and subjective conditions of social change. Even though a state of economic crisis, as traditionally understood by Marxists and others, can facilitate the spread of a critical consciousness, the struggle over subjectivity can influence our definition of what counts as a crisis, thus preventing the perception of a possible future return to more 'normal' levels of human misery and ecological destruction as an end of capitalism's crisis.

In this respect, there is a twofold relationship between the strategy of economic democratization and capitalist crisis. Developments consistent with this strategy, such as the growth of the cooperative movement in Argentina, are often a response to the kind of economic crisis that Marxist theory has always emphasized. At the same time, however, economically democratizing responses to economic crises differ from more traditional responses, such as a greater role of the government in managing the macroeconomy. They do so because they can create a different kind of human subject, one with needs and aspirations that capitalism cannot satisfy. Thus, while helping people to cope with the destructive impact of capitalism's economic contradictions, economically democratizing reforms can also highlight how intolerably undemocratic and irrational capitalism is even in periods of relative economic prosperity.

Capitalism's irrationality, along with its inhumanity and environmental destructiveness, is evident in the configurations of scarcity that it creates. These configurations are the outcome of multiple economic, political, and cultural processes. The 'social construction' of scarcity by these processes does not imply that scarcity is an illusion. Instead, it points to the fact that the extent to which the burden of scarcity is felt by various groups in a given society, as well as the forms that scarcity takes, crucially depend on the various economic, political, and cultural processes that shape people's aspirations and needs, as well as the availability of material means on which the satisfaction of these aspirations and needs depends. The multiplicity of social and economic positions within capitalism means that the configurations of scarcity facing different individuals and social groups are not the same. These configurations are the objects of economic, political, and cultural struggles, as different groups attempt to improve the configurations of scarcity facing themselves in ways that may adversely affect the configurations facing others.

Leading to extreme inequalities, unprecedented ecological devastation, and an inability to translate ever-rising levels of technological development into drastic reductions of human suffering and a richer human life, the configurations of scarcity that capitalism generates are crucially shaped by the logic of profit that drives this system forward. In this sense, these configurations emerge out of the interaction of capital's pursuit of profit and the multiple socio-economic struggles that this pursuit triggers.

In criticizing these configurations, this work is also a critique of the neoclassical approach to scarcity that dominates the discipline of economics. In its neglect of the economic processes that contribute to the formation of consumer preferences, neoclassical economics also obscures the contribution of the capitalist system to the consumerist culture informing individual preferences. This is an important failing since, as many scholars have pointed out, this consumerist culture undermines human well-being and contributes to capitalism's environmental destructiveness and its inability to translate technological advances into a richer and more satisfying life for all. This means that by glossing over the demand side of the configurations of scarcity that capitalism generates, neoclassical economics also obscures capitalism's responsibility for the immense toll that consumerism exacts on human beings and the planet. This book discusses this toll, and connects it to the exploitative nature of the capitalist system. In making this connection, I have highlighted a qualitative implication of exploitation that has escaped the attention of more traditional Marxist approaches. By this I mean the fact that capitalism does not only deny workers the surplus that they produce, but also uses this surplus to build a consumerist culture that makes it impossible for them to maximize the enjoyment they derive even from the part of their product that returns to them in the form of wages and salaries.

I have also discussed the supply side of the configurations of scarcity that capitalism generates. This dimension has to do not with people's socially produced desires but with the resources that they can deploy in their pursuit of satisfaction. Here the vast inequalities and immense (as well as unnecessary) human suffering that have characterized capitalism since its beginnings bear witness to this system's inhumanity. While economic redistribution could in theory reduce capitalism's inequalities, Marxist economists, like E. K. Hunt (2002: 387), correctly point out that the effect of these inequalities on the political system makes such redistribution unlikely.

As I show in Chapter 7, the economic inequalities at the basis of the capitalist system also vitiate the neoclassical belief in the fundamental efficiency of capitalist markets. Just as capitalist elites can use the political power they derive from their economic position to prevent redistribution, they can also increase profits by imposing negative externalities on the rest of society, and especially on vulnerable social groups that lack the political power or knowledge to mount an effective resistance. In this respect, capitalism aggravates the configurations of scarcity confronting the groups that capitalism's serious social and economic problems burden the most. The accelerating ecological degradation that accompanies the normal operation of the capitalist system is a prime example of the link between the pervasive economic externalities capitalism generates and the increasingly dangerous configurations of scarcity confronting humanity in general, and the poorest of the world in particular.

As Chapter 7 also demonstrates, however, we have to go even further than pointing out the link between the power implications of capitalist social relations and the pervasiveness of externalities that pose a threat to the ecological integrity of the planet. The very interpretation of externalities as obstacles to economic efficiency legitimizes capitalism by assuming that the overriding goal of that system is to serve consumers. Thus, in neoclassical economics, the deepening ecological crisis appears as an aberration that runs counter to the fundamental logic of the system. Against this view, I have argued that the fundamental goal of the capitalist system is not to serve consumers but to promote profit by any means necessary. This means that the imposition of environmental and other negative externalities on humanity, the poor and future generations is an efficient means of implementing this goal rather than an instance of inefficiency that runs counter to capitalism's operational logic.

In other words, the deepening ecological crisis is not the product of inefficiencies that appropriate government action is likely to remove, but a manifestation of the fact that in an undemocratic socio-economic system like capitalism, the only economic goal that is pursued efficiently is that of profit. The fact that the efficient pursuit of this goal creates configurations of scarcity that exact an intolerable toll on billions of human beings and the planet also heightens the urgency of an economically democratic alternative to a system that has proven as dangerous as it is dynamic.

HUMOROUS APPENDIX:
AUSTERITY NUT AND HIS MESSAGE

Ever since the outbreak of the current crisis, I have written journal and newspaper articles, been interviewed for television and radio programs around the world, and completed the book that you have in your hands. I have analyzed various dimensions of the crisis in Greece (where I was born), in the United States (where I live), and beyond. Carrying out this analysis is essential. I am coming to the realization, however, that to really highlight the absurdity and injustice of the austerity policies currently afflicting many countries around the world, notably in Europe, as well as most of the states in the United States, it is necessary to complement serious analysis with mockery pure and simple.

What follows is the text of an agitprop stunt I have performed in New York City subways. Partly inspired by the American comedian Steve Colbert, who exposes the stupidity of American conservatives by posing as an earnest conservative himself, this stunt questions, in an indirect and humorous rather than a direct and angry way, the use of the current crisis to attack working people and the poor. The anger below the surface is obvious, but the tone is meant to capture the attention of people who feel demoralized and cannot take any more bad news. In this respect, making the points that have to be made in a way that makes people laugh has its advantages.

This text can be adjusted to fit the specific circumstances at the locality in which it is performed. I invite my readers to perform it in any appropriate public place, and to share their experience with me at upliftingmessage@gmail.com. The response I have had from my audience has certainly been encouraging. People listen to me, take the script of the stunt that I distribute, and many of them read it very carefully and send me their appreciative comments at the email address I include. Once I even had a very spirited response by some teenage girls who thought that the whole thing was hilarious and who showered me with questions: "Are you a Democrat or a Republican?" "What do you want?" and so on. My routine is also received with great enthusiasm when I perform it at union meetings and rallies. Without further ado, here it is:

Good morning my friends. Don't worry, I'm not gonna ask for money. I do have a job, at least for the time being. My name is Austerity Nut and I preach the virtues of budget cuts. We are in a terrible crisis, my friends, because you, I, and all other working people have for too long been too comfortable and too greedy. The rich, on the other hand, are falling further and further behind, because they are being denied their fair share of the wealth produced in this country. If this trend continues, not even all the tax breaks, bailouts, and generous corporate welfare they receive from our government will be enough to save our rich from utter destitution and misery.

This is why all of us, working people, should welcome the opportunity to lend a helping hand to our rich as well as to our suffering brothers and sisters on Wall Street. As our governor and mayor rightly point out, we need to cut wasteful spending on education, health care, and other social services. These cuts are inevitable because we surely don't want to tax the bonuses of our suffering brothers and sisters on Wall Street. Our mayor and governor are right to reduce their taxes. After all, our brothers and sisters in Wall Street are the reason why our economy is in such a great shape right now.

Now it's true that sometimes things get hard for you and me. But it's surely not fair to blame the rich for our own failings or to get angry at our wonderful capitalist system. Now more than ever, my friends, we must trust our politicians and the rich. They are good people – and, I promise you, they stay up at night making sure that every New Yorker has a well-paid job that comes with good benefits; that no child goes to bed hungry at night; that no New Yorker is homeless; and that every New Yorker can afford to go to college. So let us all accept tuition hikes at our public universities and fare hikes in our public transportation system. Let us accept that we don't need to spend so much money on schools and hospitals, and that we don't need unions, pay raises, or decent pensions.

And now, firm believer in free enterprise that I am, I will make this message available to you at the recession-proof price of zero dollars and zero cents. Please spread this uplifting message to everyone you know. Show it to your friends, family, and neighbors, even your boss, if you so desire. Photocopy it, perform it, and distribute it as you please. And above all remember: ask not what the billionaires in your country can do for you; ask what you can do for the billionaires in your country.

Austerity Nut would love to hear from you. Send him your

comments and reactions to his email address, upliftingmessage@
gmail.com.

Austerity Nut would also like to take this opportunity to thank
the Committee to Screw New York, and Bernie Crook, the
leading tax avoidance specialist on Wall Street (Bernie's motto:
"If Bank of America and General Electric do not pay any taxes,
why should you?"). Without their generous support, printing and
distributing this uplifting message would have been impossible.

NOTES

1 CAPITALISM, SCARCITY, AND ECONOMIC DEMOCRACY

1 On this point also see Steger and Roy (2010).
2 On the toll of the current crisis and of austerity policies on Ireland, see Alderman (2010).
3 On the situation in Greece see Bello (2010), Epitropoulos (2010), and Panayotakis (2010a, 2010b).
4 The possibility of abolishing scarcity through socialism is one that I have in the past entertained myself – see Panayotakis (2003, 2004, 2005).

2 THE NEOCLASSICAL APPROACH TO SCARCITY

1 This definition of economics in terms of scarcity is common in textbooks. David Laidler and Saul Estrin (1989: 1) open their micro-economics textbook by declaring that "Economics is about scarcity." Heinz Kohler (1970) has written a textbook entitled *Economics: The Science of Scarcity*, while Robert Frank's (2003: 3) textbook stressed the centrality to microeconomics of choice "under conditions of scarcity." In their own textbook Krugman et al. (2007: 6–7) name scarcity as the first of the "[f]our economic principles [that] underlie the economics of individual choice." Other examples of defining economics in terms of scarcity include Boyes and Melvin (2005: 7) and Dasgupta (2007: 12–13).
2 On this point, also see Wolff and Resnick (1987: 51–2).
3 This example is used by Robin Hahnel (2002: 37).
4 This refers both to a possibility of a reallocation of productive resources that would increase the output of the productive units involved and the possibility of a reallocation of productive resources that would "produce a different mixture of outputs more to consumers' tastes" (Hahnel 2002: 38).
5 Hunt provides both a comprehensive list of the conditions for Pareto optimality and a powerful critique of the project of neoclassical welfare economics. I discuss and criticize the neoclassical analysis of externalities in Chapter 7.
6 See Robertson (1990: 33), Wolff (2009, 2010). Wolff uses the concept of oscillations between policy regimes to explain the move from the period of an interventionist state in the post-war period to the neoliberal counter-revolution of the last 30 years.

7 This statement by Weintraub agrees with my own experience as an undergraduate student of economics in the early 1990s. Sensing my incipient discomfort with the neoclassical orthodoxy, my advisor at the time warned me that the department's token Marxist professor was not taken seriously by anyone else in the department. This incident highlights the paradox (or is it hypocrisy?) of a theoretical perspective that praises competition between different laundry detergents to high heaven, even as it is allergic to any meaningful competition of ideas. On the cleansing of American economics departments from even "strong liberals or mild radicals," see Dowd (2000: 165, 284 endnote 49).

3   SCARCITY AND CAPITAL ACCUMULATION

1 On this point, see Wolff and Resnick (1987: 135).
2 For a brief overview of the rapid and wide-ranging social, economic and technological changes that capitalism has brought about, see Bowles, Edwards, and Roosevelt (2005: Chapter 1).
3 On the ways that ruling classes in the past used the surplus, see Bowles et al. (2005: Chapter 7) and Mandel (1968: 133). On reinvestment of the surplus as a condition of continued competitiveness, see Bowles et al. (2005, ch.11).
4 Note, however, that, given the prodigious productivity of capitalist society, even the small part of the surplus that capitalists consume is still sufficient to provide them with luxurious lifestyles that far outstrip those of ruling classes in the past.
5 For typologies of the different Marxist theories of crisis, see Sweezy (1942), Wright (1975), and Attewell (1984, especially ch. 4).
6 Because of its inability to increase production by putting all available physical resources to use when limited demand makes any extra ouput hard to sell, J. Kornai (1979: 804) describes capitalism as "a demand-constrained system." Note, however, that constraints on the supply side are becoming increasingly central to capitalism, as it increasingly overtaxes the planetary ecosystems necessary for production and human survival alike. I discuss capitalism's violation of ecological limits in Chapter 7 .
7 On this point also see Frey and Stutzer (2002: 99).
8 It goes without saying that the toll that capitalist crises inflict on human beings involves much more than the serious mental and physical health impact of unemployment and economic insecurity on the population of affluent countries, such as the United States. UN food officials were expecting that "[a]s a result of the crisis, an additional 104 million people are likely to go hungry" – see Associated Press (2009).
9 In an article on the "[m]onumental job losses in America," Clive Crook reported that "[i]n April [of 2010] the number of Americans looking for work for more than six months rose to 6.7m, roughly half of all those unemployed. Such a high proportion is unprecedented: the long-term

share has previously reached a quarter at most." This is a disturbing development because of "the likelihood that lengthening spells of unemployment become self-perpetuating, as skills erode or grow irrelevant" – see Crook (2010).

10 For Baran and Sweezy's discussion of why these outlets are not forthcoming, see Chapter 4 of their book.

11 In fact, their analysis of the capitalist economic system has been used by their followers in *Monthly Review* to understand the present crisis. See Foster and Magdoff (2008), Foster (2009a, 2010), McChesney et al. (2009), and Foster and McChesney (2009, 2010).

12 For a recent discussion of the continuing relevance of Baran and Sweezy's analysis of the role of military expenditure in contemporary American capitalism, see Foster, Holleman, and McChesney (2008).

13 The question of ecological limits and the deepening ecological crisis is discussed in greater detail in Chapter 7.

14 On this point see Schor (1991), Frank (1999), Basso (2003).

15 That such a scenario may not be utopian is affirmed by Michael Albert's rough esimate that the model of participatory economy that he and Robin Hahnel have devised could, by today, have reduced the workweek to as little as 13 hours a week if it had been adopted 50 years ago – see Albert (2003: 242–3).

16 The class and social struggles which interact with the logic of capital accumulation and which contribute to the formation of capitalism's configurations of scarcity are discussed in greater detail in Chapter 5 of this book.

17 For this point also see Sarkar (1999).

18 Also see Schweickart (1993: 188).

19 On this point also see Schweickart (1993: 188).

20 On the "profoundly distorting effect" of capitalist aggression on "actually existing socialism," also see Schweickart (1993: 220–1).

21 On the contribution of the Soviet regime to modernization, see Lewin (2005: especially Chapters 22, 23). For the ecological devastation wrought by the Soviet model of industrial development, see Sarkar (1999) and Kovel (2002: 203–6).

22 For a discussion of the strong libertarian impulse that imbued the Russian revolution in its early stages but was later repressed, see Guerin (1970).

4   SCARCITY, CAPITALIST EXPLOITATION, AND CONSUMPTION

1   Unwittingly, because "Lerner was a lifelong socialist" (Scitovsky 1990: 155).

2   See my discussion of Robbins in Chapter 2 of this book.

3   Although Sahlins does not discuss why societies around the world came to abandon hunting and gathering, the prevailing view among scholars is that the gradual shift to horticulture came as a result of climatic changes,

population growth, and "advances in weapons technology that led to the rapid depletion and extinction of many species of big-game animals that previously had been important sources of food" (Nolan and Lenski 1998: 120).

4 Note, however, that, according to Norbert Elias, the nobility sought to protect its prestige not simply through consumption but by joining the courtly society formed around European monarchs. In the courtly context "money was indispensable and wealth desirable as a means of living, but certainly not, as in the bourgeois world, the basis of prestige as well" (Elias 1994: 473).

5 On this point also see Bourdieu (1984: 165).

6 On this point see Frank (1999) and Schor (1998: 63).

7 On this point see Klein (2000) and Barber (2007).

8 Similarly, in his account of the rise of advertising and consumer culture in the United States, Ewen (1977: 108) concludes that "[c]onsumerism was a world view, a 'philosophy of life'."

9 On these points, see Wolff (2009, 2010) and Mishel et al (2005).

10 For example, a Reuters article in April 2009 was reporting that "General Growth Properties Inc ... the second largest U.S. mall owner ... filed for bankruptcy ...making it one of the biggest real estate bankruptcies in U.S. history." See Jonas and Chasan (2009).

11 Barber is quoting here from a *Chicago Tribune* article by Gregory Karp.

12 The discussion that follows builds on Juliet Schor's (1991: 2) claim that "[e]very time productivity increases, we are presented with the possibility of either more free time or more money."

13 There is both a demand-side and a supply-side rationale to capital's preference for longer work hours coupled with higher levels of consumption. The supply-side rationale stems from capital's attempt to control workers in the workplace by paying them wages that afford workers an 'employment rent.' This employment rent increases discipline by making workers value their job more, but also gives them an incentive to work longer hours – see Schor (1991). The demand-side rationale has to do with capitalists' fears of overproduction, which have historically led them to devise new ways of boosting consumption – see Hunnicutt (1988: 42).

5 ECONOMIC DEMOCRACY AND THE MULTIPLICITY OF SOCIAL INEQUALITIES AND STRUGGLES

1 On this point see Bowles et al (2005: 334–6), Folbre (1993: 18–20), and Hahnel (2002: 251–3).

2 In fact, Folbre (1993) devotes the second part of her book to a comparison of the "histories of social reproduction" in Northwestern Europe, the United States, and Latin America and the Caribbean. These histories describe the interaction between capitalism and patriarchal social

relationships and the impact of this interaction on the institution of the family.

3 Fraad, Resnick, and Wolff in fact argue that even households themselves are sites of class struggle, but that aspect of their analysis has met with some criticism from other feminist economists and social theorists. See the debate in Fraad et al. (1994).

4 According to Harriet Fraad (2008: 25), "[i]n 1970, 40% of US women were in the labour force, many part time. By the year 2000, 77% of US women were in the labour force, most full time."

5 A recent article in *The New York Times* reports, for example, that this inequality has not disappeared and that "[w]hen both husband and wife work outside the home, the woman spends about 28 hours a week on housework. Her husband can claim only about 16 hours, according to the National Survey of Families and Households from the University of Wisconsin" (Parker-Pope 2010).

6 On this point also see Milani (2000: 16).

7 For Schor's detailed development of this argument, see Chapter 3 of *The Overworked American*.

8 On the labor movement's abandonment of the short hours issue, see Roediger and Foner (1989: 262–3), Hunnicut (1988: 3), and Schor (1991: 81–2). On the rising number of hours worked by Americans, see Schor (1991) and Wolff (2008: 20).

9 In the United States, for example, "union workers in 2007 earned $1.50 an hour more than non-union workers, a wage premium of 14.1 percent … The union premium was even greater for benefits: 28.2 percent for health insurance, 53.9 percent for pensions, 26.6 percent for vacations, and 14.3 percent for holidays" (Yates 2009: 18).

10 This debate between the neoclassical and neo-Marxist views of discrimination was discussed earlier in this chapter.

11 On this point see Federici (2009).

6 CAPITALISM, SCARCITY, AND GLOBAL INEQUALITIES

1 On the role that state policy has historically played in promoting national economic development, see Desai (2009) and MacEwan (2009a, 2009b).

2 For a discussion of Rostow's contribution to the post-war debates on development as well as a detailed overview and critique of the major figures within the modernization school of thought, see Peet and Hartwick (2009, ch. 2) and Desai (2009).

3 Having cleared the 1 billion people mark, world hunger was at a 'historic high' by summer 2009. See Rizzo (2009).

4 On this point see Lappe (1998) and Magdoff (2008).

5 This quotation is reproduced in an article on global inequality by David Schweickart. To reach this conclusion, Pogge "add[ed] up the figures for

some 284 'mega-death events of violence and repression' that occurred during the century just past, among them World War I, World War II, the atrocities of Stalin and Mao, and some 281 other calamities. The total for the century is a quarter less than the poverty deaths since the end of the Cold War" (Schweickart 2008: 472).

6 One should add here, however, that international aid is no substitute for the kind of autonomous economic development, which is denied by the neoliberal straitjacket often imposed on countries in the global South by the IMF and the World Bank, even though it represents the only viable way to improve the ability of people in the global South to meet their needs and have greater control over their social and economic destiny.

7 According to a United Nations report, "Americans spend more on cosmetics, $8 billion annually, and Europeans on ice cream, $11 billion, than it is estimated it would cost to provide basic education ($6 billion) or water and sanitation ($9 billion) to the more than 2 billion people worldwide who go without schools and toilets" (Crossette 1998).

8 On this point also see Dowd (2000: 170). For a work that questions the usefulness of the term globalization, see Hirst and Thompson (1996).

9 For variations on this theme see Rodrik (1997), Gilpin (2000), Stiglitz (2003), and Frieden (2006).

10 Others have made the same point. See, for example, Stiglitz (2001) and Pettifor (2001: 48–9).

11 For a classic statement of the thesis that the pursuit of equity could compromise efficiency and the size of the economic pie to be distributed, see Okun (1975).

12 Working conditions in China have recently made headlines as a result of the series of suicides by workers at Foxconn, "the world's largest contract electronics manufacturer" – see Barboza (2010).

13 On this connection, see Robertson (1990: 149) and Bagchi (2005: 267).

14 Note, however, that since China's population is four times larger than that of the United States, its per capita emissions are still much lower.

15 For example, President Obama (2009) chastised the protestors at the G20 summit held in Pittsburgh for opposing capitalism and "object[ing] to the existing global financial system … [and] free markets." Having made it clear that he does not oppose any of those things, he also claimed that the protestors were not paying attention to what the political elites of the G20 were supposedly doing inside the conference, namely regulating the free markets that the ignorant protestors had the nerve to criticize. Apparently oblivious of the self-contradictory nature of his diatribe, President Obama did not even consider the possibility that those protesting not only pay attention but actually perceive the contradictions that President Obama himself is either unable or unwilling to notice.

16 On the connection between the bankruptcy of neoliberal policies and the growth of the cooperative movement in Argentina, see Howarth (2007, especially ch. 1 and pp. 39–40) and Ranis (2010).

17 For analysis of the situation in Greece and Europe, see Ewing (2010a, 2010b), Epitropoulos (2010), Bello (2010), and Panayotakis (2010a, 2010b).

18 On a personal level, this blurring of the distinction between the global North and the global South has become especially clear to me as a result of the vicissitudes of my country of origin, Greece. Having taught a course on globalization for years, I had never imagined that the IMF's brutal structural adjustment programs that I have long discussed in my classes would so soon become so commonplace in one of the main pillars of the global North, the European Union.

7 SCARCITY AND THE DEEPENING ECOLOGICAL CRISIS

1 And by the time I was revising this chapter less than a year later the entire world was watching another major environmental catastrophe unfold, as the massive earthquake and tsunami in Japan disabled the Daiichi nuclear plants in Fukushima, leading to the leaking of radiation into the environment.

2 WWF's conclusion is based on calculations of the ecological footprint of human activity, a concept that refers to the amount of land, water, and natural resources necessary to support the average lifestyle in different nations and in the world as a whole.

3 It would take about five times the resources available on the planet to allow the entire world's population to live like people in the United States do, and about 2.5 times the planet's resources to allow the entire world's population to live like Germans do (BBC News 2006). For information regarding the 'ecological footprint' of other nations, see http://www.foot-printnetwork.org/en/index.php/GFN/page/footprint_for_nations/.

4 For the serious environmental risks and potential for global conflict that capitalism's ecological unsustainability implies, see Dixon (1993), Klare (2001), and Foster (2009).

5 For capitalism's tendency to increase humanity's destructive as well as productive powers, see Enzensberger (1996) and Meszaros (1995).

6 On this point also see Longfellow (2006: 4), Brunnengraber (2006: 217–18), and Sachs et al. (1998: 72–3).

7 In this respect, Ariel Salleh is certainly right to point out that "climate change is gendered and racialised in its causes, effects, and solutions" (2009: ix).

8 For a more detailed and slightly more technical discussion of externalities, see Hahnel (2002: 85–8). As Hahnel points out, it has been "estimated that when external effects are taken into account the true social costs of a gallon of gasoline consumed in the US may be as high as $15" (2002: 88), which is many times higher than the cost that motorists currently have to pay.

9 For a more detailed discussion of the Coase theorem, see Daly (2003: 176–80).

10 Also see Vidal (2010).

11 On this role see Bowles (1991).

12 For examples of such gaming, see Bond et al. (2007).

13 Of course many, though certainly not all, neoclassical economists still deny the necessity of taking immediate and serious action against climate change. On this point see Ackerman (2009).

14 On this point, see Bowles et al (2005: 56–7) and Sackrey et al (2002: vii–viii).

15 Similarly, John Roemer (1994b) argues that market socialism might be better positioned than capitalism to promote economic efficiency by facilitating the provision of public goods and discouraging the generation of public bads, such as pollution.

16 Note, however, that even the quality of mathematics employed by neoclassical economics has been questioned. See, for example, Keen (2001: 6).

17 Indeed, *Webster's New World College Dictionary* (4th edition) defines efficiency as the "ability to produce a desired effect, product, etc. with a minimum of effort, expense, or waste."

18 As Heather Rogers (2006) has shown, greenwashing was already practiced as early as in the 1950s and has by now spread to a number of industries, from packaging to retail, as well as to a number of leading corporations such as McDonald's, Dell, Whole Foods, Toyota, and Ford. On corporate greenwashing, also see Cato (2009: 92–3), Charkiewicz et al. (2001: 60), and Wallis (2008: 27–8). For the ways in which taxation systems encourage environmental destruction, see Cato (2009: 158).

19 On this point see Lane (2000) and Layard (2005).

8   IMAGINING ECONOMIC DEMOCRACY: TWO MODELS

1 See, for example, Nove (1983); Schweickart (1993: 69).

2 Albert and Hahnel have developed these ideas in a number of works. See Albert (2003), Hahnel and Albert (1990), and Hahnel (2005). For a brief overview of the attempt to implement participatory local planning in the Indian state of Kerala, see Franke (2008). One difference of Kerala's People's Plan Campaign from Hahnel and Albert's conception of participatory planning is that the latter does not seek to supplement but to supplant markets altogether. Nonetheless, Franke's account is instructive because it discusses both the accomplishments of this attempt, with its economic and political empowerment of women and oppressed minorities, and some of the weaknesses, such as the uneven success that the campaign had in providing people with the technical skills they needed to participate effectively. Participatory planning, along with participatory budgeting, are examples of the attempt to democratize the state, which, as I will argue in Chapter 9, has to be an integral element of any political strategy aimed at democratizing the economy.

3 For some of these models and their reception by critics, see Nove (1983), Roemer (1994), Roosevelt and Belkin (1994), and Ollman (1998).

4 See Schweickart (2006b), which forms part of an exchange between Michael Albert and David Schweickart on the merits of Albert and Hahnel's model of a participatory economy. This exchange was posted on the website of Z Magazine and also includes Schweickart (2006a) and Albert (2006).

5 Schweickart's model would not completely eliminate the inequalities that result from the class division between employers and employees because it provides for "[a] quasi-capitalist sector comprised of small businesses and perhaps a sector of entrepreneurial capitalist firms" (Albert and Schweickart 2008: 51).

6 Schweickart's claim in this respect is borne out by the remuneration practices of the Mondragon cooperatives – see Azevedo and Gitahy (2010: 18–19).

7 For more detailed discussion of the distributive principles that Albert and Hahnel favor and those that they do not, see Hahnel (2002, 2004, 2005), Albert and Hahnel (1991), and Albert (2003). These works, which form the basis of my discussion below, provide a discussion of all the values that, in Albert and Hahnel's view, economic systems should advance.

8 Hahnel and Albert defend the market abolitionist position in all their different works, including Albert (2003, 2008b, 2008c) and Hahnel (2005). The paragraphs that follow summarize some of the recurring themes in their critique of markets.

9 For a philosophical discussion of the serious ethical questions that this opacity raises, see Schwartz (2010).

10 This assessment is consistent with Moshe Lewin's description of the development of the Soviet Union's bureaucracy into an autonomous force that escaped the control of its nominal political superiors – see Lewin (2005: esp. pp. 342–60).

11 The paragraphs that follow summarize Albert and Hahnel's description of their model in Albert (2003), Hahnel (2002), and Albert and Hahnel (1991, 1992).

12 This is a weakness that other market socialists, such as John Roemer, share. See Simon (1996) and Folbre (1996).

13 Interestingly, John Roemer's model of market socialism has also met with criticism that it does not pay sufficient attention to gender and racial inequality. See Satz (1996).

9 THE WAY FORWARD

1 Doug Henwood (2009) has leveled this criticism against Albert and Hahnel's "off the shelf [utopia]," while David Miller (1994: 263) has expressed the same concern regarding market socialism.

2 For a discussion of Obama's cabinet picks, in general, and his economic team, in particular, see Chomsky (2009: 22–4).

3 Originating in the work of J. Sarasua and A. Udaondo, this concept is discussed in Azevedo and Gitahy (2010: 8).

4 For a good concise overview of the various ways in which political and economic elites either paved the road to the crisis or failed to react in a timely fashion, see Bello (2008a).

5 Richard Wolff (2010c) is right when he points out that this polarity may to some extent obscure the complicity of Main Street business interests in the practices that paved the road to the current crisis. At the same time, the resonance of this polarity with the public does have a basis in reality, namely the increasing domination of the economy by the financial sector in the years leading up to the crisis. This domination became manifest both in the drastic increase, in the years leading up to the crisis, of the proportion of corporate profits going to the financial sector, and in the social shift whereby the 1960s slogan that "what is good for General Motors is good for the US" had, by the 1990s, been superseded by the slogan that "what is good for Wall Street is all that matters" (Harvey 2005: 33).

6 Naomi Klein and Avi Lewis (2007: 9) emphasize the lessons that emancipatory theory can draw from the Argentine experience when they point out that "[i]n Argentina, the theorists are chasing after the factory workers, trying to analyze what is already in noisy production."

7 See Lavaca Collective (2007), which collects the experiences of workers from a number of recuperated factories in Argentina, and Trigona (2008). The discussion that follows draws from both of these works, as well as from Ranis (2010), Sitrin (2006), and Magnani (2009).

8 The cooperative sector in the Imola region of Italy offers one example of the positive impact that producer cooperatives can have on local community life. See Hancock (2008).

9 Encompassing "106 cooperatives, with 92,773 workers and a total invoice of 15.6 billion euros," the Mondragon network was, in the course of 50 years, able to grow from "one cooperative to a network of cooperatives that was the first entrepreneurial group in the Basque Country and the seventh in all of Spain in 2006" (Azevedo and Gitahy 2010: 5).

10 On the need for democratic participation in the definition of development and in the determination of indicators of welfare, also see Milani (2000: 173); Nayak (2009: 118); Waring (2009: 177). On the problems with treating GDP as a measure of welfare, see Layard (2005: 133–7); Cato (2009: 113–16).

11 Peter Ranis (2010: 77) has linked "[c]ontemporary Argentine industrial and enterprise worker cooperatives ... to the social and economic crisis that offered little alternative to laborers and employees but unemployment and poverty." As Melanie Howarth (2007: 40) notes, moreover, the link between economic crisis and factory recuperation movements

has been operative in other parts of the world during times of economic crisis.

12 On the evolution of European social democracy over the last 100 years, see Sassoon (1996). On the use of the European Union to restructure the European social model, see Aglietta (1998: 75), Lordon (2001: 137), and Birnbaum (2010: 26–7).

13 On this point also see Cox (1997).

14 For progressive economic policies consistent with the goal of full employment see Dugger and Peach (2009: 182–5 and all of ch. 11).

15 For a critical overview of the roles the members of this unholy trinity are playing, see Peet (2009).

16 On this point, see Sassoon (1996) and Aronowitz (2006: 84–5).

17 On the political impotence of social democrats, see Erlanger (2009) and Birnbaum (2010).

18 On the growing strength of the far right, see BBC News (2009b), Blaszczynski and Doran (2009), Seddon (2009), Mail Foreign Service (2009), Cage (2009), Kulish (2009), and Traynor (2011).

CONCLUSION

1 The same point is made by Henwood (2009).

2 For a 'green' variation of the 'breakdown' thesis, see Milani (2000: 207).

3 This conceptualization of the developments that lead to social crisis and revolution forms part of the broader theory of history that Marx articulates in his famous "Preface" to *A Contribution to the Critique of Political Economy*. I have undertaken a critique of this theory of history in Panayotakis (2004). Please note, however, that the views on scarcity that I express in that article represent an earlier stage in my thinking on that issue.

BIBLIOGRAPHY

Abunimah, Ali. 2011. "The Revolution is in our Hands." *Indypendent*, February 16–March 15, p. 10.

Ackerman, Frank. 2008. "Climate Economics in Four Easy Pieces." *Dollars and Sense*, 279 (November/December): 22–26.

Aglietta, Michel. 1998. "Capitalism at the Turn of the Century: Regulation Theory and the Challenge of Social Change." *New Left Review* I/232 (November–December): 41–90.

Ahmed, Anis. 2010. "Police and Protesters Clash in Bangladesh General Strike." Reuters, June 27<www.reuters.com/article/idUSTRE65Q0TF2 0100627> (accessed June 3, 2011).

Ahrne, Goran. 1988. "A Labor Theory of Consumption," in *The Sociology of Consumption: An Anthology*, ed. Per Otnes. Oslo: Solum Forlag and New Jersey: Humanities Press International.

Al-Atraqchi, Firas. 2011. "Egyptian Youth and New Dawn Hopes." January 29 <http://english.aljazeera.net/indepth/features/2011/01/20111 29081571546.html> (accessed June 6, 2011).

Albert, Michael. 2003. *Parecon: Life After Capitalism*. London and New York: Verso.

Albert, Michael. 2006. "Critique Without Comprehension." February 24 <http://www.zmag.org/znet/viewArticle/4346> (accessed June 3, 2011).

Albert, Michael. 2008a. "Building a Pareconish Movement," in *Real Utopia: Participatory Society for the 21st Century*, ed. Chris Spannos. Edinburgh: AK Press.

Albert, Michael. 2008b. "Parecon Today: Chris Spannos interviews Michael Albert," in *Real Utopia: Participatory Society for the 21st Century*, ed. Chris Spannos. Edinburgh: AK Press.

Albert, Michael. 2008c. "Participatory Planning in Life After Capitalism: Barbara Ehrenreich Interviews Michael Albert," in *Real Utopia: Participatory Society for the 21st Century*, ed. Chris Spannos. Edinburgh: AK Press.

Albert, Michael and Robin Hahnel. 1991. *The Political Economy of Participatory Economics*. Princeton, N.J.: Princeton University Press.

Albert, Michael and Robin Hahnel. 1992. "Socialism as it was Always Meant to Be." *Review of Radical Political Economics*, 24(3 and 4): 1–28.

Albert, Michael and David Schweickart. 2008. "There is an Alternative: Economic Democracy and Participatory Economics, a Debate," in *Solidarity Economy: Building Alternatives for People and Planet – Papers and Report from the U.S. Social Forum 2007*, ed. Jenna Allard, Carl Davidson, and Julie Matthaei. Chicago, Ill.: ChangeMaker.

Alderman, Liz. 2010. "In Ireland, a Picture of the High Cost of Austerity."

New York Times, June 28 <www.nytimes.com/2010/06/29/business/ global/29austerity.html?pagewanted=1&hpw> (accessed June 3, 2011).

Ali, Tariq. 2011a. "Libya is Another Case of Selective Vigilantism by the West," *Guardian*, March 29 <www.guardian.co.uk/commentisfree/2011/ mar/29/libya-west-tripoli-arab-world-gaddafi> (accessed June 6, 2011).

Ali, Tariq. 2011b. "Plan B for a Post-Mubarak Egypt?," *MRZine*, February 5 <http://mrzine.monthlyreview.org/2011/ali050211.html> (accessed June 6, 2011).

Allard, Jenna, Carl Davidson, and Julie Matthaei. *2008. Solidarity Economy: Building Alternatives for People and Planet – Papers and Reports from the U.S. Social Forum 2007*. Chicago, Ill.: ChangeMaker.

Altvater, Elmar. 1993. *The Future of the Market: An Essay on the Regulation of Money and Nature after the Collapse of "Actually Existing Socialism."* London and New York: Verso.

Altvater, Elmar. 2006. "The Social and Natural Environment of Fossil Capitalism," in *Coming to Terms With Nature: Socialist Register 2007*, ed. Leo Panitch and Colin Leys with Barbara Harriss-White, Elmar Altvater, and Greg Albo. London: Merlin /New York: Monthly Review Press/Halifax, N.S.: Fernwood.

Amar, Paul. 2011. "How Egypt's Progressives Won," *Indypendent*, February 16 <www.indypendent.org/2011/02/17/how-egypts-progressives-won/> (accessed June 6, 2011).

Amin, Samir. 1994. *Re-Reading the Postwar Period: An Intellectual Itinerary*. New York: Monthly Review Press.

Amin, Samir. 1996. *Capitalism in the Age of Globalization: The Management of Contemporary Society*. London: Zed.

Amin, Samir. 2011a. "What is happening in Egypt," *MRZine*, February 15 <http://mrzine.monthlyreview.org/2011/amin150211.html> (accessed June 6, 2011).

Amin, Samir. 2011b. "Movements in Egypt: The US Realigns," *MRZine*, February 3 <http://mrzine.monthlyreview.org/2011/amin030211.html> (accessed June 6, 2011).

Aronowitz, Stanley. 1992. *False Promises: The Shaping of American Working Class Consciousness*. Durham, N.C. and London: Duke University Press.

Aronowitz, Stanley. 2006. *Left Turn: Forging a New Political Future*. Boulder, Colo. and London: Paradigm.

Aronowitz, Stanley. 2011. "One, Two, Many Madisons: The War on Public Sector Workers." *New Labor Forum*, 20(2): 15–21.

Asafu-Adjaye, John. 2000. *Environmental Economics for Non-Economists*. Singapore: World Scientific.

Ashman, Sam. 2001. "India," in *Anti-Capitalism: A Guide to the Movement*, ed. Emma Bircham and John Charlton. London and Sydney: Bookmarks.

Associated Press. 2009. "World Hunger Could Soon Affect Record 1 Billion People, UN Says." May 6 <www.cbc.ca/world/story/2009/05/06/world-hunger-un006.html> (accessed June 6, 2011).

Atkin, Douglas. 2004. *The Culting of Brands: When Customers Become True Believers*. New York: Portfolio.

Attewell, Paul. 1984. *Radical Political Economy Since the Sixties: A Sociology of Knowledge Analysis*. New Brunswick, N.S.: Rutgers University Press.

Avendano, Martha Palacio. 2009. "Interview with Nancy Fraser: Justice as Redistribution, Recognition and Representation." May 16 <http://mrzine.monthlyreview.org/2009/fraser160509.html> (accessed June 6, 2011).

Azevedo, Alessandra and Leda Gitahy. 2010. "The Cooperative Movement, Self-Management, and Competitiveness: The Case of Mondragon Corporacion Cooperativa." *WorkingUSA*, 13(1) (March): 5–29.

Bagchi, Amiya Kumar. 2005. *Perilous Passage: Mankind and the Global Ascendancy of Capital*. Lanham, Md.: Rowman & Littlefield.

Bannock, Graham, R. E. Baxter, and Evan Davis. 2003. 'Pareto,' in *The Penguin Dictionary of Economics*, 7th edn, p. 292.

Baran, Paul A. and Paul M. Sweezy. 1966. *Monopoly Capital: An Essay on the American Economic and Social Order*. New York and London: Monthly Review Press.

Barber, Benjamin R. 2007. *Consumed: How Markets Corrupt Children, Infantilize Adults, and Swallow Citizens Whole*. New York and London: Norton.

Barboza, David. 2010. "A Chinese Factory Outsources Worker Dorms." *New York Times*, June 25 <www.nytimes.com/2010/06/26/technology/26foxconn.html?adxnnl=1&ref=foxconn_technology&adxnnlx=1278266414-5LTKSI7Tt7FgWhw5+mIhCQ> (accessed June 6, 2011).

Barker, Colin. 2001. "Socialists," in *Anti-Capitalism: A Guide to the Movement*, ed. Emma Bircham and John Charlton. London and Sydney: Bookmarks.

Barnet Richard J. and John Cavanagh. 1994. *Global Dreams: Imperial Corporations and the New World Order*. New York: Simon & Schuster.

Basso, Pietro. 2003. *Modern Times, Ancient Hours: Working Hours in the Twenty-First Century*. London and New York: Verso.

BBC News. 2006. "Planet Enters 'Ecological Debt'." October 9 <http://news.bbc.co.uk/2/hi/science/nature/6033407.stm> (accessed June 6, 2011).

BBC News. 2007. "Billions Face Climate Change Risk." April 6 <http://news.bbc.co.uk/2/hi/science/nature/6532323.stm> (accessed June 6, 2011).

BBC News. 2009. "Industrial Unrest in Europe." February 24 <http://news.bbc.co.uk/2/hi/europe/7869639.stm> (accessed June 6, 2011).

BBC News. 2009b. "Voters Steer Europe to the Right." June 8 <http://news.bbc.co.uk/2/hi/europe/8088309.stm> (accessed June 6, 2011).

BBC News. 2010. "Italians Stage General Strike Against Austerity." June 25 <http://news.bbc.co.uk/2/hi/world/europe/10415150.stm> (accessed

June 6, 2011).

Beaud, Michel. 2001. *A History of Capitalism, 1500–2000*. New York: Monthly Review Press.

Beck, Ulrich. 2000. *What is Globalization?* Cambridge, UK: Polity.

Beem, Christopher. 2005. "Challenges to Change: The Invasion of the Money World," in *Unfinished Work: Building Equality and Democracy in an Era of Working Families*, ed. Jody Heymann and Christopher Beem. New York and London: New Press.

Belkin, David. 1994. "Why Market Socialism? From the Critique of Political Economy to Positive Political Economy," in *Why Market Socialism? Voices from Dissent*, ed. Frank Roosevelt and David Belkin. Armonk, N.Y. and London: M. E. Sharpe.

Bello, Walden. 2008. "A Primer on Wall Street Meltdown." *Monthly Review*, October 1 <http://mrzine.monthlyreview.org/2008/bello031008. html> (accessed June 6, 2011).

Bello, Walden. 2008b. "The Coming Capitalist Consensus." *Foreign Policy in Focus*, December 24 <www.fpif.org/articles/the_coming_capitalist_consensus> (accessed June 2, 2011).

Bello, Walden. 2010. "Greece: Same Tragedy, Different Scripts." *Huffington Post*, July 14 <http://www.huffingtonpost.com/walden-bello/greece-same-tragedy-diffe_b_646401.html> (accessed June 6, 2011).

Belluck, Pam. 2009. "Recession Seeps Into Everyday Lives." *New York Times,* April 8 <www.nytimes.com/2009/04/09/health/09stress. html?scp=1&sq=recession%20anxiety%20belluck%20april&st=cse> (accessed June 6, 2011).

Berger, Johannes. 1994. "The Economy and the Environment," in *The Handbook of Economic Sociology*, ed. Neil J. Smelser and Richard Swedberg. Princeton, N.J.: Princeton University Press/New York: Sage.

Berman, Marshall. 1981. *All That Is Solid Melts into Air: The Experience of Modernity*. New York: Simon & Schuster.

Bhagwati, Jagdish. 2005. *In Defense of Globalization*. Oxford: Oxford University Press.

Bird-David, Nurit. 1997. "Beyond 'The Original Affluent Society': A Culturalist Reformulation," in *Limited Wants, Unlimited Means: A Reader on Hunter-Gatherer Economics and the Environment*, ed. John M. Gowdy. Washington, D. C. and Covelo, Calif.: Island Press.

Birnbaum, Norman. 2010. "Is Social Democracy Dead? The Crisis of Capitalism in Europe." *New Labor Forum* 19(1): 24–31.

Blaszcznski, Eva M. and Peter B. Doran. 2009. "Central Europe's Emerging Far-Right." Centre for European Policy Analysis (CEPA), June 12 <http://cepa.org/publications/view.aspx?record_id=79> (accessed June 2, 2011).

Block, Fred. 1994a. "Remaking our Economy: New Strategies for Structural Reform," in *Why Market Socialism? Voices from Dissent*, ed. Frank Roosevelt and David Belkin. Armonk, N.Y. and London: M. E. Sharpe.

Block, Fred. 1994b. "The Roles of the State in the Economy," in *The Handbook of Economic Sociology*, ed. Neil J. Smelser and Richard

Swedberg. Princeton, N.J.: Princeton University Press/New York: Sage.

Block, Fred. 2001. "Introduction," in Karl Polanyi, *The Great Transformation: The Political and Economic Origins of Our Time*. Boston, Mass.: Beacon.

Bonacich, Edna. 1972. "A Theory of Ethnic Antagonism: The Split Labor Market." *American Sociological Review*, 37 (October): 547–59.

Bond, Patrick. 2000. "Defunding the Fund, Running on the Bank," *Monthly Review* (July–August): 127–40.

Bond, Patrick. 2010. "Climate Capitalism Wins in Cancun: Everyone Else Loses." *Counterpunch*, December 13, <http://counterpunch.org/bond12132010.html> (accessed June 6, 2011).

Bond, Patrick, Rehana Dada, and Graham Erion. 2007. *Climate Change, Carbon Trading and Civil Society: Negative Returns on South African Investments*. Scottsville, South Africa: University of KwaZulu-Natal Press.

Bookchin, Murray. 1986. *Post-Scarcity Anarchism*, 2nd edn. Montreal and New York: Black Rose.

Bosman, Julie. 2009. "Newly Poor Swell Lines at Food Banks." *New York Times*, February 19 <http://www.nytimes.com/2009/02/20/nyregion/20food.html> (accessed June 6, 2011).

Bourdieu, Pierre. 1998. "A Reasoned Utopia and Economic Fatalism." *New Left Review* I/227 (January/February): 125–30.

Bousquet, Marc. 2010. "Occupy and Escalate." *Academe* 96(1): 28–33.

Bowles, Samuel. 1991. "What Markets Can – and Cannot – Do." *Challenge* (July–August): 11–16.

Bowles, Samuel. 1998. "Endogenous Preferences: The Cultural Consequences of Markets and other Economic Institutions." *Journal of Economic Literature* 36 (March): 75–111.

Bowles, Samuel and Richard Edwards. 1993. *Understanding Capitalism: Competition, Command, and Change in the U.S. Economy*, 2nd edn. New York: Harper Collins College.

Bowles, Samuel, Richard Edwards, and Frank Roosevelt. 2005. *Understanding Capitalism: Competition, Command, and Change*, 3rd edn. New York and Oxford: Oxford University Press.

Bowles Samuel and Herbert Gintis. 1986. *Democracy and Capitalism: Property, Community, and the Contradictions of Modern Social Thought*. New York: Basic Books.

Boyce, James K. 2002. *The Political Economy of the Environment*. Cheltenham, UK and Northampton, Mass.: Edward Elgar.

Boyes, William and Michael Melvin. *Microeconomics*, 6th edn. Boston, Mass. and New York: Houghton Mifflin.

Bradsher, Keith. 2010. "To Conquer Wind Power, China Writes the Rules." *New York Times*, December 14 <www.nytimes.com/2010/12/15/business/global/15chinawind.html?_r=1&scp=1&sq=china%20sets%20rules%20and%20wins%20wind&st=cse> (accessed June 6, 2011).

Brady Henry E., and Laurel Elms. 2005. "Public Opinion on Work and Family Policy: The Role of Changing Demographics and Unionization," in *Unfinished Work: Building Equality and Democracy in an Era of Working Families*, ed. Jody Heymann and Christopher Beem. New York and London: New Press.

Brenner, Robert. 1998. "Uneven Development and the Long Downturn: The Advanced Capitalist Economies from Boom to Stagnation, 1950–1998." *New Left Review* 229 (May/June).

Broder, John M. 2010. "'Cap and Trade' Loses Its Standing as Energy Policy of Choice." *New York Times*, March 25 <www.nytimes.com/2010/03/26/science/earth/26climate.html?ref=globalwarming> (accessed June 6, 2011).

Bronfenbrenner M. 1962. "The Scarcity Hypothesis in Modern Economics." *American Journal of Economics and Sociology*, 21(3) (July): 265–70.

Brown, Lester R. 2001. *Eco-Economy: Building an Economy for the Earth*. New York and London: Norton.

Brunnengraber, Achim. 2006. "The Political Economy of the Kyoto Protocol," in *Coming to Terms with Nature: Socialist Register 2007*, ed. Leo Panitch and Colin Leys with Barbara Harriss-White, Elmar Altvater, and Greg Albo. London: Merlin/New York: Monthly Review Press/Halifax, N.S.: Fernwood.

Bryner, Jeanna. 2010. "U.S. is Richest Nation, but not Happiest." *Live Science*, July 1 <http://www.livescience.com/6660-richest-nation-happiest.html> (accessed June 6, 2011).

Budd, Adrian. 2001. "Western Europe," in *Anti-Capitalism: A Guide to the Movement*, ed. Emma Bircham and John Charlton. London and Sydney: Bookmarks.

Bullard, Robert. 1994. "Environmental Racism and the Environmental Justice Movement," in *Ecology*, ed. Carolyn Merchant. Amherst, N.Y.: Humanity Books.

Bush, George W. 2008. "Transcript: President Bush's Speech to the Nation on the Economic Crisis." *New York Times*, September 24 <www.nytimes.com/2008/09/24/business/economy/24text-bush.html?scp=1&sq=september%20bush%20speech%20economic%20crisis%20transcript&st=cse> (accessed June 6, 2011).

Cage, Sam. 2009. "Swiss Minaret Ban May Signal New Right-Wing Surge." *Reuters,* November 30, <http://www.reuters.com/article/2009/11/30/us-swiss-minarets-idUSTRE5AT4M820091130> (accessed June 6, 2011).

Casciani, Dominic. 2009. "The Challenge of Policing the G20." *BBC News*, March 30, http://news.bbc.co.uk/2/hi/uk_news/7971212.stm> (accessed June 6, 2011).

Castells, Manuel. 2000. "Information Technology and Global Capitalism," in *Global Capitalism*, ed. Will Hutton and Anthony Giddens. New York: New Press.

Castle, Stephen. 2009. "Economy Slumps, but it's a Bull Market for Protesters." *New York Times*, April 3 <www.nytimes.com/2009/04/04/

world/europe/04iht-protest.html?scp=1&sq=castle%20bull%20 market%20for%20protesters&st=cse> (accessed June 6, 2011).

Cato, Molly Scott. 2009. *Green Economics: An Introduction to Theory, Policy and Practice.* London and Sterling, Va.: Earthscan.

Cave, Damien. 2010. "Students Gain After Strike in Puerto Rico." *New York Times,* June 17 <www.nytimes.com/2010/06/18/us/18students. html?hpw> (accessed June 6, 2011).

CBS News. 2010. "BP Oil Spill is Now the Largest Ever in Gulf." July 1 <http://www.cbsnews.com/stories/2010/07/01/national/main6636406. shtml> (accessed June 6, 2011).

Chang, Anita. 2011. "China Tries to Stamp Out 'Jasmine Revolution'," *cbn. com,* February 20 <http://www.cbn.com/cbnnews/world/2011/February/ China-Tries-to-Stamp-Out-Jasmine-Revolution-/> (June 3, 2011).

Charkiewicz, Eva, with Sander van Bennekom and Alex Young. 2001. *Transitions to Sustainable Production and Consumption: Concepts, Policies and Actions.* The Hague: Tools for Transition.

Charlton, John. 2001. "Events," in *Anti-Capitalism: A Guide to the Movement,* ed. Emma Bircham and John Charlton. London and Sydney: Bookmarks.

Chomsky, Noam. 2009. "Elections 2008 and Obama's 'Vision'." *Z Magazine* (February): 19–30.

Christopherson, Susan. 1991. "Trading Time for Consumption: The Failure of Working-Hours Reduction in the United States," in *Working Time in Transition: The Political Economy of Working Hours in Industrial Nations,* ed. Karl Hinrichs, William Roche, and Carmen Siriani. Philadelphia, Pa.: Temple University Press.

Clark, Brett, and Richard York. 2008. "Rifts and Shifts: Getting to the Root of Environmental Catastrophe." *Monthly Review* 60 (November): 13–24.

Cockburn, Alexander, and Jeffrey St. Clair. 2000. *Five Days that Shook the World: Seattle and Beyond.* London: Verso.

Costanza, Robert, John Cumberland, Herman Daly, Robert Goodland, and Richard Norgaard. 1997. *An Introduction to Ecological Economics.* Boca Raton, Fla.: St. Lucie.

Cox, Robert W. 1992. "Global *Perestroika,*" in *New World Order?: Socialist Register 1992,* ed. Ralph Miliband and Leo Panitch. London: Merlin.

Cox, Robert W. 1997. "Democracy in Hard Times: Economic Globalization and the Limits to Liberal Democracy," in *The Transformation of Democracy?: Globalization and Territorial Democracy,* ed. Anthony McGrew. Cambridge, UK: Polity.

Crook, Clive. "Monumental Job Losses in America." *Financial Times,* May 23 <http://www.ft.com/intl/cms/s/0/653d6036-6698-11df-aeb1-00144fea b49a,s01=1.html?ftcamp=rss> (accessed June 3, 2011).

Cross, Gary. 1988a. "Worktime and Industrialization: An Introduction," in *Worktime and Industrialization: An International History,* ed. Gary Cross. Philadelphia, Pa.: Temple University Press.

Cross, Gary. 1988b. "Worktime in International Discontinuity, 1886–1940," in *Worktime and Industrialization: An International History*, ed. Gary Cross. Philadelphia, Pa.: Temple University Press.

Cross, Gary. 2000. *An All-Consuming Century: Why Commercialism Won in Modern America*. New York: Columbia University Press.

Crossette, Barbara. 1998. "Most Consuming More, and the Rich Much More" *New York Times*, September 13 <http://www.nytimes.com/1998/09/13/world/most-consuming-more-and-the-rich-much-more.html> (accessed June 3, 2011).

Csikszentmihalyi, Mihaly. 1990. *Flow: The Psychology of Optimal Experience*. New York: Harper & Row.

Csikszentmihalyi, Mihaly. 1992a. "The Flow Experience and Its Significance for Human Psychology," in *Optimal Experience: Psychological Studies of Flow in Consciousness*, ed. Mihaly Csikszentmihalyi and Isabella Selega Csikszentmihalyi. Cambridge: Cambridge University Press.

Csikszentmihalyi, Mihaly. 1992b. "The Future of Flow," in *Optimal Experience: Psychological Studies of Flow in Consciousness*, ed. Mihaly Csikszentmihalyi and Isabella Selega Csikszentmihalyi. Cambridge: Cambridge University Press.

Csikszentmihalyi, Mihaly. 2003. "Materialism and the Evolution of Consciousness," in *Psychology and Consumer Culture: The Struggle for a Good Life in a Materialistic World*, ed. Tim Kasser and Allen D. Kanner. Washington, D.C.: American Psychological Association.

Daly Herman E. 1992. "From Empty-world Economics to Full-world Economics: Recognizing an Historical Turning Point in Economic Development," in *Population, Technology, and Lifestyle: The Transition to Sustainability*, ed. Robert Goodland, Herman E. Daly, and Salah El Serafy. Washington, D.C. and Covelo, Calif.: Island Press.

Daly, Herman E. and Joshua Farley. 2003. *Ecological Economics: Principles and Applications*. Washington, D.C.: Island Press.

Dasgupta, Partha. 2007. *Economics: A Very Short Introduction*. Oxford: Oxford University Press.

Delle Fave, Antonella and Fausto Massimini. 1992. "Modernization and the Changing Contexts of Flow in Work and Leisure," in *Optimal Experience: Psychological Studies of Flow in Consciousness*, ed. Mihaly Csikszentmihalyi and Isabella Selega Csikszentmihalyi. Cambridge: Cambridge University Press.

DeParle Jason. 2009. "Slumping Economy Tests Aid System Tied to Jobs." *New York Times*, May 31 <www.nytimes.com/2009/06/01/us/politics/01poverty.html?scp=1&sq=deparle%20slumping%20economy%20tests%20aid&st=cse> (accessed June 3, 2011).

Desai, Meghnad. 1992. "Neoclassical Economics," in *The Blackwell Dictionary of Twentieth-Century Social Thought*, ed. William Outhwaite and Tom Bottomore. Oxford, UK and Cambridge, Mass.: Blackwell.

Desai, Radhika. 2009. "Theories of Development," in *Introduction to International Development: Approaches, Actors, and Issues*, ed. Paul A.

Haslam, Jessica Schafer, and Pierre Beaudet. Toronto: Oxford University Press.

Devine, Pat. 1992. "Market Socialism or Participatory Planning?" *Review of Radical Political Economics*, 24(3 and 4): 67–89.

Dickerson, Donna. 1997. "Counting Women in: Globalization, Democratization and the Women's Movement," in *The Transformation of Democracy?: Globalization and Territorial Democracy*, ed. Anthony McGrew. Cambridge, UK: Polity.

Dodson, Lisa, and Ellen Bravo. 2005. "When There is No Time or Money: Work, Family, and Community Lives of Low-Income Families," in *Unfinished Work: Building Equality and Democracy in an Era of Working Families*, ed. Jody Heymann and Christopher Beem. New York and London: New Press.

Dowd, Douglas. 2000. *Capitalism and its Economics: A Critical History.* London and Sterling, Va.: Pluto.

Dugger, William M. and James T. Peach. 2009. *Economic Abundance: An Introduction.* Armonk, N.Y. and London: M. E. Sharpe.

Durning, Alan Thein. 1992. *How Much Is Enough? The Consumer Society and the Future of the Earth.* New York and London: Norton.

Easterlin, Richard A. 1996. "Does Satisfying Material Needs Increase Human Happiness?," in *Growth Triumphant: The Twenty-first Century in Historical Perspective.* Ann Arbor, Mich.: University of Michigan Press.

Eckersley, Robin. 1992. *Environmentalism and Political Theory: Toward an Ecocentric Approach.* Albany, N.Y.: SUNY Press.

Economist. 2011. "Oil and the Economy: The 2011 Oil Shock." March 3 <http://www.economist.com/node/18281774> (accessed June 3, 2011).

Egan, Carolyn and Michelle Robidoux. 2001. "Women," in *Anti-Capitalism: A Guide to the Movement*, ed. Emma Bircham and John Charlton. London and Sydney: Bookmarks.

Ehrenreich, Barbara, and Bill Fletcher Jr. 2009. "Rising to the Occasion." *The Nation*, March 23 <http://www.thenation.com/article/rising-occasion> (accessed June 3, 2011).

Ehrlich Paul R., and Anne H. Ehrlich. 1991. *Healing the Planet: Strategies for Resolving the Environmental Crisis.* Reading, Mass.: Addison-Wesley.

Elias, Norbert. 1994. *The Civilizing Process: The History of Manners and State Formation and Civilization.* Oxford: Blackwell.

Elliott, John E. 1980. "Marx and Engels on Communism, Scarcity, and Division of Labor." *Economic Inquiry*, 18 (April): 275–92.

Enzensberger, Hans Magnus. 1996. "A Critique of Political Ecology," in *The Greening of Marxism*, ed. Ted Benton. New York and London: Guilford.

Epitropoulos, Mike-Frank. 2010. "Greece as a Demonstration Project: Will the Black Sheep Bite Back? Will the PIIGS? What about the US?" *Dollars and Sense: Real World Economics*, 288 (May/June): 9–11.

Erber, Ernest. 1994. "Virtues and Vices of the Market: Balanced Correctives to a Current Craze," in *Why Market Socialism? Voices from Dissent*, ed. Frank Roosevelt and David Belkin. Armonk, N.Y. and London: M. E. Sharpe.

Erlanger, Steven. 2009. "Europe's Socialists Suffering Even in Downturn." *New York Times*, September 29 <www.nytimes.com/2009/09/29/world/europe/29socialism.html?scp=1&sq=steven%20erlanger%20a%20specter%20haunts&st=cse> (accessed June 3, 2011).

Erlanger, Steven. 2010. "Deflation Could Stall Efforts to Revive Greece." *New York Times*, May 2 <http://www.nytimes.com/2010/05/03/world/europe/03austerity.html> (accessed June 3, 2011).

Eshragi, Ali Reza. 2011. "Tehran Looks on Calmly as Arabs Protest." *Indypendent*, February 16–March 15, pp. 6–7, 12.

Esping-Andersen, Gosta. 1994. "Welfare States and the Economy," in *The Handbook of Economic Sociology*, ed. Neil J. Smelser and Richard Swedberg. Princeton, N.J.: Princeton University Press/New York: Sage.

Estrin, Saul and David Winter. 1989. "Planning in a Market Socialist Economy," in *Market Socialism*, ed. Julian Le Grand and Saul Estrin. Oxford: Clarendon.

Ewen, Stuart. 1977. *Captains of Consciousness: Advertising and the Social Roots of the Consumer Culture*. New York: McGraw-Hill.

Ewing, Jack. 2010a. "Fears Rise in Europe Over Potential for Deflation." *New York Times*, May 30 <www.nytimes.com/2010/05/31/business/global/31deflation.html?ref=global-home> (accessed June 3, 2011).

Ewing, Jack. 2010b. "Europe's Debt Crisis Starts to Weigh on Manufacturing." *New York Times*, June 1 <www.nytimes.com/2010/06/02/business/global/02factories.html?hpw> (accessed June 3, 2011).

Feagin, Joe R. and Robert Parker. 1996. "The Rise of Mass Rail Transit," in *Readings for Sociology*, 2nd edn, ed. Garth Massey. New York and London: Norton.

Federici, Silvia. 2009. "The Devaluation of Women's Labour," in *Eco-sufficiency and Global Justice: Women Write Political Ecology*, ed. Ariel Salleh. London and New York: Pluto/North Melbourne: Spinifex.

Fisher, John. 2001. "Africa," in *Anti-Capitalism: A Guide to the Movement*, ed. Emma Bircham and John Charlton. London and Sydney: Bookmarks.

Folbre, Nancy. 1993. *Who Pays for the Kids?: Gender and the Structures of Constraint*. London and New York: Routledge.

Folbre, Nancy. 1996. "Roemer's Market Socialism: A Feminist Critique," in *Equal Shares: Making Market Socialism Work*, ed. John E. Roemer. London and New York: Verso.

Foster, John Bellamy. 2002. *Ecology Against Capitalism*. New York: Monthly Review Press.

Foster, John Bellamy. 2008a. "Ecology and the Transition from Capitalism to Socialism." *Monthly Review* 60 (November): 1–12.

Foster, John Bellamy. 2008b. "Peak Oil and Energy Imperialism." *Monthly Review* 60(3) (July–August): 12–33.

Foster, John Bellamy. 2009a. "A Failed System: The World Crisis of Capitalist Globalization and its Impact on China." *Monthly Review* 60 (March): 1–23.

Foster, John Bellamy. 2009b. "Economy, Ecology, Empire." *The Nation*, March 10 <http://www.thenation.com/article/economy-ecology-empire> (accessed June 3, 2011).

Foster, John Bellamy. 2010. "The Age of Monopoly-Finance Capital." *Monthly Review* 61 (February): 1–13.

Foster, John Bellamy and Brett Clark. 2004. "Ecological Imperialism: The Curse of Capitalism," in *The New Imperial Challenge: Socialist Register 2004*, ed. Leo Panitch and Colin Leys. London: Merlin.

Foster, John Bellamy and Fred Magdoff. 2008. "Financial Implosion and Stagnation: Back to the Real Economy." *Monthly Review* 60 (December): 1–29.

Foster John Bellamy and Robert W. McChesney. 2009. "Monopoly-Finance Capital and the Paradox of Accumulation." *Monthly Review* 61(5): 1–20.

Foster John Bellamy and Robert W. McChesney. 2010. "Listen Keynesians, It's the System!" *Monthly Review* 61 (April): 44–56.

Foster, John Bellamy, Hannah Holleman, and Robert W. McChesney. 2008. "The Military/Industrial/Media Triangle." *Monthly Review* 60 (October): 1–19.

Fraad, Harriet, Stephen Resnick, and Richard Wolff. 1994. *Bringing it All Back Home: Class, Gender and Power in the Modern Household.* London and Boulder, Colo.: Pluto.

Fraad, Harriet. 2008. "Post Bush America: A Site of Family Disintegration and Revolutionary Personal Change." *Transform!* 3: 25–34.

Frank, Robert H. 1999. *Luxury Fever: Why Money Fails to satisfy in an Era of Excess.* New York: Free Press.

Frank, Robert H. 2003. *Microeconomics and Behavior*, 5th edn. Boston, Mass.: McGraw-Hill Irwin.

Franke, Richard W. 2008. "Local Planning: The Kerala Experiment," in *Real Utopia: Participatory Society for the 21st Century*, ed. Chris Spannos. Edinburgh: AK Press.

Frey, Bruno S. and Alois Stutzer. 2002. *Happiness and Economics: How the Economy and Institutions Affect Well-Being.* Princeton, N.J. and Oxford: Princeton University Press.

Frieden, Jeffry A. 2006. *Global Capitalism: Its Fall and Rise in the Twentieth Century.* New York and London: Norton.

Friedman, Thomas L. 1999. "Foreign Affairs; Senseless in Seattle." *New York Times*, December 1 <www.nytimes.com/1999/12/01/opinion/foreign-affairs-senseless-in-seattle.html?scp=1&sq=friedman%20seattle%20flat%20earth%20advocates&st=cse> (accessed June 3, 2011).

Friedman, Thomas L. 2000. *The Lexus and the Olive Tree.* New York: Anchor.

Gall, Gregor. 2010. "Resisting Recession and Redundancy: Contemporary Worker Occupations in Britain." *WorkingUSA*, 13(1) (March): 5–29.

Gans, Herbert J. 1972. "The Positive Functions of Poverty." *American Journal of Sociology*, 78: 275–89.

George, Kenneth D., and John Shorey. 1978. *The Allocation of Resources: Theory and Policy*. London and Boston, Mass.: Allen & Unwin.

George, Susan. 2001. "Corporate Globalization," in *Anti-Capitalism: A Guide to the Movement*, ed. Emma Bircham and John Charlton. London and Sydney: Bookmarks.

Geronimo, Sigmund. 1988. "Compensatory Consumer Behavior: Elements of a Critical Sociology of Consumption," in *The Sociology of Consumption: An Anthology*, ed. Per Otnes. Oslo: Solum Forlag/New Jersey: Humanities Press International.

Gilpin, Robert (with Jean Millis Gilpin). 2000. *The Challenge of Global Capitalism: The World Economy in the 21st Century*. Princeton, N.J.: Princeton University Press.

Glyn, Andrew. 2001. "Aspirations, Constraints and Outcomes," in *Social Democracy in Neoliberal Times: The Left and Economic Policy since 1980*, ed. Andrew Glyn. Oxford: Oxford University Press.

Gould, J. P., and C. E. Ferguson. 1980. *Microeconomic Theory*, 5th edn. Homewood, Ill.: Irwin.

Gowdy, John M. (ed.). 1997a. *Limited Wants, Unlimited Means: A Reader on Hunter-Gatherer Economics and the Environment*. Washington, D.C. and Covelo, Calif.: Island Press.

Gowdy, John M. 1997b. "Introduction: Back to the Future and Forward to the Past," in *Limited Wants, Unlimited Means: A Reader on Hunter-Gatherer Economics and the Environment*, ed. John M. Gowdy. Washington, D.C. and Covelo, Calif.: Island Press.

Gramsci, Antonio. 1971. *Selections from the Prison Notebooks of Antonio Gramsci*, ed. Quintin Hoare and Geoffrey Nowell Smith. New York: International Publishers.

Gramsci, Antonio. 1977. *Selections from Political Writings (1910–1920)*, ed. Quentin Hoare. London: Lawrence & Wishart.

Gramsci, Antonio. 1978. *Selections from Political Writings (1921–1926)*, ed. Quentin Hoare. New York: International Publishers.

Greider, William. 1997. *One World Ready or Not: The Manic Logic of Global Capitalism*. New York: Simon & Schuster.

Grimes, Peter E. 1999. "The Horsemen and the Killing Fields: The Final Contradiction of Capitalism," in *Ecology and the World-System*, ed. Walter L. Goldfrank, David Goodman, and Andrew Szasz. Westport, Conn.: Greenwood.

Guerin, Daniel. 1970. *Anarchism: From Theory to Practice*. New York: Monthly Review Press.

Hahnel, Robin. 2002. *The ABCs of Political Economy: A Modern Approach*. London and Sterling, Va.: Pluto.

Hahnel, Robin. 2004. "Economic Justice." *Review of Radical Political Economics* 37(2): 131–54.

Hahnel, Robin. 2005. *Economic Justice and Democracy: From Competition to Cooperation*. New York and London: Routledge.

Hahnel, Robin. 2011. *Green Economics: Confronting the Ecological Crisis*. Armonk, N.Y.: M. E. Sharpe.

Hahnel, Robin and Michael Albert. 1990. *Quiet Revolution in Welfare Economics*. Princeton, N.J.: Princeton University Press.

Hancock, Matt. 2008. "Competing by Cooperating in Italy: The Cooperative District of Imola," in *Solidarity Economy: Building Alternatives for People and Planet – Papers and Reports from the U.S. Social Forum 2007*, ed. Jenna Allard, Carl Davidson, and Julie Matthaei. Chicago, Ill.: ChangeMaker.

Hanieh, Adam. 2011. "Egypt's Uprising: Not Just a Question of 'Transition'," *The Bullet*, February 14 <www.socialistproject.ca/bullet/462.php> (accessed June 3, 2011).

Hardt, Michael, and Antonio Negri. 2000. *Empire*. Cambridge, Mass. and London: Harvard University Press.

Hardt, Michael, and Antonio Negri. 2001. "What the Protesters in Genoa Want." *New York Times*. July 20 <www.nytimes.com/2001/07/20/opinion/20HARDT.html?scp=1&sq=hardt%20negri%20genoa&st=cse> (accessed June 3, 2011).

Harrington, Michael. 1994. "Markets and Plans: Is the Market Necessarily Capitalist?," in *Why Market Socialism? Voices from Dissent*, ed. Frank Roosevelt and David Belkin. Armonk, N.Y. and London: M. E. Sharpe.

Harvard Working Group on New and Resurgent Diseases. 1996. "Globalization, Development, and the Spread of Disease," in *The Case Against the Global Economy and For a Turn Toward the Local*, ed. Jerry Mander and Edward Goldsmith. San Francisco, Calif.: Sierra Club.

Harvey, David. 2003. *The New Imperialism*. Oxford: Oxford University Press.

Harvey, David. 2005. *A Brief History of Neoliberalism*. Oxford: Oxford University Press.

Henry, Ray. 2010. "Scientists: Oil Leaking Up to 2.52M Gallons Daily." *Seattle Times*, June 15 <http://seattletimes.nwsource.com/html/businesstechnology/2012125335_apusgulfoilspillflow.html> (accessed June 3, 2011).

Heilbroner, Robert (ed.) 1996. *Teachings from the Worldly Philosophy*. New York and London: Norton.

Henwood, Doug. 2009. "A Post-Capitalist Future is Possible." *The Nation*, March 13 <http://www.thenation.com/article/post-capitalist-future-possible> (accessed June 3, 2011).

Hinrichs, Karl. 1991. "Work-Time Development in West Germany: Departure to a New Stage," in *Working Time in Transition: The Political Economy of Working Hours in Industrial Nations*, ed. Karl Hinrichs, William Roche, and Carmen Siriani. Philadelphia, Pa.: Temple University Press.

Hirsch, Fred. 1976. *Social Limits to Growth*. Cambridge, Mass.: Harvard University Press.

Hirst, Paul and Grahame Thompson. 1996. *Globalization in Question: The International Economy and the Possibililties of Governance*. Cambridge, UK: Polity.

Hobsbawm, Eric. 2003. *Interesting Times: A Twentieth-Century Life*. New York: Pantheon.

Holland, Joshua. 2009. "The Whole World is Rioting as the Economic Crisis Worsens – Why Aren't We?" AlterNet, February 4 <www.alternet.org/story/124836/> (accessed June 3, 2011).

Homer-Dixon, Thomas F. 1993. *Environmental Scarcity and Global Security*, No. 300 (Fall). Foreign Policy Association.

Hoogvelt, Ankie. 1997. *Globalization and the Postcolonial World: The New Political Economy of Development*. Baltimore, Md.: Johns Hopkins University Press.

Human Experience. 2011. "Labor Rebuilds a Nation," *Indypendent*, February 16 <http://www.indypendent.org/2011/02/17/labor-rebuilds-a-nation/> (accessed June 3, 2011).

Hunnicutt, Benjamin Kline. 1988. *Work Without End: Abandoning Shorter Hours for the Right to Work*. Philadelphia, Pa.: Temple University Press.

Hunt, E. K. 2002. *History of Economic Thought: A Critical Perspective*, 2nd edn. Armonk, NY and London: M. E. Sharpe.

Ira, Kumaran. 2008. "Amid Fears Greek Demonstrations Could Spread Government Postpones French High School Reform." World Socialist website, December 19 <http://www.wsws.org/articles/2008/dec2008/fran-d19.shtml> (accessed June 3, 2011).

Isaac, T. M. Thomas and Richard W. Franke. 2007. "Local Democracy and Development in Kerala," in *Real World Globalization: A Reader in Business, Economics, and Politics from Dollars and Sense*, 9th edn, ed. Betsy Racocy, Alejandro Reuss, Chris Sturr, and the *Dollars and Sense* Collective. Boston, Mass.: Economic Affairs Bureau.

Jackson, Kenneth T. 1987. *Crabgrass Frontier: The Suburbanization of the United States*. New York: Oxford University Press.

Jacobs, Andrew. 2011. "China Issues Warning on Climate and Growth." *New York Times*, February 28 <www.nytimes.com/2011/03/01/world/asia/01beijing.html?_r=1&scp=2&sq=china%20environment&st=cse> (accessed June 3, 2011).

Jameson, Fredric. 2000. "Globalization and Political Strategy." *New Left Review*, 4 (July–August): 49–68.

Jonas, Ilaina and Emily Chasan. 2009. "General Growth Files for Bankruptcy Protection." Reuters, April 17 <http://uk.reuters.com/article/idUKTRE53F68P20090416> (accessed June 3, 2011).

Kanner, Allen D. and Renee G. Soule. 2003. "Globalization, Corporate Culture, and Freedom," in *Psychology and Consumer Culture: The Struggle for a Good Life in a Materialistic World*, ed. Tim Kasser and Allen D. Kanner. Washington, D.C.: American Psychological Association.

Kasser, Tim. 2002. *The High Price of Materialism*. Cambridge, Mass. and London: MIT Press.

Kasser, Tim and Allen D. Kanner. 2003. *Psychology and Consumer Culture: The Struggle for a Good Life in a Materialistic World*. Washington, D.C.: American Psychological Association.

Katsiaficas, George. 1987. *The Imagination of the New Left: A Global Analysis of 1968*. Boston, Mass.: South End.

Katsiaficas, George. 2006. *The Subversion of Politics: European Autonomous Social Movements and the Decolonization of Everyday Life*. Edinburgh: AK Press.

Keen, Steve. 2001. *Debunking Economics: The Naked Emperor of the Social Sciences*. Annandale: Pluto Press Australia/London and New York: Zed.

Kelleher, James B. 2011. "Up to 100,000 Protest Wisconsin Law Curbing Unions." Reuters, March 12 <www.reuters.com/article/2011/03/13/usa-wisconsin-idUSN1227540420110313> (accessed June 3, 2011).

Kilbourne, Jean. 2003. "'The More You Subtract, the More You Add': Cutting Girls Down to Size," in *Psychology and Consumer Culture: The Struggle for a Good Life in a Materialistic World*, ed. Tim Kasser and Allen D. Kanner. Washington, D.C.: American Psychological Association.

Kirkpatrick, David D., and Mona El-Naggar. 2011. "Rich, Poor and a Rift Exposed by Unrest," *New York Times*, January 30 <www.nytimes.com/2011/01/31/world/africa/31classwar.html?scp=1&sq=rich,%20poor%20and%20a%20rift&st=cse> (accessed June 3, 2011).

Klare, Michael T. 2001. *Resource Wars: The New Landscape of Global Conflict*. New York: Metropolitan Books.

Klein, Naomi. 2000. *No Logo*. New York: Picador.

Klein, Naomi and Avi Lewis. 2007. "Foreword," in *Sin Patron: Stories from Argentina's Worker-Run Factories*, Lavaca Collective. Chicago, Ill.: Haymarket.

Klein, Naomi and Avi Lewis. 2009. "The Cure for Layoffs: Fire the Boss." *The Nation*, May 15 <http://www.thenation.com/article/cure-layoffs-fire-boss> (accessed June 3, 2011).

Kohler, Heinz. 1970. *Economics: The Science of Scarcity*. Hinsdale, Ill.: Dryden.

Kornai, Janos. 1979. "Resource-Constrained versus Demand-Constrained Systems." *Econometrica*, 47(4) (July): 801–19.

Kotz, David M. 2007. "Contradictions of Economic Growth in the Neoliberal Era: Accumulation and Crisis in the Contemporary U.S. Economy." *Review of Radical Political Economics*, 40(2) (Spring): 174–88.

Kotz, David M. 2008. "Crisis and Neoliberal Capitalism." *Dollars and Sense* 279 (November/December): 13–15.

Kovel, Joel. 2002. *The Enemy of Nature: The End of Capitalism or the End of the World?* Nova Scotia: Fernwood/London and New York: Zed.

Kozol, Jonathan. 1992. *Savage Inequalities: Children in America's Schools*. New York: Harper Perennial.

Krugman, Paul. 2009a. "Betraying the Planet." *New York Times*, June 28 <www.nytimes.com/2009/06/29/opinion/29krugman.html?scp=1&sq=krugman%20betraying%20the%20planet&st=cse> (accessed June 3, 2011).

Krugman, Paul. 2009b. "Financial Policy Despair." *New York Times*, March 22 <www.nytimes.com/2009/03/23/opinion/23krugman.html?scp=1&sq=krugman%20financial%20policy%20despair&st=cse> (accessed June 3, 2011).

Krugman, Paul. 2009c. "Cassandras of Climate." *New York Times*, September 27 <www.nytimes.com/2009/09/28/opinion/28krugman.html?_r=1> (accessed June 3, 2011).

Krugman, Paul. 2011. "The Forgotten Millions." *New York Times*. March 17 <www.nytimes.com/2011/03/18/opinion/18krugman.html?src=ISMR_AP_LO_MST_FB> (accessed June 3, 2011).

Krugman, Paul, Robin Wells, and Martha L. Olney. 2007. *Essentials of Economics*. New York: Worth.

Kuhnhenn, Jim. 2009. "Bush Overpaid Banks in Bailout, Watchdog Says." BlueRidgeNow.Com, February 6 </www.blueridgenow.com/article/20090206/NEWS/902060289/1151/NEWS?Title=Bush_over paid_banks_in_bailout__watchdog_says> (accessed June 3, 2011).

Kulish, Nicholas. 2009. "As Economic Turmoil Mounts, so do Attacks on Hungary's Gypsies." *New York Times*, April 26 <www.nytimes.com/2009/04/27/world/europe/27hungary.html?scp=1&sq=kulish%20as%20economic%20turmoil%20mounts&st=cse> (accessed June 3, 2011).

La Botz, Dan. 2008. "World's Labor Federations React to Financial Crisis with Proposals from Re-regulation to Socialism." *MRZine*, October 24 <http://mrzine.monthlyreview.org/2008/labotz241008p.html> (accessed June 3, 2011).

La Botz, Dan. 2011. "A New American Workers Movement has Begun." *MRZine*, February 18 <http://mrzine.monthlyreview.org/2011/labotz 180211.html> (accessed June 3, 2011).

LaFranniere, Sharon. 2009. "China Puts Joblessness for Migrants at 20 Million." *New York Times*, February 2 <http://www.nytimes.com/2009/02/03/world/asia/03china.html> (accessed June 3, 2011).

Lamy, Rodolphe. 2009. "Clashes Exacerbate Strike in French Caribbean." *Fox News*, February 16 <www.foxnews.com/wires/2009Feb16/0,4670,CBFrenchCaribbeanUnrest,00.html> (accessed June 3, 2011).

Landy, Joanne. 2009. "I Love Bill Moyers, but He's Wrong about Socialism." *The Nation*, April 1 <http://www.thenation.com/article/i-love-bill-moyers-hes-wrong-about-socialism> (accessed June 3, 2011).

Lane, Robert E. 2000. *The Loss of Happiness in Market Democracies*. New Haven, Conn. and London: Yale University Press.

Lapoint Velma D. and Priscilla J. Hambrick-Dixon. 2003. "Commercialism's Influence on Black Youth: The Case of Dress-Related Challenges," in *Psychology and Consumer Culture: The Struggle for a Good Life in a Materialistic World*, ed. Tim Kasser and Allen D. Kanner. Washington, D.C.: American Psychological Association.

Lappe Frances Moore, Joseph Collins, and Peter Rosset (with Luis Esparza). 1998. *World Hunger: Twelve Myths*, 2nd edn. New York: Grove.

Lavaca Collective. 2007. *Sin Patron: Stories from Argentina's Worker-Run Factories*. Chicago, Ill.: Haymarket.

Lawler, James. 1998. "Marx as Market Socialist," in *Market Socialism: The Debate Among Socialists*, ed. Bertell Ollman. New York and London: Routledge.

Layard, Richard. 2005. *Happiness: Lessons from a New Science*. New York: Penguin.

Lee, Richard. 1997. "Foreword," in *Limited Wants, Unlimited Means: A Reader on Hunter-Gatherer Economics and the Environment*, ed. John M. Gowdy. Washington, D.C. and Covelo, Calif.: Island Press.

Lee, Su-Hoon and David A. Smith. 1999. "The Emergence of South Korean Environmental Movements: A Response (and Challenge?) to Semiperipheral Industrialization," in *Ecology and the World-System*, ed. Walter L. Goldfrank, David Goodman, and Andrew Szasz. Westport, Conn.: Greenwood.

Lefebvre, Henri. 2003. *The Urban Revolution*. Minneapolis, Minn. and London: University of Minnesota Press.

Le Grand, Julian and Saul Estrin. 1989. *Market Socialism*. Oxford: Clarendon.

Leite, Jose Correa. 2005. *The World Social Forum: Strategies of Resistance*. Chicago, Ill.: Haymarket.

Leonhardt, David. 2010. "A Good Report, with Two Dark Linings." *New York Times* blog, June 4 <http://economix.blogs.nytimes.com/2010/06/04/a-good-report-with-two-dark-linings/> (accessed June 2, 2011).

Lerner, Abba P. 1972. "The Economics and Politics of Consumer Sovereignty." *American Economic Review*, 62(1/2) (March): 258–66.

Levine, Diane E. and Susan Linn. 2003. "The Commercialization of Childhood: Understanding the Problem and Finding Solutions," in *Psychology and Consumer Culture: The Struggle for a Good Life in a Materialistic World*, ed. Tim Kasser and Allen D. Kanner. Washington, D.C.: American Psychological Association.

Lewin, Moshe. 2005. *The Soviet Century*. London: Verso.

Li, Minqi. 2008. "Climate Change, Limits to Growth, and the Imperative for Socialism." *Monthly Review*, 60(3): 51–67.

Lichtenstein, Nelson. 2001. *State of the Union: A Century of American Labor*. Princeton, N.J. and Oxford: Princeton University Press.

Lomborg, Bjorn. 2001. *The Skeptical Environmentalist: Measuring the Real State of the World*. Cambridge and New York: Cambridge University Press.

Longfellow, Brenda. 2006. "Weather Report: Images from the Climate Crisis," in *Coming to Terms With Nature: Socialist Register 2007*, ed. Leo Panitch and Colin Leys with Barbara Harriss-White, Elmar Altvater, and Greg Albo. London: Merlin/New York: Monthly Review Press/Halifax, N.S.: Fernwood.

Lordon, Frederic. 2001. "The Logic and Limits of *Desinflation Competitive*," in *Social Democracy in Neoliberal Times: The Left and Economic Policy since 1980*, ed. Andrew Glyn. Oxford: Oxford University Press.

Lukacs, Georg. 1971. *History and Class Consciousness: Studies in Marxist Dialectics*. Cambridge, Mass.: The MIT Press.

MacEwan, Arthur. 2009a. "The Gospel of Free Trade," in *Real World Globalization: A Reader in Economics, Business and Politics from Dollars and Sense*, ed. Ravi Bhandari and Chris Sturr. Cambridge, Mass.: Economic Affairs Bureau.

MacEwan, Arthur. 2009b. "Free Markets, International Commerce, and Economic Development," in *Real World Globalization: A Reader in Economics, Business and Politics from Dollars and Sense*, ed. Ravi Bhandari and Chris Sturr. Cambridge, Mass.: Economic Affairs Bureau.

Magdoff, Fred. 2008. "World Food Crisis: Sources and Solutions." *Monthly Review* 60(1): 1–15.

Magnani, Esteban. 2009. *The Silent Change: Recovered Businesses in Argentina*. Buenos Aires: Teseo.

Mail Foreign Service. 2009. "The Neo-Nazi Surge: Right-Wing Parties Sweep to Power in the European Parliament as Turnover Plummets to Record Low." *Daily Mail*, June 11 <www.dailymail.co.uk/news/worldnews/article-1191533/Right-wing-parties-sweep-power-European-Parliament-voter-turnout-plummets-record-low.html?ITO=1490> (accessed June 3, 2011).

Mandel, Ernest. 1968. *Marxist Economic Theory*, Vol. I. New York and London: Monthly Review Press.

Marchand Marianne H. and Anne Sisson Runyan. 2001. "Feminist Sightings of Global Restructuring: Conceptualizations and Reconceptualizations," in *Globalization and Development Studies: Challenges for the 21st Century*, ed. Frans J. Schuurman. London and Thousand Oaks, Calif.: Sage.

Marglin, Stephen A., and Juliet B. Schor (eds.) 1990. *The Golden Age of Capitalism: Reinterpreting the Postwar Experience*. Oxford: Clarendon.

Marshall, Lorna. 1997. "Sharing, Talking, and Giving: Relief of Social Tensions Among the !Kung," in *Limited Wants, Unlimited Means: A Reader on Hunter-Gatherer Economics and the Environment*, ed. John M. Gowdy. Washington, D C. and Covelo, Calif.: Island Press.

Martinez-Alier, Joan. 2006. "Social Metabolism and Environmental Conflicts," in *Coming to Terms With Nature: Socialist Register 2007*, ed. Leo Panitch and Colin Leys with Barbara Harriss-White, Elmar Altvater and Greg Albo. London: Merlin/New York: Monthly Review Press/Halifax, N.S.: Fernwood.

Martinez-Alier, Joan, with Klaus Schlupmann. 1987. *Ecological Economics: Energy, Environment and Society*. Oxford and New York: Blackwell.

Marx, Karl. 1964. *The Economic and Philosophic Manuscripts of 1844*, ed. Dirk J. Struik. New York: International Publishers.

Marx, Karl. 1970. *A Contribution to the Critique of Political Economy*, ed. Maurice Dobb. New York: International Publishers.

Marx, Karl. 1973. *Grundrisse: Foundations of the Critique of Political Economy*. New York: Vintage.

Marx, Karl. 1977. *Capital: A Critique of Political Economy*, Vol. 1. New York: Vintage.

Marx, Karl. 1978a. "Speech at the Anniversary of the *People's Paper*," in *The Marx–Engels Reader*, 2nd edn, ed. Robert C. Tucker. New York and London: Norton.

Marx, Karl. 1978b. "Critique of the Gotha Program," in *The Marx–Engels Reader*, 2nd edn, ed. Robert C. Tucker. New York and London: Norton.

Marx, Karl. 1981. *Capital: A Critique of Political Economy*, Volume 3 London: Penguin in association with New Left Review.

Marx, Karl, and Friedrich Engels. 1978. "Manifesto of the Communist Party," in *The Marx–Engels Reader*, 2nd edn, ed. Robert C. Tucker. New York and London: Norton.

Marx, Karl, and Friedrich Engels. 1978b. "The German Ideology: Part I," in *The Marx–Engels Reader*, 2nd edn, ed. Robert C. Tucker. New York and London: Norton.

Marzouki, Nadia. 2011. "An Economic Nightmare," *Indypendent*, February 16 <www.indypendent.org/2011/02/21/an-economic-nightmare/> (accessed June 3, 2011).

Max, Arthur. 2007. "UN Panel Gives Dire Warming Forecast." *Huffington Post*, November 17 <http://www.huffingtonpost.com/huff-wires/20071117/climate-change-conference/> (accessed June 3, 2011).

McChesney, Robert W., John Bellamy Foster, Inger L. Stole, and Hannah Holleman. 2009. "The Sales Effort and Monopoly Capital." *Monthly Review*, 60 (April): 1–23.

McCormack, Gowan. 1999. "Modernism, Water, and Affluence: The Japanese Way in East Asia," in *Ecology and the World-System*, ed. Walter L. Goldfrank, David Goodman, and Andrew Szasz. Westport, Conn.: Greenwood.

McCracken, Grant. 1988. *Culture and Consumption: New Approaches to the Symbolic Character of Consumer Goods and Activities*. Bloomington and Indianapolis, Ind.: Indiana University Press.

McMichael, Philip. 2004. *Development and Social Change: A Global Perspective*, 3rd edn. Thousand Oaks, Calif.: Pine Forge.

McNally, David. 2011a. "Mubarak's Folly: The Rising of Egypt's Workers," *The Bullet*, February 11 <www.socialistproject.ca/bullet/460.php> (accessed June 3, 2011).

McNally, David. 2011b. "Night in Tunisia: Riots, Strikes and a Spreading Insurgency," *PM Press*, January 18 <www.pmpress.org/content/article.php/20110118130924392> (accessed June 3, 2011).

Meadows, Donella H., Dennis L. Meadows, and Jorgen Randers. 1992. *Beyond the Limits: Confronting Global Collapse, Envisioning a Sustainable Future*. White River Junction, Vt.: Chelsea Green.

Menser, Michael and Juscha Robinson. 2008. "Participatory Budgeting:

From Porto Alegre, Brazil to the U.S.," in *Solidarity Economy: Building Alternatives for People and Planet – Papers and Reports from the U.S. Social Forum 2007*, ed. Jenna Allard, Carl Davidson, and Julie Matthaei. Chicago, Ill.: ChangeMaker.

Merton, Robert K. 1967. "Manifest and Latent Functions." In *On Theoretical Sociology: Five Essays, Old and New*. New York: Fress/ London: Collier Macmillan.

Meszaros, Istvan. 1995. *Beyond Capital: Towards a Theory of Transition*. New York: Monthly Review Press.

Michaels, Walter Benn. 2006. *The Trouble with Diversity: How We Learned to Love Identity and Ignore Inequality*. New York: Metropolitan Books.

Midgley, Jane. 2007. "Gender Responsive Budgeting," in *Real World Globalization: A Reader in Business, Economics, and Politics from Dollars and Sense*, 9th edn, ed. Betsy Racocy, Alejandro Reuss, Chris Sturr, and the *Dollars and Sense* Collective. Boston, Mass.: Economic Affairs Bureau.

Mies, Maria. 1998. *Patriarchy and Accumulation on a World Scale: Women in the International Division of Labor*. London: Zed.

Milani, Brian. 2000. *Designing the Green Economy: The Postindustrial Alternative to Corporate Globalization*. Lanham, Md., Boulder, Colo., New York, and Oxford, UK: Rowman & Littlefield.

Milanovic, Branko. 2005. *Worlds Apart: Measuring International and Global Inequality*. Princeton, N.J. and Oxford: Princeton University Press.

Miller, David. 1994. "A Vision of Market Socialism: How It Might Work – And Its Problems," in *Why Market Socialism? Voices from Dissent*, ed. Frank Roosevelt and David Belkin. Armonk, N.Y. and London: M. E. Sharpe.

Mills, C. Wright. 1961. *The Sociological Imagination*. New York: Grove.

Mishel, Lawrence, Jared Bernstein, and Sylvia Allegretto. 2005. *The State of Working America 2004/2005*. Ithaca, N.Y. and London: ILR.

Mitchell, Richard G. 1992. "Sociological Implications of the Flow Experience," in *Optimal Experience: Psychological Studies of Flow in Consciousness*, ed. Mihaly Csikszentmihalyi and Isabella Selega Csikszentmihalyi. Cambridge: Cambridge University Press.

Moody, Kim. 2001. "Unions," in *Anti-Capitalism: A Guide to the Movement*, ed. Emma Bircham and John Charlton. London and Sydney: Bookmarks.

Moraes, Andrea, and Patricia E. Perkins. 2009. "Deliberative Water Management," in *Eco-sufficiency and Global Justice: Women Write Political Ecology*, ed. Ariel Salleh. London and New York: Pluto/North Melbourne: Spinifex.

Mulberg, Jon. 1995. *Social Limits to Economic Theory*. London and New York: Routledge.

Murphy, Teresa. 1988. "Work, Leisure, and Moral Reform: The

Ten-Hour Movement in New England, 1830–1850," in *Worktime and Industrialization: An International History*, ed. Gary Cross. Philadelphia, Pa.: Temple University Press.

Nagourney, Adam, and Carl Hulse. 2010. "Tea Party Pick Causes Uproar on Civil Rights." *New York Times*, May 20 <www.nytimes.com/2010/05/21/us/politics/21paul.html?scp=5&sq=rand%20paul%20segregation&st=cse> (accessed June 3, 2011).

Nash, June. 1988. "Cultural Patterns of Sexism and Racism in the International Division of Labor," in *Racism, Sexism, and the World-System*, ed. Joan Smith, Jane Collins, Terence K. Hopkins, and Akbar Muhammad. New York: Greenwood.

Nayak, Nalini. 2009. "Development for Some is Violence for Others," in *Eco-sufficiency and Global Justice: Women Write Political Ecology*, ed. Ariel Salleh. London and New York: Pluto/North Melbourne: Spinifex.

Negri, Antonio, in conversation with Raf Valvola Scelsi. 2008. *Goodbye Mr. Socialism*. New York: Seven Stories.

Newton, Scott. 2004. *The Global Economy, 1944–2000: The Limits of Ideology*. London: Arnold.

New York Times. 2008. "The First Presidential Debate." September 26 <http://elections.nytimes.com/2008/president/debates/transcripts/first-presidential-debate.html> (accessed June 3, 2011).

New York Times. 2009. "Copenhagen Climate Talks." December 18 <http://topics.nytimes.com/top/reference/timestopics/subjects/u/united_nations_framework_convention_on_climate_change/index.html?scp=1&sq=copenhagen%20accord&st=cse> (accessed June 3, 2011).

New York Times. 2010. "Gulf of Mexico Oil Spill." June 25 <http://topics.nytimes.com/top/reference/timestopics/subjects/o/oil_spills/gulf_of_mexico_2010/index.html?scp=5&sq=bp%20explosion%20dead%20oil%20workers&st=cse> (accessed June 3, 2011).

New York Times. 2011. "Global Warming." January 13 <http://topics.nytimes.com/top/news/science/topics/globalwarming/index.html?scp=1&sq=global%20warming%20january%2013%20cancun&st=cse#> (accessed June 3, 2011).

Nolan, Patrick and Gerhard Lenski. 1998. *Human Societies: An Introduction to Macrosociology*, 8th edn. New York: McGraw-Hill College.

Nossiter, Adam. 2010. "Far From Gulf, a Spill Scourge 5 Decades Old." *New York Times*, June 16 <www.nytimes.com/2010/06/17/world/africa/17nigeria.html?ref=global-home> (accessed June 3, 2011).

Nove, Alec. 1983. *The Economics of Feasible Socialism*. London: George Allen & Unwin.

Nove, Alec. 1990. "Socialism," in *The New Palgrave: Problems of the Planned Economy*, ed. John Eatwell, Murray Milgate, and Peter Newman. New York and London: Norton.

O'Connor, James. 1996. "The Second Contradiction of Capitalism," in *The Greening of Marxism*, ed. Ted Benton. New York and London: Guilford.

O'Connor, James. 1998. *Natural Causes: Essays in Ecological Marxism*. New York and London: Guilford.

O'Hara, Sabine U. 2009. "Feminist Ecological Economics in Theory and Practice," in *Eco-sufficiency and Global Justice: Women Write Political Ecology*, ed. Ariel Salleh. London and New York: Pluto/North Melbourne: Spinifex.

Obama, Barack. 2009. "Remarks by the President at G20 Closing Press Conference". White House press release, September 25 <www.whitehouse. gov/the_press_office/Remarks-by-the-President-at-G20-Closing-Press-Conference/> (accessed June 3, 2011).

Okello, Christina. 2010. "French Strike Over Plans to Raise Retirement Age." *Seattle Times*, June 24 <http://seattletimes.nwsource.com/ html/nationworld/2012201487_franceretire25.html?syndication=rss> (accessed June 6, 2011).

Okun, Arthur M. 1975. *Equality and Efficiency: The Big Tradeoff*. Washington, D.C.: Brookings Institution.

Ollman, Bertell. 1979. *Social and Sexual Revolution: Essays on Marx and Reich*. Boston, Mass.: South End.

Ollman, Bertell. 1988. "Market Mystification in Capitalist and Market Socialist Societies," in *Market Socialism: The Debate Among Socialists*, ed. Bertell Ollman. New York and London: Routledge.

Ollman, Bertell. (ed.) 1998. *Market Socialism: The Debate Among Socialists*. New York and London: Routledge.

Ophuls, William. 1976. *Ecology and the Politics of Scarcity: Prologue to a Political Theory of the Steady State*. San Francisco, Calif.: Freeman.

Pan, Philip P. 2009. "Economic Crisis Fuels Unrest in E. Europe: Shaky Governments Face Growing Anger." *Washington Post*, January 26, A1.

Panayotakis, Costas. 2003. "Capitalism's 'Dialectic of Scarcity' and the Emancipatory Project." *Capitalism Nature Socialism* 14 (March): 88–107.

Panayotakis, Costas. 2004. "A Marxist Critique of Marx's Theory of History: Beyond the Dichotomy Between Scientific and Critical Marxism." *Sociological Theory*, 22(1): 123–39.

Panayotakis, Costas. 2005. "Environmental Ethics and Capitalism's Dialectic of Scarcity." *Environmental Ethics*, 27 (Fall): 227–44.

Panayotakis, Costas. 2009a. "Reflections on the Greek Uprising." *Capitalism Nature Socialism*, 20 (June): 97–101.

Panayotakis, Costas. 2009b. "Individual Differences and the Potential Tradeoffs Between the Values of a Participatory Economy." *Review of Radical Political Economics*, 41(1): 23–42.

Panayotakis, Costas. 2010a. "Meltdown Greek Style." April 21 <http:// www.indypendent.org/2010/04/21/meltdown-greek-style/> (accessed June 3, 2011).

Panayotakis, Costas. 2010b. "Greece and the Global Capitalist Crisis." *Z Magazine* (June): 18–19.

Panayotakis, Costas. 2010c. "Capitalism, Socialism, and Economic

Democracy: Reflections on Today's Crisis and Tomorrow's Possibilities." *Capitalism Nature Socialism*, 21(4): 7–33.

Panayotakis, Costas. 2011. "Youth in Revolt." *Indypendent*, 165, May 18–June 7: 6 <http://www.indypendent.org/2011/05/20/youth-in-revolt/> (accessed June 3, 2011).

Panayotakis, Costas. (forthcoming). "Democracy and the Capitalist Crisis: The Case of Greece." *International Journal of Pluralism and Economics Education*.

Panitch, Leo and Ralph Miliband. 1992. "The New World Order and the Socialist Agenda," in *New World Order? Socialist Register 1992*, ed. Ralph Miliband and Leo Panitch. London: Merlin.

Papandreou, George A. 2009. "The Challenge of Global Governance." *The Nation*, April 23 <http://www.thenation.com/article/challenge-global-governance> (accessed June 3, 2011).

Parker-Pope, Tara. 2010. "Now, Dad Feels as Stressed as Mom." *New York Times*, June 18 <http://www.nytimes.com/2010/06/20/weekinreview/20parkerpope.html?hpw> (accessed June 3, 2011).

Peet, Richard. 2009. *Unholy Trinity: The IMF, World Bank and WTO*, 2nd edn. London and New York: Zed.

Peet, Richard, and Elaine Hartwick. 2009. *Theories of Development: Contentions, Arguments, Alternatives*, 2nd edn. New York and London: Guilford.

Perelman, Michael. 2008. "How to Think About the Crisis." *Radical Notes*, October 7 <http://radicalnotes.com/content/view/73/39/> (accessed June 3, 2011).

Pettifor, Ann. 2001. "Debt," in *Anti-Capitalism: A Guide to the Movement*, ed. Emma Bircham and John Charlton. London and Sydney: Bookmarks.

Pineiro Harnecker, Camila. 2010. "Workplace Democracy and Social Consciousness: A Study of Venezuelan Cooperatives." *Science and Society* 73(3): 309–39.

Piven, Frances Fox, and Richard A. Cloward. 1987. "The Contemporary Relief Debate," in *The Mean Season: The Attack on the Welfare State*, ed. Fred Block, Richard A. Cloward, Barbara Ehrenreich, and Frances Fox Piven. New York: Pantheon.

Pogge, Thomas. 2002. *World Poverty and Human Rights*. Cambridge, UK: Polity.

Polanyi, Karl. 2001. *The Great Transformation: The Political and Economic Origins of Our Time*. Boston, Mass.: Beacon.

Pomeranz, Kenneth. 2000. *The Great Divergence: China, Europe, and the Making of the Modern World Economy*. Princeton, N.J. and Oxford: Princeton University Press.

Ponting, Clive. 1991. *A Green History of the World: The Environment and the Collapse of Great Civilizations*. New York: St. Martin's.

Prins, Nomi. 2011. "The Egyptian Uprising is a Direct Response to Ruthless Global Capitalism." *Alternet*, February 4 <www.alternet.org/

story/149793/the_egyptian_uprising_is_a_direct_response_to_ruthless_global_capitalism> (accessed June 3, 2011).

Rabin, Roni Caryn. 2009. "Unemployment may be Hazardous to your Health." *New York Times*, May 8 <www.nytimes.com/2009/05/09/health/09sick.html?scp=1&sq=rabin%20unemployment%20hazardous%20health&st=cse> (accessed June 3, 2011).

Ranis, Peter. 2010. "Argentine Worker Cooperatives in Civil Society: A Challenge to Capital-Labor Relations." *WorkingUSA,* 13(1): 77–105.

Rasmussen Reports. 2009. "Just 53% Say Capitalism Better Than Socialism." April 9 <www.rasmussenreports.com/public_content/politics/general_politics/april_2009/just_53_say_capitalism_better_than_socialism> (accessed June 3, 2011).

Resnick, Stephen A., and Richard D. Wolff. 2002. *Class Theory and History: Capitalism and Communism in the U.S.S.R.* New York and London: Routledge.

Resnick, Stephen, and Richard Wolff. 2003. "Exploitation, Consumption, and the Uniqueness of US Capitalism." *Historical Materialism,* 11(4): 209–26.

Reuters 2010. "Document Shows BP Estimates Spill up to 100,000 bpd," June 20 <http://www.reuters.com/article/2010/06/20/us-oil-spill-markey-idUSTRE65J1WI20100620> (accessed June 3, 2011).

Rist, Gilbert. 1997. *The History of Development: From Western Origins to Global Faith.* London and New York: Zed.

Ritzer, George. 2005. *Enchanting a Disenchanted World: Revolutionizing the Means of Consumption,* 2nd edn. Thousand Oaks, Calif.: Pine Forge.

Rizzo, Alessandra. 2009. "World Hunger Reaches the 1 billion people mark." *Faith and Aids,* June 19 <http://faithandaids.wordpress.com/2009/06/19/ap-reports-world-hunger-reaches-the-1-billion-people-mark/> (accessed June 3, 2011).

Robbins, Lionel. 1962. *An Essay on the Nature and Significance of Economic Science,* 2nd edn. London: Macmillan.

Robbins, Richard H. 2005. *Global Problems and the Future of Capitalism,* 3rd edn. Boston, Mass.: Pearson.

Robertson, James. 1990. *Future Wealth: A New Economics for the 21st Century.* New York: Bootstrap.

Rodrik, Dani. 1997. *Has Globalization Gone Too Far?* Washington, D.C.: Institute for International Economics.

Roediger, David R. and Philip S. Foner. 1989. *Our Own Time: A History of American Labor and the Working Day.* London and New York: Verso.

Roemer, John. 1992. "The Morality and Efficiency of Market Socialism." *Ethics,* 102(3): 448–64.

Roemer, John. 1994a. "Market Socialism, a Blueprint: How such an Economy Might Work," in *Why Market Socialism? Voices from Dissent,* ed. Frank Roosevelt and David Belkin. Armonk, N.Y. and London: M. E. Sharpe.

Roemer, John. 1994b. *A Future for Socialism.* Cambridge, Mass.: Harvard University Press.

Rogers, Heather. 2006. "Garbage Capitalism's Green Commerce," in *Coming to Terms With Nature: Socialist Register 2007*, ed. Leo Panitch and Colin Leys with Barbara Harriss-White, Elmar Altvater and Greg Albo. London: Merlin/New York: Monthly Review Press/Halifax, N.S.: Fernwood.

Roosevelt, Frank, and David Belkin (eds.) 1994. *Why Market Socialism? Voices from Dissent*. Armonk, N.Y. and London: M. E. Sharpe.

Rostow, W. W. 1990. *The Stages of Economic Growth: A Non-Communist Manifesto*. Cambridge and New York: Cambridge University Press.

Rupert, Mark, and M. Scott Solomon. 2005. *Globalization and International Political Economy*. Lanham, Md.: Rowman & Littlefield.

Sachs, Wolfgang. 1996. "Neo-Development: 'Global Economic Management'," in *The Case Against the Global Economy and For a Turn Toward the Local*, ed. Jerry Mander and Edward Goldsmith. San Francisco, Calif.: Sierra Club.

Sachs, Wolfgang. 1999. *Planet Dialectics: Explorations in Environment and Development*. London: Zed.

Sachs, Wolfgang, Reinhard Loske, and Manfred Linz. 1998. *Greening the North: A Post-Industrial Blueprint for Ecology and Equity*. London and New York: Zed.

Sackrey, Charles and Geoffrey Schneider (with Janet Knoedler). 2002. *Introduction to Political Economy*. 3rd edn. Cambridge, Mass.: Economic Affairs Bureau.

Sahlins, Marshall. 1972. *Stone Age Economics*. Chicago, Ill.: Aldine Atherton.

Salleh, Ariel. 2009. *Eco-sufficiency and Global Justice: Women Write Political Ecology*. London and New York: Pluto/North Melbourne: Spinifex.

Sarkar, Saral. 1999. *Eco-socialism or Eco-capitalism? A Critical Analysis of Humanity's Fundamental Choices*. London and New York: Zed.

Sassoon, Donald. 1996. *One Hundred Years of Socialism: The West European Left in the Twentieth Century*. New York: New Press.

Satz, Debra. 1996. "Status Inequalities and Models of Market Socialism," in *Equal Shares: Making Market Socialism Work*, ed. John E. Roemer. London and New York: Verso.

Schaeffer, Robert K. 1999. "Success and Impasse: The Environmental Movement in the United States and Around the World," in *Ecology and the World-System*, ed. Walter L. Goldfrank, David Goodman, and Andrew Szasz. Westport, Conn.: Greenwood.

Schifferes, Steve. 2008. "World Poverty 'More Widespread.'" *BBC News*. August 27 <http://news.bbc.co.uk/2/hi/business/7583719.stm> (accessed June 3, 2011).

Schifferes, Steve. 2009. "G20 Leaders Seal $1tn Global Deal". *BBC News*, April 2 <http://news.bbc.co.uk/2/hi/business/7979484.stm> (accessed June 3, 2011).

Schnaiberg, Allan. 2005. "The Economy and the Environment," in *The Handbook of Economic Sociology*, 2nd edn, ed. Neil J. Smelser and Richard Swedberg. Princeton, N.J. and Oxford: Princeton University Press/New York: Sage.

Schor, Juliet B. 1991. *The Overworked American: The Unexpected Decline of Leisure*. New York: Basic Books.

Schor, Juliet B. 1998. *The Overspent American: Upscaling, Downshifting, and the New Consumer*. New York: Basic Books.

Schwartz, David T. 2010. *Consuming Choices: Ethics in a Global Consumer Age*. Lanham, Md.: Rowman & Littlefield.

Schweickart, David. 1992. "Socialism, Democracy, Market, Planning: Putting the Pieces Together." *Review of Radical Political Economics*, 24(3/4): 29–45.

Schweickart, David. 1993. *Against Capitalism*. Cambridge, UK: Cambridge University Press/Paris: Editions de la Maison des Sciences de l'Homme.

Schweickart, David. 2006a. "Nonsense on Stilts." *Z Magazine*, February 24 <www.zmag.org/znet/viewArticle/4348> (accessed June 3, 2011).

Schweickart, David. 2006b. "I Still Think it's Nonsense." *Z Magazine*, March 15 <www.zmag.org/znet/viewArticle/4227> (accessed June 3, 2011).

Schweickart, David. 2006c. "China: Market Socialism or Capitalism?," in *GSA Papers 2006: Alternative Globalizations*, ed. Jerry Harris. Chicago, Ill.: ChangeMaker.

Schweickart, David. 2008. "Global Poverty: Alternative Perspectives on What We Should Do – and Why." *Journal of Social Philosophy*, 39(4): 471–91.

Scitovsky, Tibor. 1990. "Abba Ptachya Lerner," in *Problems of the Planned Economy*, ed. John Eatwell, Murray Millgate, and Peter Newman. New York and London: Norton.

Scitovsky, Tibor. 1992. *The Joyless Economy: The Psychology of Human Satisfaction*, rev. edn. New York and Oxford: Oxford University Press.

Screpanti, Ernesto. 2007. *Libertarian Communism: Marx, Engels and the Political Economy of Freedom*. New York: Palgrave Macmillan.

Seddon, Mark. 2009. "Europe's Far Right on the March." *Al Jazeera*, April 27 <http://english.aljazeera.net/news/europe/2009/04/2009421183245814501.html> (accessed June 3, 2011).

Shannon, Thoman R. 1996. *An Introduction to the World-System Perspective*, 2nd edn. Boulder, Colo.: Westview.

Shooter, Helen. 2001. "China," in *Anti-Capitalism: A Guide to the Movement*, ed. Emma Bircham and John Charlton. London and Sydney: Bookmarks.

Silver, Beverley and Giovanni Arrighi. 2000. "Workers North and South," in *Working Classes, Global Realities: Socialist Register 2001*, ed. Leo Panitch, Colin Leys, Greg Albo, and David Coates. New York: Monthly Review Press.

Simms, Andrew. 2005. *Ecological Debt: The Health of the Planet and the Wealth of Nations*. London and Ann Arbor, Mich.: Pluto.

Simon, William H. 1996. "Inequality and Alienation in the Socialist Capital Market," in *Equal Shares: Making Market Socialism Work*, ed. John E. Roemer. London and New York: Verso.

Singer, Peter. 2006. "What Should a Billionaire Give – And What Should You?" *New York Times*, December 17 <www.nytimes.com/2006/12/17/

magazine/17charity.t.html?pagewanted=1&_r=1&sq=what should a billionaire give&st=cse&scp=1> (accessed June 3, 2011).

Siriani, Carmen. 1991. "The Self-Management of Time in Postindustrial Society," in *Working Time in Transition: The Political Economy of Working Hours in Industrial Nations*, ed. Karl Hinrichs, William Roche, and Carmen Siriani. Philadelphia, Pa.: Temple University Press.

Sitrin, Marina (ed.) 2006. *Horizontalism: Voices of Popular Power in Argentina*. Edinburgh: AK Press.

Skidelsky, Robert. 2008. "Farewell to the Neo-classical Revolution," September 16 <http://www.skidelskyr.com/site/article/farewell-to-the-neo-classical-revolution/> (accessed June 3, 2011).

Sklair, Leslie. 2002. *Globalization: Capitalism and its Alternatives*. Oxford: Oxford University Press.

Slackman, Michael. 2011. "Bullets Stall Youthful Push for Arab Spring." *New York Times*, March 17 <www.nytimes.com/2011/03/18/world/middleeast/18youth.html?src=me&ref=world> (accessed June 3, 2011).

Slater, Don. 1997. *Consumer Culture and Modernity*. Cambridge, UK: Polity.

Smith, Adam. 1909. *An Inquiry Into the Nature and Causes of the Wealth of Nations*. New York: Collier.

Solnit, Rebecca. 2009. "The Revolution has Already Occurred." *The Nation*, March 23 <www.thenation.com/article/revolution-has-already-occurred> (accessed June 3, 2011).

Spitzner, Meike. 2009. "How Global Warming is Gendered: A View from the EU," in *Eco-sufficiency and Global Justice: Women Write Political Ecology*, ed. Ariel Salleh. London and New York: Pluto/North Melbourne: Spinifex.

Starr, Amory, and Luis Fernandez. 2007. "Post-Seattle Social Control," in *GSA Papers 2007: Contested Terrains of Globalization*, ed. Jerry Harris. Chicago, Ill.: Global Studies Association.

Steger, Manfred B. 2003. *Globalization: A Very Short Introduction*. Oxford: Oxford University Press.

Steger, Manfred B. and Ravi K. Roy. 2010. *Neoliberalism: A Very Short Introduction*. Oxford: Oxford University Press.

Steinberg, Stephen. 1989. *The Ethnic Myth: Race, Ethnicity, and Class in America*. Boston, Mass.: Beacon.

Stiglitz, Joseph E. 2001. "Foreword," in Karl Polanyi's *The Great Transformation: The Political and Economic Origins of Our Time*. Boston, Mass.: Beacon.

Stiglitz, Joseph E. 2003. *Globalization and Its Discontents*. New York and London: Norton.

Stiglitz, Joseph E. 2009. "Obama's Ersatz Capitalism." *New York Times*. March 31 <www.nytimes.com/2009/04/01/opinion/01stiglitz.html? scp=1&sq=stiglitz%20ersatz%20capitalism&st=cse> (accessed June 3, 2011).

Stillman, Peter G. 1983. "Scarcity, Sufficiency, and Abundance: Hegel and Marx on Material Needs and Satisfactions." *International Political Science Review*, 4(3): 295–310.

Sweezy, Paul M. 1942. *The Theory of Capitalist Development: Principles of Marxian Political Economy*. New York: Monthly Review Press.

Sweezy, Paul M. 2004. "Capitalism and the Environment." *Monthly Review*, 56(5).

Tabb, William K. 2001. *The Amoral Elephant: Globalization and the Struggle for Social Justice in the Twenty-First Century*. New York: Monthly Review Press.

Tabb, William K. 2008a. "Four Crises of the Contemporary World Capitalist System." *Monthly Review*, 60(5) (October): 43–59.

Tabb, William K. 2008b. "The Current Situation of the United States Economy." *MR Zine*, September 12 <http://mrzine.monthlyreview.org/2008/tabb120908.html> (accessed June 3, 2011).

Tabuchi, Hiroko. 2010. "Walkout Closes Another Toyota Supplier in China." *New York Times*, June 18 <http://www.nytimes.com/2010/06/19/business/global/19iht-strike.html> (accessed June 3, 2011).

Tarleton, John. 2011. "Is It Algeria's Turn?" *Indypendent*, February 16–March 15, p. 10.

Thrasher, Steven. 2010. "Inside a Divided Upper East Side Public School." *Village Voice*, February 23 <www.villagevoice.com/2010-02-23/news/inside-a-divided-nyc-public-school/1> (accessed June 3, 2011).

Ticktin, Hillel. 1998. "The Problem is Market Socialism," in *Market Socialism: The Debate Among Socialists*, ed. Bertell Ollman. New York and London: Routledge.

Tilly, Chris and Marie Kennedy. 2007. "From Resistance to Production in Argentina," in *Real World Globalization: A Reader in Business, Economics, and Politics from Dollars and Sense*, 9th edn, ed. Betsy Racocy, Alejandro Reuss, Chris Sturr, and the *Dollars and Sense* Collective. Boston, Mass.: Economic Affairs Bureau.

Traynor, Ian. 2011. "Eurosceptic True Finns Party Surpise Contender in Finnish Election." *Guardian*, April 15 <www.guardian.co.uk/world/2011/apr/15/eurosceptic-true-finns-contender-finnish-election> (accessed June 3, 2011).

Trigona, Marie. 2008. "Fasinpat (Factory Without a Boss): An Argentine Experience in Self-Management," in *Real Utopia: Participatory Society for the 21st Century*, ed. Chris Spannos. Edinburgh: AK Press.

Tucker, Richard. 2002. "Environmentally Damaging Consumption: The Impact of American Markets on Tropical Ecosystems in the Twentieth Century," in *Confronting Consumption*, ed. Thomas Princen, Michael Maniates, and Ken Conca. Cambridge, Mass. and London: MIT Press.

Twitchell, James. 2000. "Two Cheers for Materialism," in *The Consumer Society Reader*, ed. Juliet B. Schor and Douglas B. Holt. New York: New Press.

Vartiainen, Juhana. 2001. "Understanding Swedish Social Democracy: Victims of Success?," in *Social Democracy in Neoliberal Times: The Left and Economic Policy since 1980*, ed. Andrew Glyn. Oxford and New York: Oxford University Press.

Vasudevan, Ramaa. 2009. "The Credit Crisis: Is the International Role of the Dollar at Stake?" *Monthly Review*, 60 (April): 24–35.

Vasudevan, Ramaa. 2010. "Financialization: A Primer," in *The Economic Crisis Reader: Readings in Economics, Politics, and Social Policy from Dollars and Sense*, ed. Gerald Friedman, Fred Moseley, Chris Sturr, and the *Dollars and Sense* Collective. Boston, Mass.: Dollars and Sense.

Vidal, John. 2010. "Climate Aid Threat to Countries that Refuse to Back Copenhagen Accord." *Guardian*, April 11 <www.guardian.co.uk/environ ment/2010/apr/11/climate-aid-threats-copenhagen-accord> (accessed June 3, 2011).

Wallerstein, Immanuel. 1979. *The Capitalist World-Economy*. New York: Cambridge University Press.

Wallerstein, Immanuel. 1999. "Ecology and Capitalist Costs of Production," in *Ecology and the World-System*, ed. Walter L. Goldfrank, David Goodman, and Andrew Szasz. Westport, Conn.: Greenwood.

Wallerstein, Immanuel. 2008. "The Depression: A Long-Term View." *Monthly Review*, October 16 <http://mrzine.monthlyreview.org/2008/ wallerstein161008.html> (accessed June 3, 2011).

Wallis Victor. 2008. "Capitalist and Socialist Responses to the Ecological Crisis." *Monthly Review*, 60 (November): 25–40.

Waring, Marilyn. 2009. "Policy and the Measure of Woman: Revisiting UNSNA, ISEW, HDI, and GPI," in *Eco-sufficiency and Global Justice: Women Write Political Ecology*, ed. Ariel Salleh. London: Pluto/North Melbourne: Spinifex.

Waters, Malcolm. 2001. *Globalization*, 2nd edn. London/New York: Routledge.

Weaver, Stuart. 1988. "The Political Ideology of Short Time: England, 1820–1850," in *Worktime and Industrialization: An International History*, ed. Gary Cross. Philadelphia, Pa.: Temple University Press.

Weber, Max. 1949. *The Methodology of the Social Sciences*, ed. Edward A. Shils and Henry A. Finch. New York: Free Press.

Weintraub, E. Roy. 2002. "Neoclassical Economics," in *The Concise Encyclopedia of Economics*, <www.econlib.org/library/Enc1/Neoclass icalEconomics.html> (accessed June 3, 2011).

Weisskopf, Thomas E. 1992. "Toward a Socialism for the Future in the Wake of the Demise of the Socialism of the Past." *Review of Radical Political Economics*, 24(3/4): 1–28.

Wen, Dale and Minqi Li. 2006. "China: Hyper-Development and Environmental Crisis," in *Coming to Terms With Nature: Socialist Register 2007*, ed. Leo Panitch and Colin Leys with Barbara Harriss-White, Elmar Altvater, and Greg Albo. London: Merlin/New York: Monthly Review Press/Halifax, N.S.: Fernwood.

Wetzel, Tom. 2008. "Workers' Power and the Russian Revolution," in *Real Utopia: Participatory Society for the 21st Century*, ed. Chris Spannos. Edinburgh: AK Press.

Whitesides, John. 2010. "U.S. Liberals: Time to Make Obama Uncomfortable." Reuters, June 7 <http://www.reuters.com/article/2010/

06/07/us-usa-politics-liberals-idUSTRE6565RA20100607> (accessed June 3, 2011).

Wilkinson, Richard. 2005. *The Impact of Inequality: How to Make Sick Societies Healthier*. New York and London: New Press.

Williams, Colin C. 2005. *A Commodified World? Mapping the Limits of Capitalism*. London and New York: Zed.

Wolff, Richard D. 2008. "Capitalism Hits the Fan." *Dollars and Sense*, 279 (November/December):15–17.

Wolff, Richard D. 2009. "Economic Crisis from a Socialist Perspective." *Socialism and Democracy* 23(2) (July): 3–20.

Wolff, Richard D. 2010a. *Capitalism Hits the Fan: The Global Economic Meltdown and What to Do About It*. Northampton, Mass.: Olive Branch.

Wolff, Richard D. 2010b. "Taking Over the Enterprise: A New Strategy for Labor and the Left." *New Labor Forum* 19(1):8–12.

Wolff, Richard D. 2010c. "Wall Street vs Main Street: Finger Pointing vs. System Change," in *Capitalism Hits the Fan: The Global Economic Meltdown and What to Do About It*. Northampton, Mass.: Olive Branch.

Wolff, Richard D. 2011. "Bonuses for Bankers, Bankruptcy for Public Services: Goldman Sachs Sets Aside $15bn for Pay; the State of California Cuts 1.5bn from Education. What's Wrong with this Picture?" *Guardian*, January 20, <www.rdwolff.com/content/bonuses-bankers-bankruptcy-public-services> (accessed June 3, 2011).

Wolff, Richard D. and Stephen A. Resnick. 1987. *Economics: Marxian versus Neoclassical*. Baltimore, Md. and London: Johns Hopkins University Press.

Wong, Edward. 2010. "As China Aids Labor, Unrest is Still Rising." *New York Times*, June 20 <www.nytimes.com/2010/06/21/world/asia/21chinalabor.html?pagewanted=1&ref=global-home> (accessed June 3, 2011).

World Commission on Environment and Development. 1987. *Our Common Future*. Oxford and New York: Oxford University Press.

World Wildlife Fund. 2010. *Biodiversity, Biocapacity and Development: 2010 Living Planet Report*. <http://wwf.panda.org/about_our_earth/all_publications/living_planet_report/> (accessed June 3, 2011).

Wright Erik O. 1975. "Alternative Perspectives in the Marxist Theory of Accumulation and Crisis." *The Insurgent Sociologist*, 6 (Fall): 5–40.

Xenos, Nicholas. 1989. *Scarcity and Modernity*. London and New York: Routledge.

Yadav, Stacey Philbrick. 2011. "No Pink Slip for Yemen's Salih." *Indypendent*, February 16–March 15, pp. 11–12.

Yates, Michael D. 2009. "Why Unions Still Matter." *Monthly Review*, 60 (February): 18–28.

Zerzan, John. 1997. "Future Primitive," in *Limited Wants, Unlimited Means: A Reader on Hunter-Gatherer Economics and the Environment*, ed. John M. Gowdy. Washington, D.C. and Covelo, Calif.: Island Press.

Zizek, Slavoj. 2009. *First as Tragedy, Then as Farce*. London and New York: Verso.

INDEX